Hide 'n' Seek Kids

Volume 1
Core Curriculum, ESV
(Units 1-4)

THE PRAISE FACTORY

manufacturers of active minds, noisy joy, and prayerful hearts since 1997

Curriculum for preschool and elementary age children,
training tools, music and other resources
are available for download or to order at:
www.praisefactory.org

Table of Contents

Getting to Know the Hide 'n' Seek Curriculum

Hide 'n' Seek Kids Resources 5

Hide 'n' Seek Kids Overview Flyer 6

Session Prep 7

Learning More about Hide 'n' Seek Kids Curriculum, by Resource ... 9

Learning More about Hide 'n' Seek Kids Curriculum, by Activity ... 10

Customizing the Curriculum: Know Yourself to Know What You Need ... 12

Customizing the Curriculum: Build-Your-Own-Curriculum Sandwich ... 17

Common Customizations: by Age Groups 18

Common Customizations: Teaching Situations 19

Maiden Voyage: Testing Out the Curriculum 22

The Real Launch: Implementing the Curriculum in Your Situation ... 23

Protect Your Investment: Tips on Storing the Curriculum for Future Use ... 24

Master Supplies List for All Hide 'n' Seek Kids Games 25

VBS, Camps and Other Programs 29

The Praise Factory Bible Truths across the Three Curriculums ... 32

Comparison Chart of the 3 Praise Factory Curriculums ... 37

CORE CURRICULUM

Unit 1: The God Who Reveals Himself 41

Session Prep 42

Unit Overview Sheet 43

Track Numbers 44

Lesson Plan 45

Bible Story 55

Discussion Sheet 61

Unit 2: God's Wonderful Word, the Bible 63

Session Prep 64

Unit Overview Sheet 65

Track Numbers 66

Lesson Plan 67

Bible Story 77

Discussion Sheet 83

Unit 3: The Good News of God 85

Session Prep 86

Unit Overview Sheet 87

Track Numbers 88

Lesson Plan 89

Bible Story 99

Discussion Sheet 105

Unit 4: The God Like None Other 107

Session Prep 108

Unit Overview Sheet 109

Track Numbers 110

Lesson Plan 111

Bible Story 121

Discussion Sheet 127

APPENDIX A: Songs — 129

Index of Songs — 130

General Classroom Songs (Used every lesson, every unit) — 133
Lyrics — 135
Sheet Music — 139

Unit 1 Songs — 143
Track Numbers — 144
Lyrics — 145
Sheet Music — 153

Unit 2 Songs — 161
Track Numbers — 162
Lyrics — 163
Sheet Music — 171

Unit 3 Songs — 179
Track Numbers — 180
Lyrics — 181
Sheet Music — 188

Unit 4 Songs — 195
Track Numbers — 196
Lyrics — 197
Sheet Music — 206

APPENDIX B: Games — 213
Games Index — 214
Master Supplies List for All Hide n' Seek Kids Games — 215
Bible Verse Games — 219
Music, Movement & Memory Activities — 232
Bible Story Review Games — 245

APPENDIX C: Crafts and Take Home Sheets — 259
Crafts Index — 260
Unit 1 Crafts — 261
Unit 2 Crafts — 289
Unit 3 Crafts — 317
Unit 4 Crafts — 345

APPENDIX D: Free Time Activity Suggestions — 373

APPENDIX E: Resources to Make or Buy — 379
Making a Big Question Box/Briefcase — 381
Making a Flannelgraph Storyboard — 382
Making Durable Storyboard Pictures — 382
Making the Hide 'n' Seek Kids Bible Folder — 383

Getting Started with Hide 'n' Seek Kids

Get It

NOTE: Most 2 & 3 year olds do best simply learning the Big Question & Answer, a simple version of the Bible story, and maybe the Bible Verse. Use other activities, as time and attention span allow. Your session prep need only include

Order the **Praise Factory Tour: Extended Version** (or download it from the website in the Getting Started with Hide 'n' Seek Kids section). It is going to be your easiest, most visual way to learn about this curriculum. Order/download the **Hide 'n' Seek Kids Core Curriculum (ESV/NIV)** and the **Hide 'n' Seek Kids Visual Aids books (Small Format/Large Format pictures/Simple Story Scenes)** resources.

Tour It....Three Times

1 **1. Read through the whole Praise Factory Tour: Extended Version book once.**
Learn how each curriculum in the Praise Factory family is related to each other. Pay special attention to the section on Hide 'n' Seek Kids.

2 **2. Go back and read through just the section on Hide 'n' Seek Kids in the Tour book again.**

3 **3. Now go back and read the Hide 'n' Seek section of the Tour book a third time, only this time, get out your two resource books (Hide 'n' Seek Kids Core Curriculum and Hide 'n' Seek Kids Visual Aids books) and follow along.**
This will help you see how the curriculum flows and where to find each of the resources visualized in the Tour Book.

Rip It Up

The **Hide 'n' Seek Kids Visual Aids book** is meant to be taken apart. These will be made into your visual aids and storyboard pictures used in each lesson.

You May Want to Second It

The **Hide 'n' Seek Kids Core Curriculum book** contains resources you will probably want to photocopy--such as, the lesson plans, the crafts/take home sheets, and the music for the songs. **For this reason, you might want to print out a second copy (from online) or buy a second copy of the book.** This will allow you to take apart one copy for easy photocopying and still have another one intact for reference. Or, you can photocopy a copy from your original and keep that on hand.

Choose It

Choose how you want to use the curriculum resources with your kids and your setting. There is a questionaire and other resources in the Getting Started section of the praisefactory.org website that can help you make the best custom fit for your situation. You may want to follow the curriculum as written and use them all. Or, you may want to pick and choose. Do what is best for your situation.

Prepare It and Protect It

Cut out and laminate the Big Question Box resources (Big Question and Answer; Bible Verse; and, Listening Assignment signs) as well as the Simple Story Scenes or the storyboard pictures from the **Hide 'n' Seek Kids Visual Aids book.** Stick velcro on the back of the storyboard pictures to get them ready to be used on the storyboard and in the Story Review games. **More information about making storyboard pictures can be found in Appendix E of the Core Curriculum books.**

Download It

Download the **zip file of unit songs** from the website. Or, download the sheet of QR codes.

Getting Started with Hide 'n' Seek Kids, continued

Make It... Before You Get Started

There are a few more resources that Hide 'n' Seek Kids uses that you will need to make/buy before you use the curriculum. You need to purchase/make a **Big Question Box; a HSK "Bible" folder; and a flannelgraph storyboard**. Directions for making these are found in the **back of the Core Curriculum books in Appendix E.**

Are You Game?

Hide 'n' Seek Kids is a very active curriculum, with a number of different games suggested for each lesson. The good news is that they are used in a rotation throughout the curriculum. That means, once you make these games, you store them and use them over and over (and for years to come!).

While you only need to make whatever games you choose to use with each lesson, **I strongly recommend that you make all the games before you start using the curriculum.** Get the prep work over with at the beginning and coast your way through years of enjoyment!

Store them in ziploc bags or baskets and pull them out when needed. So simple! Your teachers will love how easy it is to have an engaging learning session with so little work for them to do! Happy teachers are more likely to be repeat teachers! **A full list of the games and the supplies needed to make them can be found in the back of the Core Curriculum books in Appendix B with the instructions for all the games.**

Session Prep

Prepare the curriculum for your teachers. Largely, this will mean making copies of the lesson plan, the crafts and take home sheets...especially if you have already assembled the games. We give the teachers a **basket of curriculum and materials they will use to teach the class each session.** This has worked very well for us.

Don't Ignore It, Store It!

This is a curriculum that keeps on giving, year after year. If you do a good job of storing the curriculum, it will serve your church well and at little cost for many years. We store the resources for each unit in **manilla envelopes and magazine storage boxes.**

Learn More

There are many more resources online that may help you customize the curriculum to fit your learning situation. These are listed online in the Praise Factory Resources section, as well as in the Getting Started section.

Two you might especially want to look at are:
- **From the Ground Up** (Making a Great Start in Children's Ministry and with the Praise Factory Family of Curriculum)
- **Classroom Management Suggestions for Teaching Preschoolers**

These are available for download or to order through Amazon.com.

See It in Action

visit us in Washington, D.C.

Three times a year (the third Saturday/Sunday of March, May and September), we hold a **free lunch, learn-and-look workshop and observation time here at Capitol Hill Baptist Church in Washington, D.C.**

On the Saturday, we gather for lunch and talk philosophy, child protection policy, encouraging parents, dealing with discipline issues, etc. and, of course, curriculum. After finishing up our group session, we are happy to talk to individual churches about their particular situations. Then on Sunday, we offer an opportunity to see Hide 'n' Seek Kids and the other Praise Factory curriculum in action in our classes. The registration form for these workshops can be found on the Praise Factory website.

Hide 'n' Seek Kids Curriculum Overview Flyer

This (and the Praise Factory Tour: Extended Version book) is great to give to church leaders or other prospective teachers who want to know more.

Hide 'n' Seek Kids Session Overview

Session Format: Circle Times, Free Play and Your Choice of Activities

Each session is structured around Circle Time and Free Play Time. Circle Times are used to introduce and review the concept, Bible verse, Bible story, and the ACTS prayer. (A prayer including **A**doration, **C**onfession, **T**hanksgiving, and **S**upplication related to the Bible truth they are learning.) Free play is not only enjoyable, but helps to replenish attention spans and prepare the children for more group listening later in the session. However, every session includes response activities that you may choose to use during free play time to add as much reinforcement as best suits your children. Each Hide 'n' Seek Kids session follows the same four-part format, as described here:

PART 1: Getting Started
A time to welcome the children to the class, enjoy free play, music, and/or play a Bible verse game.

PART 2: Opening Circle Time
The children are gathered together for their primary teaching time. The Big Question (and related songs) are introduced. A listtening assignment* is given; the Bible story told; then, the listening assignment answered at the end of story time.

PART 3: Free Play/Activity Time
The children participate in free play and/or response activities.

PART 4: Closing Circle Time
The children gather together for a brief review of what they have learned and a closing prayer. Teachers give out take home sheets as children are dismissed.

*As with the other two Praise Factory curriculums, Hide 'n' Seek Kids has a few detective-ish elements to it: (1) There is the "Big Question Briefcase" that contains the key concept visual aids and the Bible storyboard pictures that the teacher uses as he teaches. And (2), Each story is called "The Case of the ...." and comes with "Detective Dan's Listening Assignements." These are listening assignments to be solved as the children listen to the story. There are 5 different listening assignments--one for each of the 5 sessions of curriculum included with each Hide 'n' Seek Kids unit. These questions are especially good for use with three-year-olds or older preschoolers.

Session Length
The resources for each Hide 'n' Seek Kids session-- as described in the lesson plan--are designed for a 60 to 90 minutes session. However, they can easily be tailored to fit a shorter or longer session.

Hide 'n' SEEK KIDS

we use with ages 2-3,
often used with ages 2-5

the first of 3 curriculums
in the Praise Factory family

downloads and hard-copies
available through
praisefactory.org

16 Big Bible Truths
to Hide in
Little Hearts

Hide 'n' SEEK KIDS... at a glance

- Teaches the 16 Biblical (theological) themes used in all three Praise Factory curriculum in its simplest form.

- Each of the 16 themes are taught as a simple Big Question & Answer, set to the music of a simple nursery rhyme.

- One Bible truth, one Bible story, and one Bible verse are used with each of the 16 themes. All Bible verses are set to music, which can be a great aid in learning and remembering the verses.

- There are five sessions of curriculum per theme. Use as few or as many as you want. Each is jam-packed with activities.

- The multiple sessions for each theme give children the time they need to really learn it. The new activities keep the learning fresh each session.

- The curriculum for each theme comes with a fully-scripted lesson plan, beautiful storyboard pictures, games, crafts, take-home sheets, and lots of music.

- The curriculum is flexible and is easily adaptable to many different teaching settings.

- Both downloads and hard copies are available.

Hide 'n' Seek Kids Curriculum Overview Flyer, back side

Hide 'n' SEEK KIDS Scope & Sequence

UNIT	BIBLE RESOURCES	UNIT	BIBLE RESOURCES
Unit 1: The God Who Reveals Himself Q: How Can I Know What God Is Like? A: He Shows Me What He's Like!	Bible Verse: Amos 4:13 Story: The Case of the Old Man Who Looked for God Luke 2:25-32	**Unit 9: Jesus Christ, Immanuel, God with Us** Q: What Did Jesus Come to Do? A: Jesus Came to Bring Us to God!	Bible Verse: 1 Peter 3:18 Story: The Case of the The Son Who Came Down The Gospels
Unit 2: God's Wonderful Word, the Bible Q: What's So Special about the Bible? A: It Alone Is God's Word!	Bible Verse: Psalm 18:30, 46 Story: The Case of the Women's Best Gift 1 Timothy	**Unit 10: The Holy Spirit: The Indwelling God** Q: What Does the Holy Spirit Do in God's People? A: He Changes Their Hearts!	Bible Verse: Ezekiel 36:26-27 Story: The Case of the Heart Helper Acts 1-2
Unit 3: The Good News of God, the Gospel Q: What Is the Gospel? A: Salvation through Faith in Jesus Christ!	Bible Verse: John 3:16 Story: The Case of the Stranger's Very Good News Acts 8:1-8	**Unit 11: The God Who Saves** Q: How Can We Be Saved? A: It Is God's Free Gift!	Bible Verse: Romans 6:23 Story: The Case of the Most Important Question Acts 16
Unit 4: The God Like None Other Q: Can Anybody Tell Me What the LORD Is Like? A: He's Not Like Anyone Else!	Bible Verse: 1 Kings 8:23 Story: The Case of the Big Showdown Exodus 1-12	**Unit 12: God's People Live for Him** Q: How Should God's People Live? A: They Should Live Like Jesus!	Bible Verse: Ephesians 5:1-2 Story: The Case of the Runaway Who Came Back Philemon
Unit 5: God, the Good Creator Q: Can You Tell Me What God Made? A: God Made All Things Good!	Bible Verse: Genesis 1:1, 31 Story: The Case of the Wild and Wonderful Words Genesis 1-2	**Unit 13: The Sustaining God** Q: Why Do God's People Keep Believing in Him? A: It Is God's Sustaining Grace!	Bible Verse: Psalm 55:22 Story: The Case of the Terrible Trouble Acts 17, 1 & 2 Thessalonians
Unit 6: God, the Just and Merciful Q: How Did Bad Things Come into God's Good World? A: Bad Things Came Through Sin!	Bible Verse: Romans 5:12 Story: The Case of the Terrible, Terrible Day Genesis 3-4	**Unit 14: The God Who Delights in Our Prayers** Q: How Does God Want Us to Pray? A: Every Night and Day!	Bible Verse: Philippians 4:5,6 (ESV), Luke 18:1 (NIV) Story: The Case of the Man with Big Teeth Daniel 6
Unit 7: The Law-Giving God Q: What Are God's Laws Like? A: God's Laws Are Perfect!	Bible Verse: Psalm 19:7, 9,11 Story: The Case of the Big Voice Exodus 19-20, 24	**Unit 15: God's People Gather Together** Q: Why Do God's People Go to Church? A: To Worship God and Love One Another!	Bible Verse: Hebrews 10:24-25 Story: The Case of the People Who Loved a Lot Acts 2
Unit 8: The God Who Loves Q: What Is God's Love for His People Like? A: It's More than They Could Ever Deserve!	Bible Verse: 1 Chronicles 16:34 Story: The Case of the Eager Enemy's End Acts 7-9	**Unit 16: Jesus, the Returning King** Q: What Will Happen When Jesus Comes Back? A: God Will Make Everything New!	Bible Verse: Revelation 21:5-7 Story: The Case of the Wonderful Ending 2 Peter 3

Session Prep (especially good for newbies!)

Pray! *NOTE: Most 2 & 3 year olds do best simply learning the Big Question & Answer, a simple version of the Bible story, and maybe the Bible Verse. Use other activities, as time and attention span allow. Your session prep need only include what you use.*

Pray for the Holy Spirit to be at work in your heart and the children's hearts.

Review

If new to the curriculum, look at the **Getting Started with Hide 'n' Seek Kids section of this book** (p.5) It will be especially helpful to read through the Hide 'n' Seek Kids section of **The Praise Factory Tour: Extended Version Book.** This is a visual way to understand what goes on in the classroom. (A pdf of the book is found in the samples section on the website.)

Look through and Learn the Lesson

Read over **lesson plan**. Practice any **songs or action rhymes** you are using. Choose/make up motions to go with these. Choose less with younger children and more with older preschoolers. **Practice the lesson with the visual aids** and using the Big Question Box/Briefcase.

Read and Rehearse the Bible Story with Pictures

Read the Bible story from the Bible. Read the curriculum version. Practice telling it with the storyboard pictures. (If you have not previously laminated the story pictures, do that now.) Or, rehearse it from the Simple Story Scenes, if you are using those.

Let There Be Music

Download the music and listen to the songs. Choose which of the songs you will use with the children. If using live musicians, make sure they have the sheet music (found in Appendix A).

Put the Props in Place

1. Prepare your Visual Aids. Put the Bible Verse, Listening Assignment, Bible Story in one side of the Bible folder. Keep out the Big Question sign.

2. Get out your storyboard. If using Simple Story Scenes, put these in your BIble Folder. Or, if using the individual storyboard figures, put all background pictures in place (they have a BG by the number). Put the rest of the storyboard pictures (these have a SB by the number) in order of use in the other side of the Bible folder.

3. Put the HSK Bible Folder as well as the Big Question sign in the Big Question Box/Briefcase and shut it. If your box/briefcase has locks and you want to use the unlocking the box as part of your session, lock it now....but make sure you have the key or know the code first.

4. Prepare the music CD or sheet music or mp3 device for use in your session.

Set Out Free Play Activities

Choose and set up free time activities you will use with the children. Choose a variety of different activities that will be enjoyed by different types of children. Rotate the activities you provide to keep them interesting and fresh to your children. (Suggestions in Appendix D, Core Curriculum books.)

Prepare Any Activities

Choose which (if any) of the unit games and crafts activities you want to use in the session. Bear in mind your time frame as well as the developmental abilities/attention span of your children as you decide what/how many to prepare. **Look over the Discussion Sheet** and choose a few questions you might use to spark discussion with the children as they do their activities (especially good for ages 3's+). Pray for God to give you opportunities to talk about these things with the children.

Let Them Take It with Them

Make copies of the craft/take home sheets, if you are not already using them as one of your activities. You may also want to make copies of the story (see take-home version of each story included in Appendix C with the other take home resources) to have for parents to use with their children at home. There's a link on each craft/take home sheet to the story, if you don't make hard copies.

Store It

After your session is over, collect the resources and store them for future use.
This curriculum can be used over and over for years to come.

Learning More about Hide 'n' Seek Kids Curriculum, by Resource

The extra-depth information starts here! This section will describe important features of the Hide 'n' Seek Kids curriculum. Look at them in the Hide 'n' Seek Kids Core Curriculum and Visual Aids books as you read below. **This first section takes a look at the major resources used in presenting the curriculum.**

Scripted Lesson Plan *Resources found in the Core Curriculum book*	There are **five lessons of curriculum** provided for each unit. Since much of the text is the same for all five lessons, **only one lesson plan is needed**. The different activities for each lesson are noted where they occur. The lesson plans are fully-scripted. This helps even the most inexperienced teacher to know what to say and do. train your teachers in what to say and do, every step of the way. Notice **the green squares with numbers** found in the left side bar of the lesson plan. These are references to the visual aids the teacher can use with the children as she teaches.
Visual Aids *Resources found in the Hide 'n' Seek Kids Visual Aids books*	Visual aids are very important in the Hide 'n' Seek Kids curriculum. They help the children learn, and keep them focused and interested. Visual aids also help even the newest teacher teach with greater ease. All of the visual aids are used with the **Big Question Box/Briefcase and are revealed as the lesson progresses.** They include the Big Question and Answer sign, the Bible Verse sign, the Listening Assignments (used as the children listen to the Bible story), and the storyboard pictures used with the Bible story. The storyboard pictures are available in 2 sizes.
Big Question Box/ Briefcase *Directions for making this found in the back of the Hide 'n' Seek Core Curriculum books*	**The Big Question Box/Briefcase** is a simple box with a lid that you buy or make; or, you can use a briefcase with a combination lock (kids love this!). Inside the Big Question Box/Briefcase are the props for key teaching concepts (Big Question and Answer; Bible verse; Listening Assignments and Bible story.) While not absolutely necessary, the Big Question Box adds a lot of interest to the lesson.
Hide 'n 'Seek Kids "Bible" Folder *Directions for making this found in the back of the Hide 'n' Seek Core Curriculum books and the Hide 'n' Seek Kids Visual Aids books*	The Hide 'n' Seek Kids "Bible" Folder is a large, homemade folder **made from a 22" x 28" piece of poster board.** Images for the front and back of this mock Bible can be glued in place. 8.5" x 11" front and back cover images are included in the Hide 'n' Seek Kids Visual Aids in the back. Larger versions of the front and back covers are found online for download with the resources for each unit. Inside this over-sized folder, the teacher places the Bible Verse, the Listening Assignment for the Bible story, the text to the Bible story and the Storyboard pictures. The point of this Bible folder is for children to begin to grasp that the truths they are learning come from the Bible.
Simple Story Scenes, Storyboard and Storyboard Pictures  *Directions for making these found in Appendix E in the back of the Hide 'n' Seek Core Curriculum books*	Beautiful **storyboard pictures** have been created for you to put up on a feltboard to bring the story alive. (These figures are also used in the **Bible Story Review Game**.) The storyboard pictures are found in the **Hide 'n' Seek Kids Visual Aids Book** for each unit. **See Core Curriculum Appendix E for preparation instructions.** **Simple Story Scenes** are the easiest way to use the pictures. Each story is simply told in 6-9 scenes. If you want a more traditional flannelgraph approach, choose the **Storyboard Pictures.** These are individual figures that let you build your own scene and allow kids to help put up the pictures. Fun, but they are more work. There are **two, different sizes of storyboard pictures** you can choose from. Small Format for the smaller class or home setting. Large Format, for a larger class.

Learning More about Hide 'n' Seek Kids Curriculum, by Resource

Hide 'n' Seek Kids Music  *Songs for each unit found in the back of the Core Curriculum book*	Lyrics and sheet music for the songs used with each unit are actually included within the Hide 'n' Seek Kids Core Curriculum books in Appendix A.
Hide 'n' Seek Kids Audio mp3's *Resources found online only with the resources for each unit*	The audio music for each unit are **included in a zip file** found on the Praise Factory website with the resources for each Hide 'n' Seek Kids unit. Download the zip file from the website to a desired location on your computer. Open the zip file by choosing the "extract" option (often shows up when you right click your mouse over the file.) Once they are extracted, you can access them. You also can play the songs right off of the website from the Hide 'n' Seek Kids "Just Music" section. And, there are QR code sheets that you can print out and access the songs via your phone's camera.

Learning More about Hide 'n' Seek Kids Curriculum, by Activity

This section describes the activities offered in the Hide 'n' Seek Kids curriculum, in order of use. Look at them in the Hide 'n' Seek Kids Core Curriculum and Visual Aid books as you read below.

Intake Activities 	These are activities that help the children settle in their class and get ready for learning. They are open-ended so that any child can join in as they are checked in to class. **Younger children** typically do a free time activity. **Older children** typically play a Bible Verse Memory Game or take part in the Sing-along Music Time. Adding the Music, Movement & Memory Activity to the singing can be especially enjoyable for these children. Both the **Bible Verse Memory Game** and the **Music, Movement & Memory Activity** are some of the games included in the Response Activities section of the lesson plan. There are five sets of these games suggested, enough for a new set of games for each of the five lessons included with each unit. **Game directions are found in Appendix B of the Core Curriculum book.**
The Classroom Song 	Transitions between activities can be difficult, particularly for preschoolers. The Classroom Song is a simple song with four verses used at transition times to make transitions easy and fun. **Verse 1: The Gathering Verse** invites the children to gather together to worship God. **Verse 2: The Go and Play Verse** dismisses the children to play time. **Verse 3: Time to Go & Tell Verse** transitions the children to Closing Circle Time,. It is used not only to hel them remember what they have learned in class , but also to go and tell others what they've learned **Verse 4: What's Our Big News Verse** asks the children to think about what they will go and tell others as they are dismissed. **The lyrics to the Classroom Song are included in the lesson plan. Large format lyrics and sheet music are included in Appendix A of each Hide 'n' Seek Kids Core Curriculum book. An audio version of each verse is included in the unit music.**
The Hide 'n' Seek Kids Theme Song	Circle Time opens with the curriculum theme song. It reminds the children what their learning time is about. **The lyrics to the Classroom Song are included in the lesson plan. Large format lyrics and sheet music are included in Appendix A of each Hide 'n' Seek Kids Core Curriculum book. The song audio included with the rest of the unit songs.**
The Classroom Rules Song 	A major challenge and important goal with 2's and 3's is teaching them how to act in a more formal, group teaching setting. Remember this and do not let yourself become frustrated. Your work with the children now will make way for easier teaching as they get older. Reviewing simple and clear classroom rules, then praying for God's help with the children is a great way to start every session. During the rest of the session, you may want to refer back to the rules, praising the children when they are keeping them well or reminding them of the rules when addressing problems. The Classroom Rules Song provides a simple, fun to sing/say chant of class rules. It helps remind children of the behavior expected of them in class. **The lyrics to the Classroom Rules Song are included in the lesson plan. Large format lyrics and sheet music are included in Appendix A of each Hide 'n' Seek Kids Core Curriculum book. The audio for this song is included in the unit music.**

Prayers 	**Two prayers** are used in each session: **an Opening Prayer and an Unit ACTS** prayer. **The Opening Prayer** stays the same for every session of Hide 'n' Seek Kids. It is a prayer asking for God's help to keep the class rules and to learn about Him. The Opening Prayer can be introduced with the **"Let's Pray!" Song/rhyme.** **The ACTS Prayer** changes with each unit. It is called an ACTS prayer because it incorporates four elements of prayer: Adoration (praising God for who He is); Confession (asking forgiveness for our sins); Thanksgiving (thanking God for what He's done, especially through Jesus); and, Supplication (asking God to do great things). It centers around the unit theme. The Unit ACTS prayer can be introduced by the **ACTS Prayer Song**, which helps familiarize the children with the four elements of prayer represented by A,C,T, and S. The lyrics to "Let's Pray" and the "ACTS Prayer Song" **are included in the lesson plan. Large format lyrics and sheet music are included in Appendix A of each Hide 'n' Seek Kids Core Curriculum book. An audio version of each song is included in the unit music.**
The Big Question & Answer  **The Big Question Box Song** 	The Big Question and Answer is introduced by the use of a 8 ½" x 11" two-sided **Big Question and Answer sign.** This sign is hidden in **The Big Question Box/Briefcase**, a simple box with a lid you can buy or make; or, a briefcase. (Suggestions for making or buying one included in the Core Curriculum books in Appendix E). The children sing/say the **Big Question Box/Briefcase Song**, then the teacher or a designated child opens the box/briefcase and gives it to the teacher to hold up and read to the children. The teacher and children then sing the **Big Q & A Song**: the Big Question and Answer set to the tune of a familiar nursery rhyme. The words to the Big Question Box Song **are included in the lesson plan. Large format lyrics and sheet music are included in Appendix A of each Hide 'n' Seek Kids Core Curriculum book. The audio for this song is included in the unit music.**
Big Question Action Rhyme and Song 	The meaning of the Big Question and Answer is explained by use of an action rhyme. The action rhyme includes actions that you can do as you say it. Use as few or as many of the actions as you deem appropriate for your children. Or, you can sing the **Big Question Song**, which incorporates the same concepts into a song. The lyrics to the Big Question Song **are included in the lesson plan. Large format lyrics and sheet music are included in Appendix A of each Hide 'n' Seek Kids Core Curriculum book. The audio for this song is included in the unit music.**
The Bible Chant Song 	The kids prepare to hear teaching from the Bible by singing/saying **the Bible Chant Song.** This is a simple jingle that reminds the kids that the Bible is very special because it alone is God's Word. The lyrics to the Bible Chant **are included in the lesson plan. Large format lyrics and sheet music are included in Appendix A of each Hide 'n' Seek Kids Core Curriculum book. The audio for this song is in the unit music.** After singing this song, the teacher/designated child pulls out the **Hide 'n' Seek Kids "Bible" Folder** from the **Big Question Box/Briefcase.**

The Hide 'n' Seek Kids "Bible" Folder	As explained previously, the point of this Bible folder is for children to begin to grasp that the truths they are learning come from the Bible. The Hide 'n' Seek Kids "Bible" Folder is a large, homemade folder made from a 22" x 28" piece of poster board. Images for the front and back of this mock Bible can be glued in place. Inside this over-sized folder, the teacher places **the Bible Verse, the Listening Assignment for the Bible story, the text to the Bible story and the storyboard pictures.**
The Bible Verse and Song 	**The first thing the teachers pulls out of the "Bible" folder in the Bible verse.** **Only one Bible verse is taught with each unit.** This gives the children four or five lessons to really learn the verse and its meaning--not just hear it and forget it. The Bible verse is reinforced even more through **the Bible Verse Song.** This song is used as part of the regular teaching time in Circle Time, as well as in the **Music, Movement and Memory activities,** described next. These activities provide even more opportunities for learning the verse. The lyrics to the Bible Verse Song **are included in the lesson plan. Large format lyrics and sheet music are included in Appendix A of each Hide 'n' Seek Kids Core Curriculum book. The audio for this song is included the unit music.**
The Bible Story and Resources	**Only one Bible story is used in each unit.** Instead of tiring of hearing the same story for the four/five lessons, the children are delighted to have mastered it by the end of the unit. **Optional actions/questions are woven into the story text.** Use the Simple Story Scenes to tell the story; or, use the **storyboard pictures** to put up on a homemade storyboard board to bring the story alive. (These figures are also used in the **Bible Story Review Game.**) The storyboard pictures are found in the **Hide 'n' Seek Kids Visual Aids books. Two sizes of pictures are available for smaller or larger storyboards.** Directions for making a homemade storyboard board and for making durable storyboard pictures are found in the Core Curriculum books in Appendix E. While the same Bible story is used for all five lessons, there is a different listening assignment for each lesson. These are called **Detective Dan's Listening Assignments.** (These listening assignments will probably be **too much for two year olds**; can be **useful in developing a three year olds listening skills; and great for children older than this.** The story ends with the answers to the listening assignment; sharing the gospel, and praying the ACTS (Adoration, Confession, Thanksgiving, Supplication) prayer; and, two response songs.
Story Response Songs 	There is a hymn and a praise song that you may choose to close Opening Circle Time with. Each unit features a different pair of response songs, related to the unit Big Question and Answer. This gives the children many lessons to learn these songs. A short unit tie-in description is included with each song. The words to these two songs **are included in the lesson plan. Large format lyrics and sheet music are included in Appendix A of each Hide 'n' Seek Kids Core Curriculum book. The audio for this song is included in the unit music.**
Response Activities: Games and Crafts 	After Opening Circle Time, the children can either enjoy free play **(see Core Curriculum Appendix D for suggestions)** or one of the many game or craft activities. The games and crafts can help reinforce the truths the children have just learned in Circle Time. There are **three, different games suggested for each lesson:** the Bible Verse Game, the Bible Story Game, and the Music, Movement & Memory Activity. And, there is a **simple coloring craft/take home sheet for each lesson, as well as three extra crafts that can be used anytime.** **Because there are so many response activities, some teachers like to incorporate some of them as Intake Activities at the beginning of a session.** Let's look at each of these activities, starting on the next page.

Response Activities: Games

When Opening Circle Time ends, the children can either enjoy free play or one of the many game or craft activities. **The games are referenced in the lesson plans, but are listed in Appendix B at the back of each Hide 'n' Seek Kids Curriculum book. The crafts are referenced in the lesson plan, but instructions and any pages to be photocopied are found in Appendix C at the back of each Hide 'n' Seek Kids Curriculum book.**

Let's look at the games, then the crafts.

The Bible Verse Game

The Bible Verse Game helps the children learn the Bible verse and think about what it means. **The Bible verse games are referenced in the curriculum, but listed in Appendix B in each Hide 'n' Seek Kids Core Curriculum book.**

The Bible Story Review Game

The **Bible Story Review Game** helps the children think about what they learned in the story. It uses the **Storyboard Pictures** from the Bible story. **The Bible Story games are referenced in the curriculum, but listed in Appendix B in each Hide 'n' Seek Kids Core Curriculum book.**

Music, Movement & Memory Activity

The Music, Movement & Memory Activities have the children do certain movement or use **simple homemade (or store bought) musical instruments,** as they sing songs or say the Bible verse. A **simple hymn** and **praise song** as well as the **Bible Verse Songs** and **Big Question Song** are suggested for use. A short blurb describing how each song ties in with the unit is given. **The Music, Movement & Memory Activities are referenced in the curriculum, but listed in Appendix B in each Hide 'n' Seek Kids Core Curriculum book.**

The lyrics and music to these songs are included in the Core Curriculum books (Appendix A). The audio for these songs is found with each unit's music.

All three of these activities are part of a **collection of games that can be assembled ahead of time, then stored** for use throughout the curriculum on a rotation basis. This makes it easy to keep each lesson active and fun, but with less prep work. **A complete list of supplies need to make the games is included in Appendix B with the games.**

Response Activities: Crafts

Coloring Pages/ Take Home Sheets

There are both coloring pages/take home sheets as well as a few extra crafts available with each unit. **The crafts are referenced in the lesson plan, but instructions and any pages to be photocopied are found in Appendix C at the back of each Hide 'n' Seek Kids Core Curriculum book.**

A coloring page is provided for each of a unit's five lessons. On the back of each are the key concepts, a few questions; an ACTS prayer; and, a song/s for parents to use with their children that act as a take home sheet. There is a different emphasis for each lesson's coloring sheet that corresponds with the listening assignment for the lesson:

Lesson 1 Coloring Sheet Emphasis: The Unit Bible Truth
Lesson 2 Coloring Sheet Emphasis: The Unit Bible Verse
Lesson 3 Coloring Sheet Emphasis: The Bible Story and the Story Clues
Lesson 4 Coloring Sheet Emphasis: The Unit ACTS Prayer
Lesson 5 Coloring Sheet Emphasis: The Gospel Tied into the Unit

While these are simple coloring sheets, they can be easily turned into something more. Upgrade your coloring sheet to a more interesting craft by offering simple embellishments, such as jiggly eyes, craft sand, glitter, glitter glue, colored paper dots (made with a hole punch), fabric scraps, etc. Make cut-to-size glued-on clothes, hair, etc. for characters by using a copy of the coloring sheet, cutting out the selected portions and making them the patterns for whatever you want to cut out of fabric, paper, foil, etc.

Response Activities: Crafts **Extra Crafts**	With each unit, there are three extra crafts included for use at any time. These are a **Go-and-Tell Craft**; a **Bible Story Coloring Picture and a Bible Story Puzzle** (which is the Storyboard Picture Placement page from the story, which you can cut out into the appropriate number of puzzle pieces for your children, then re-assembled by them). **Like the other crafts in the curriculum, these extra crafts are referenced in the lesson plan, but instructions and any pages to be photocopied are found in Appendix C at the back of each Hide 'n' Seek Kids Core Curriculum book.**
Response Activities: Discussion Sheet	The discussion sheet contains questions about the key concepts used in the unit. These can be used to spark good conversation as the children are coloring. They can also be used as part of the games and other activities to add even more depth. They are most appropriate for use with children ages 3 and up.
Take Home Resources **Coloring Pages/ Take Home Sheets** **Take Home Version of the Bible Story**	The **back side of the each coloring page is the take home sheet**. Each lesson has a different emphasis. Each includes the key concepts; a few questions; a song/songs and an ACTS prayer. It tells the parents where they can find the full script to Bible story on the Praise Factory website (in the parents' resources), if they want to use it at home with their children. **These coloring pages/take home sheets are referenced in the lesson plan, but the pages to be photocopied are found in Appendix C at the back of each Hide 'n' Seek Kids Core Curriculum book.** There is also a **take home version of the story** that you can give out along with the take home sheets. This is also available online in the Hide 'n' Seek parents' resources section. **This take home version of the Bible story is referenced in the lesson plan, but included in Appendix C at the back of each Hide 'n' Seek Kids Core Curriculum book with the other take home resources.**
Music Resources **Lyrics and Sheet Music** **audio mp3's of the songs**	**Lyrics and sheet music for the songs used with each unit are included within the Hide 'n' Seek Kids Core Curriculum books.** Each leson plan includes the lyrics to the core songs used with each unit. Large format lyrics and sheet music for the songs is included in Appendix A of each Core Curriculum book. Frequently, the lesson plan references extra songs. The lyrics and sheet music to these extra songs are only found in Appendix A with the other unit songs. The songs can be downloaded from the praisefactory.org website. There are 16 zip files of mp3s of songs, one for each of the 16 Hide 'n' Seek Kids units. Or, you can listen to them straight from the website in the Hide 'n' Seek Kids "Just Music" section.

Customizing the Curriculum: Know Yourself to Know What You Need

A good, curriculum custom-fit starts with thinking carefully about those involved. Here are six, key factors to consider. (The Children's Ministry Questionnaire will guide you through these issues in much greater depth.)

Your Children's Abilities

+ readers/pre-readers?
+ age groupings in the same class
+ attention span
+ exposure to the gospel?
+ etc.

Your Teachers' Agility

+ teaching experience
+ experience with children
+ classroom experience
+ their own spiritual maturity
+ etc.

Your Time Capacity

+ Thirty minutes or one hour?
+ Once a week/five days a week?
+ A camp session/a V.B.S
+ School year/a full year?
+ etc.

Who are we?

What do we need?

What can we do?

What should we do?

Your Teaching Locality

+ Home, church or school?
+ Urban, suburban or rural?
+ Storage space available?
+ Classroom size?
+ etc.

Your Ministry Priorities

+ Who gives you spiritual oversight?
+ What do they want you to teach?
+ Are they willing to look over the curriculum/help find and screen teachers?
+ etc.

Your Practicalities

+ What is your budget?
+ Who will prepare the curriculum?
+ How much time do they have?
+ Is there anyone willing/able to oversee the start up and implementation of a new curriculum?

Customizing the Curriculum: Build-Your-Own-Curriculum Sandwich

You've thought about who you are, what you need, what you can do, and what you can should do. Now it's time to customize your own curriculum version. We like to think of this process as similar to creating your favorite sandwich. Start with what you know has to be there, then add in extras until you get just what you want. You might be a "meat-only" sandwich, needing only the very basics of the curriculum. Or, you want "the works"--the whole curriculum, just as it is written. Many people use something in between. The important thing is to keep in mind the specifics of your teachers; your children; your time constraints; and, your ministry situation. Then build the cusrom version of Hide 'n' Seek Kids that works best for you. Bon appetit!

1. Start with the Meat: Core Curriculum	Resources: • Big Question and Answer • Bible Verse • Bible Story	These are the backbone of biblical truth for the curriculum. You really only have to have these. Everything else is extra!
2. Choose Your Cheese: Response Activities	Resources: • Bible Memory Game • Bible Story Review Game • Music, Movement & Memory • Crafts	Response activities are second in importance only to the "meat." They are enjoyable, hands-on activities that help the children learn and retain the "meat" of biblical truths.
3. Add the Lettuce: Intake Activities	Resources: • Free Play • Activity Centers • Unit Songs • Bible Memory Game	Intake Activities are a nice addition to your curriculum "sandwich", but you don't have to have them. They often help the children settle better in class and prepare them for learning.
4. Throw on Extra Veggies: Zesty Extras	Resources: • Hide 'n' Seek Kids Song • Classroom Rules Chant • The Big Question Box Song • The Bible Song • Let's Pray Song • ACTS Prayer Song	These are few extras that add zest to the curriculum. The Classroom Rules Song is especially helpful for reminding the children of expected classroom behavior in a fun way.
5. Spread on Condiments: Transitions	Resources: • The Classroom Song (4 verses)	Harnessing the transition points in your curriculum can make teaching much easier for your teachers and actually fun for your kids. The Hide 'n ' Seek Kids curriculum uses music to structure and teach the children through every transition.
6. Choose Your Bread: Curriculum Presentation Features	Resources: • Big Question Box/Briefcase • Storyboard Pictures	These are resources that are used to present the curriculum to the children. They help keep the children focus and make the learning more visual and interactive.
7. Prepare It for Carry Out Take Home Resources	Resources: • Coloring Sheet/Take Home Sheet for each lesson • Take Home version of each	Take home resources are a great way for parents to know what their children are learning and to provide them with a tool for further discussion.

Common Customizations: By Age Groups

Having considered these questions, put this information to work to build your version of the curriculum.

Here are some ways we have customized the curriculum or seen it customized by others:

CUSTOMIZE BY: Age Group	
2 year olds	**GENERAL OBSERVATIONS:** You are doing well just to get these children to begin to sit as a group. Build up to this, as they get adjusted to a classroom setting. Set your expectations LOW! Helping the children learn how to be a group prepares them for learning more later and even more being able to join in the church service better. This, by itself, is a job well-done. **NUMBER OF LESSONS OF A UNIT USED:** Four or five--based on how many Sundays in a month. Repetition is great for these kids! **It will take 16 months to complete the curriculum at this rate.** **SUGGESTIONS FOR HOW TO USE THE CURRICULUM:** **Opening Activity Time:** • Free play time as they come to class • You can have unit music playing in the background • Use the Classroom Songs to begin to teach them about transitions **Opening Circle Time:** • Use the Big Question Box/Briefcase • Teach them the Big Question • Sing the Big Question Song (short, nursery rhyme version) • Tell them the Bible Verse (maybe sing the song) • Tell the Bible story, using the storyboard • Do not expect these children to be able to do the listening assignment. • End with the ACTS prayer or an even shorter prayer, if attention is lagging. **Response Activity Time:** • Dismiss to free play time. • You can have unit music playing in the background. • Offer the coloring sheet/take home sheet craft after they have played for a while. • You MIGHT be able to weave a few of the discussion questions into your conversations with the children as they play or do their coloring sheet... but don't count on it. It's just fine if they don't! They are only two years old! **Closing Circle Time:** • Use the Classroom Songs to gather them back together. • Ask them the Big Question and Answer and sing the short Big Question Song again. • End with the ACTS prayer or an even shorter prayer, if attention is lagging. **Dismissal:** • Give out the take home version of the Bible Story, the day you start a new unit. • Give out coloring sheet/take home sheet for the lesson.

Common Customizations: Age Groups

CUSTOMIZE BY: Age Group	
3 year olds	**GENERAL OBSERVATIONS:** This curriculum is geared especially for this age group. If the children have been exposed to it as two-year-olds in the previous year, the curriculum really begins to bear a lot of fruit as they repeat it as 3 year olds.. **NUMBER OF LESSONS OF A UNIT USED:** Four or five--based on how many Sundays in a month. Repetition is great for these kids! It will take 16 months to complete the curriculum. **HOW TO USE THE CURRICULUM:** As written, except... the listening questions will be a new concept to this children of this age. This is the new skill you will be working on to give the children. It may take a while to get them used to holding on to a question or two as they listen. You might even want to remind them of the questions as you read the story. (This is another way we help these children prepare to gather with the congregation and be ready to learn from a sermon.
4-5 year olds OR 2-5 year olds as one class	**GENERAL OBSERVATIONS:** **4-5 year olds:** The concepts of the curriculum are still very good for this age group, but three years repeating it (if you use it with 2's and 3's, too) is a bit much. I would move on to Deep Down Detectives, if I was using Hide 'n' Seek Kids already with 2's and 3's. However, if this curriculum is being introduced with this age group, it will be great for them. **2-5 year olds as one class:** You are combining children with fairly different developmental abilities. While one teacher is teaching, the other teacher may need to be quietly tending to the 2 year olds as their attention span fades. **NUMBER OF LESSONS OF A UNIT USED:** These older children will do best with 2-3 lessons of the five included with each unit. You will probably bore them if you repeat beyond this point. We do two concepts per month of Sundays. That 2 lessons from one unit, then 2 lessons from the next unit. Or, in months with five Sundays, you would choose to do 2 lessons from one unit and 3 lessons from the next. **You will complete the curriculum in 8 months at this rate.** **HOW TO USE THE CURRICULUM:** As written. Definitely introduce the longer, full Big Question Songs, not just the short nursery songs with these groups. And, for those who have combined 2-5 year olds, having the children do the suggested actions that go with the full, Big Question Songs can be a great chance for the little 2-year-olds to get some wiggles out.

Common Customizations: Age Groups

CUSTOMIZE BY: Age Group	
pre-K & K	**GENERAL OBSERVATIONS:** The concepts of the curriculum are still very good for this age group, if you are not using it with younger classes, too. I would move on to Deep Down Detectives, if I was using Hide 'n' Seek Kids with the younger children. However, if this curriculum is being introduced with this age group, it will be great for them. **NUMBER OF LESSONS OF A UNIT USED:** These older children will do best with 2-3 lessons of the five included with each unit. You will probably bore them if you repeat beyond this point. We do two concepts per month of Sundays. That means 2 lessons from one unit, then 2 lessons from the next unit. Or, in months with five Sundays, you would choose to do 2 lessons from one unit and 3 lessons from the next. You will complete the curriculum in 8 months. **HOW TO USE THE CURRICULUM:** As written. Definitely introduce the longer, full Big Question Songs, not just the short nursery songs with this group.
K-2nd grade	**GENERAL OBSERVATIONS:** The concepts of the curriculum can still very good for this age group, but you are bumping up against its outer limits. I would move on to Deep Down Detectives, if I was using Hide 'n' Seek Kids with the preschoolers. However, if this curriculum is being introduced with this age group, it will be great for them. **NUMBER OF LESSONS OF A UNIT USED:** These older children will do best with 1 to 2 lessons of the five included with each unit. You will probably bore them if you repeat beyond this point. **HOW TO USE THE CURRICULUM:** Definitely introduce the longer, full Big Question Songs, not just the short nursery songs with this group. I would either do: two, full lessons per unit; OR, I would do one full lesson per unit, then use the Opening Activity time of the next session to review the previous session's concepts by playing the Bible Story game/ Bible Verse Review Game/singing the songs). I would then introduce the next unit's concepts in Opening Circle Time.

Common Customizations: Teaching Situations

CUSTOMIZE BY: Teaching Situation	How to Structure the Curriculum
Single Session One, 60-90 minute session on a lesson, in one day, once a week examples: Sunday School, Church Hour, Mid-week programs	As written. If you do not really have 60 minutes of actual teaching time, you will need to choose what not to use. Choose what you think is most important to have in your session, then continue to add in elements until you have filled up your time budget.
Double Session Two 60-90 minute sessions, on the same lesson, in one day, once a week examples: Sunday School PLUS Church Hour OR, Sunday Morning PLUS Sunday Evening OR, Sunday Morning PLUS Wednesday Evening	*(This is how we use the curriculum here at CHBC)* **First session of the Double:** • Use Opening Activity • Opening Circle Time • And choose an activity • Fill in extra time with free play activities snack and potty break **Second session of the Double:** • Review Opening Circle Time • Choose another activity • Fill in extra time with free play activities
Daycare/Schools Bible Class	Schools vary in how many days they teach Bible. Some will have a daily Bible class. Others, will have it only certain days. Here's a suggestion for one unit a month, 5 days a week Bible class for preschoolers: Typically, each session you will be: • Reminding the children of the Big Question and Bible verse; • Telling them the Bible story (or asking them questions to review it); • Singing the songs; and, • Following up with a response activity. There are five lessons in each unit, with a listening assignment for each lesson. each with a coloring page, and three games; plus, three extra crafts. • That makes 20 activities, plus the three extra crafts. Plenty for even a month of Bible classes for little preschoolers. • You could read the story on the first day of each of the four/five weeks in a month using a different listening activity each time. • The coloring sheet corresponds to the listening activity. Give them that activity on the Monday. • Then, the other four days of the week, use the games to review what they have learned. With 16 units, this gives you 16 months (or two academic years) of curriculum.
Camps, VBS and Short-term Missions Trips	Since camps, VBS and mission trips usually involve both preschoolers and elementary school children, you will do best use two or three of the Praise Factory family of curriculum to meet everyone's needs. At the end of this introduction section (starting on page 32), we provide suggested schedules for these ministry situations. We also have included how the Bible Truths across all three curriculums line up so you can coordinate the truths you are teaching across all of the age groups/curriculums.

Maiden Voyage: Testing Out the Curriculum

Making a Test Run	At last it's time to try out the curriculum on your kids. As mentioned before, our favorite way to try out a new curriculum is with a smaller group of children (of the more-likely-to-be-well-behaved variety), when there is an opportunity to do so. This gives the curriculum its best test-run. Ideally, you want to give any curriculum a few sessions trial period. New curriculum is new curriculum. Teachers will be getting used to it as will the kids. You may choose to dive in the deep end and introduce the whole curriculum to the children at once. As you introduce the curriculum to your children, also remember that everything will be new to them at first. New ideas and structures use up a lot more attention and energy than when they are familiar and routine...and it takes time for them to become routine. Be patient! Expect this! Or, you may take the gradual approach, deciding on lesson elements to introduce gradually, then adding more in as you go. Think about the routine the children are used to in your classroom already. What works? What doesn't work? Slot Hide 'n' Seek Kids resources into the parts of your current framework that work best with your children, then gradually build from there. For example, you might want to start with just the Bible story and Bible verse the first lesson, adding other elements the second lesson, and so on. Also, realize that the children will be doing a lot more watching and a lot less direct participation at first as they are learning the routine. Give yourself and the children a few lessons to settle into the routine before deciding what is the right amount of activities to include each week. As the children get used to the lesson routine, you will find the children have more attention and energy to devote to the learning activities.
Evaluate and Adjust It	As you test-run the curriculum, you will probably want to evaluate and make changes. Reflect on how the teaching session goes, after each of your test runs and make any necessary changes. As you get closer to a good fit, add in more conditions like the typical classroom--such as your crazier kids, etc.. See how the curriculum works with these new elements. Make more changes until you feel good about your fit.

The Real Launch: Implementing the Curriculum in Your Situation

Sign Post It	Once you have figured out what works best for your children and those teaching the curriculum, put sign posts in place in the classroom. If you found that certain activities work better in a certain part of the room (such as games or craft time), put up a sign on the wall near that area indicating that. Or, put down a rug where you want to have Circle Time.
Choose and Train Your Load-Bearers	If the curriculum follows a set time schedule, display the schedule on the wall in large print so a teacher can with just a glance know what he/she should be doing. Signpost where you store your curriculum resources (games, curriculum, music, craft supplies, etc), too, so that even the newest teacher can easily find what he/she needs. Once you feel that you have adjusted the curriculum to a good fit for teacher and children, begin to train others in how to teach it, too. Ideally, this starts as a mentoring experience between you and another teacher (preferably two). You are looking for people who are willing to learn the curriculum inside-out until they can teach it well themselves and can later train others in it, too. I call these teachers, "load-bearers," because they will share the weight of implementing the new curriculum. First, have your load-bearers come observe you as you teach the curriculum. Have them read the introductory materials and the curriculum lesson plan before they observe. After class, de-brief with them about the session. Have them continue to come for a number of session, gradually handing over the teaching responsibilities until they are comfortable and confident.
Bring the Parents Up to Speed	Make sure to include parents in your launch! Communicate with them about the change in curriculum that is happening. Hold a meeting. Send out an email. Hand out the Hide 'n' Seek Kids flyer (pgs. 7-8, Core Curriculum books). Ask them to parents. Invite their feedback. Make them your partners, after all, it is them and their kids you hope to help.
Add Others	With your load-bearers in place and confident in the curriculum, you can now begin to look for more potential teachers to be trained. The load-bearers will then follow the same steps as you took with them: having them observe, then gradually take teaching responsibilities, de-briefing after each session. Continue until they are confident.
Want to See More?	Three times a year (the third Saturday/Sunday of March, May and September), we hold a free lunch, learn-and-look workshop and observation time here at Capitol Hill Baptist Church in Washington, D.C. On the Saturday, we gather for lunch and talk philosophy; child protection policy; encouraging parents; recruiting teachers; dealing with discipline issues; etc; and, of course, curriculum. After finishing up our group session, we are happy to talk to individual churches about their particular situations. Then, on Sunday, we offer an opportunity to see Hide 'n' Seek Kids and the other Praise Factory curriculum in action in our classes. This can be a great way to help others understand and get excited about the curriculum. The registration form for these workshops can be found on the Praise Factory website.

Protect Your Investment: Tips on Storing the Curriculum for Future Use

This is a curriculum that keeps on giving year after year. Everything is re-used. If you do a good job storing the curriculum, it will serve your church well and at little cost for many years.

Here are two ideas to help you:

Idea #1: If you are teaching only a small group of children:

Visual aids, (except for Storyboard Pics)

Lesson plan, story, and other paper resources you can re-use

CD's, Song Track Lists, Lyrics & Sheet Music

Bible Storyboard Pictures, Pictures Key, & Placement Guide

Crafts and Take Home Sheets (paper resources you will have to photo copy again)

Then, store all of these resources together in a magazine file

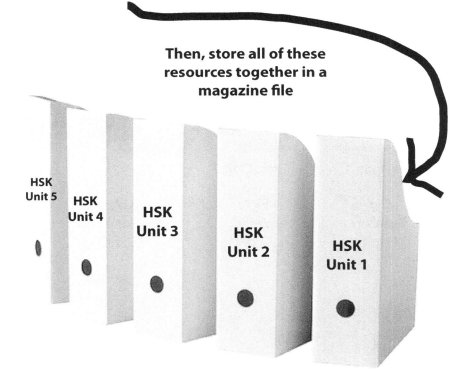

Protect Your Investment: Tips on Storing the Curriculum for Future Use

Idea #2: If you are teaching a large group of children (like we do at CHBC), you may want to have a separate envelope for each resource type.

Copies of
Unit Lesson Plan,
and Story
with Listening
Assignments

CD's,
Song Track Lists,
Lyrics &
Sheet Music

Bible Story
Storyboard
Pictures,
Pictures Key and
Placement Guide

Discussion Sheet

Visual aids,
(except for Bible
Storyboard Pics)

Craft/Take Home
Sheet 1

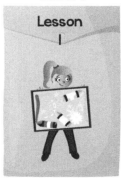

Craft/Take Home
Sheet 2

Craft/Take Home
Sheet 3

Craft/Take Home
Sheet 4

Craft/Take Home
Sheet 5

Extra Craft 1

Extra Craft 2

Extra Craft 3

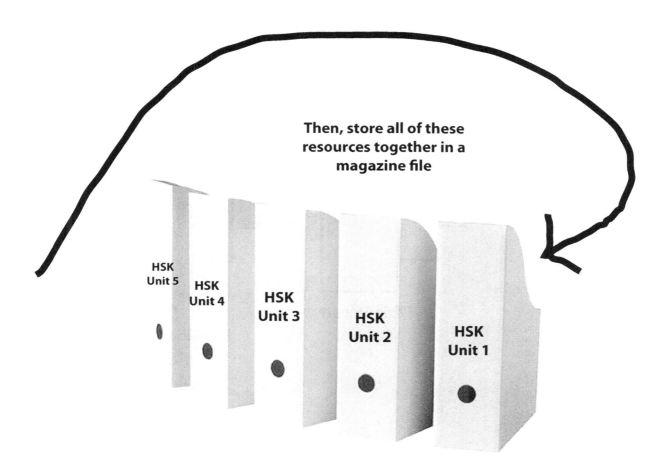

Then, store all of these resources together in a magazine file

Protect Your Investment: Tips on Storing the Curriculum for Future Use

Store your games in separate ziploc bags and put them in bins.

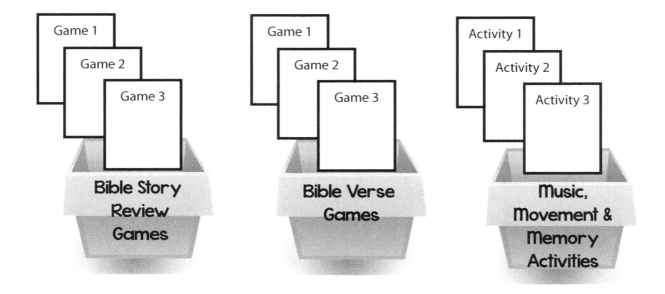

Master Supplies List for all Hide 'n' Seek Kids Games

Hide 'n' Seek Kids uses many games. The good news is, they are simply made and they are re-used throughout the whole curriculum. Make sure you save the games you make and it will save you a lot of time later.

This is the full list of the games and the supplies needed in the Hide 'n' Seek Kids Curriculum. While you only need to make whatever games you choose to use with each lesson, **I strongly recommend that you make all the games before you start using the curriculum.** Get the prep work over with at the beginning and coast your way through years of enjoyment! Store them in ziploc bags or baskets and pull them out when needed. So simple!

Bible Verse Games

Lily Pad Jump
- Cube-shaped cardboard box,
- paper,
- glue,
- marker

Animal Cube
- Cube-shaped cardboard box,
- paper,
- glue,
- marker

Simon Says How
- Cube-shaped Cardboard box
- Paper, glue, and a marker

Bean Bag Catch
- 1 bean bag per every 2 children (or every child)
- NOTE: Can also fill socks with beans and tie open end to make beanbags.

Slap, Clap and Stack
- 10 or 12 Blocks or other stackable objects

Freeze 'n' Say
- Music and CD/Tape player

Fill 'er Up
- 1 bean bag per child
- NOTE: Can also fill socks with beans and tie open end to make beanbags.
- Cardboard box or laundry basket
- Carpet squares, 1 per child

Bible Verse Games

Loud and Soft, Big and Little
- none

Roll 'n' Toss
- Cube-shaped Cardboard box
- Paper, glue, and a marker
- 1 bouncy ball per 2 children

Duck, Duck, Goose
- none

Detective Mission Madness Practice
- Detective Gear, such as a trench coat, sunglasses, and a hat

Master Supplies List for all Hide 'n' Seek Kids Games, continued

Music, Movement & Memory

Thumping Drums
- 1 Oatmeal container/coffee can with lid per drum
- Tape
- Popcorn, rice, beans, etc.
- Wooden spoons, dowels, unsharpened pencils, if desired, for mallets

Say, Spring Up and Shout
- Bean bags, one per child

Freeze Frame
- Some kind of fun hat or clothing for the leader to wear

Egg Shakers
- Empty Easter eggs
- Rice, beans, buttons, pennies, popcorn, beads, small nails or bolts, etc.
- Glue and glue gun OR strong packing tape

Jingle Bell Hands
- 1 6" piece of sturdy string
- 4 or 5 jingle bells, available in most craft shops

Big Voice, Little Voice
- none

Music, Movement & Memory
- 1 oatmeal container/coffee can with lid per drum
- Tape
- Popcorn, rice, beans, etc.
- Wooden spoons, dowels, unsharpened pencils, if desired, for mallets

Bottle Shakers
- 1 empty 16 oz. soda bottle per shaker
- Rice, beans, buttons, pennies, popcorn, beads, small nails or bolts, etc.
- Glue and glue gun OR strong packing tape

Clap, Tap and Say
- none

Music, Movement & Memory

March 'n' Say
- Optional: A fun hat for the leader of the march, or for everyone in the march

Block Clappers
- 2 wooden blocks per child, preferably about 3"x 2", as found in many children's block sets

Master Supplies List for all Hide 'n' Seek Kids Games, continued

Story Review Games

Who's Inside?
- 10 different containers with lids

Look Who's Coming Down the Tracks
- Two shoe boxes
- 6' or so of rope
- Optional: Engineer's hat

Going Fishing
- One long wooden dowel, yardstick, etc. per fishing pole
- Yarn
- Paper clip per fishing pole
- Rope
- Two chairs
- Blanket
- Box/bucket/container
- Bucket

Pony Express
- Small manila envelopes, one per storyboard picture
- Kid's small backpack or a tote bag with a strap
- Basket
- Cowboy hat
- Stick horse or a broom

Clothespin Line Up and Drop
- Rope
- Clothespins, the hinged type
- Shoe box
- Tape

Missing in Action
- None

Hide 'n' Seek Kids Detective Clue Hunt
- Variety of interesting items that have one or more places to hide a storyboard picture
- Detective Hat
- 4 False Clues (included on the next page)
- CD Player and Hide 'n' Seek Kids Theme Song

Take Me Through the Tunnel
- Chairs or Table
- Sheet or blanket
- Box

Story Review Games

Who's in the Basket?
- Blanket
- Basket

Run to the Grocery Store
- Grocery bag or kid's grocery cart
- Empty food cartons

Treasure Hunt
- 10 small lidded plastic containers or boxes (like from a jewelry store) or wooden, hinged boxes from a craft store
- Various decorating supplies, such as fake craft jewels, glitter, glitter glue, foil paper, gold spray paint
- glue

VBS, Camps and other Programs

Programs like camps, VBS and short-term missions Children's Ministry usually involve such a wide, age-range of children that it's best to use two or three curriculums, instead of just one, to meet everyone's learning level. This is easy to do with the Praise Factory family of curriculum, since you are using the same, sixteen Big Question Units in all three curriculums.

There are so many ways to do these programs. Here are the most common ones I've heard of:
- One, half day
- One, full day
- One evening
- Friday Night-Saturday
- Five, half days
- Five, full days
- Five evenings in a row
- Five one-day evenings (such as five Wednesday nights in a row)
- Two, five-day weeks in a row

Although these programs take place at many different times, they typically run one of three, standard lengths of time:
- 1 1/2 hour programs
- 2 1/2 hour programs
- 6 hour programs

Here are session suggestions for each of these three lengths of programs:

 NOTE: I have put some place holder times in schedules. You change them to your actual times.

1 1/2 Hour Multi- Age Programs

1 1/2 Hour Program (for 2 year olds):
- 9:00   Free Play/Activity Centers
- 9:15   Opening Circle Time (Singing, Big Question, Bible Verse and Bible Story)
- 9:30   Free Play/Activity Centers
- 9:45   Activities: Game, Craft and/or Music
- 10:20 Closing Circle Time
- 10:30 Dismissal

1 1/2 Hour Program (for ages 3-5):
Hide 'n' Seek Kids or Deep Down Detectives Session, as written

1 1/2 Hour Program (for elementary age kids):
Praise Factory Investigators Session, as written

VBS, Camps and other Programs: 1 1/2 Hour Schedule

1 1/2 Hour Program (for 2 year olds): (Hide 'n' Seek Kids or Deep Down Detectives)
- (9:15 – Early Arriver Activity – a few puzzles or paper and crayons on a table)
- 9:30 – Activity Centers
- 9:40 – Clean Up Toys
- 9:45 – Opening Circle Time (Add actions to songs to make this time more active)
- 10:05 – Craft Time (Use one of the Extra Crafts)
- 10:15 – Play with Toys /Check Diapers/Potty Break
- 10:25 – Clean Up Toys
- 10:30 – Memory Verse Time: Music, Movement & Memory; Bible Verse Review Game
- 10:40 – Snack Time
- 10:50 – Closing Time/Take Home Sheet/Coloring Time (Ask them the Closing Time questions as they are coloring at the tables)
- 11:00 – Parents come

1 1/2 Hour Program (for 3-preK 5 year olds): (Hide 'n' Seek Kids or Deep Down Detectives)
- (9:15 – Early Arriver Activity – a few puzzles or paper and crayons on a table)
- 9:30 – Activity Centers
- 9:40 – Clean Up Toys
- 9:45 – Opening Circle Time (Add actions to songs to make this time more active)
- 10:05 – Craft Time (Use one of the Extra Crafts)
- 10:15 – Play with Toys /Check Diapers/Potty Break
- 10:25 – Clean Up Toys
- 10:30 – Memory Verse Time: Music, Movement & Memory; Bible Verse Review Game
- 10:40 – Snack Time
- 10:50 – Closing Time/Take Home Sheet/Coloring Time (Ask them the Closing Time questions as they are coloring at the tables)
- 11:00 – Parents come

1 1/2 Hour Program--elementary school (Praise Factory Investigators)
- 9:00 Opening Large Group Time: Welcome, Singing
- 9:15 Opening Large Group Time: Big Question, Bible Truth, Bible Verse and Bible Story
- 9:45 Small Group Activities (Discussion and Games/Music/Craft Activities) If desired, each small group can prepare their activity for Small Group Presentations in Closing Large Group.
- 10:15 Closing Large Group Time: Small Group Presentations and/or Singing
- 10:30 Dismissal

VBS, Camps and other Programs: 2 1/2 Hour Schedule

2 1/2 Hour Program (for 2 year olds): (Hide 'n' Seek Kids or Deep Down Detectives)
- (8:45 Early Arriver Activity – a few puzzles or paper and crayons on a table)
- 9:00 Activity Centers (first set)
- 9:10 Clean Up Toys
- 9:15 Opening Circle Time (Add actions to songs to make this time more active)
- 9:25 Activity Centers (first set)
- 9:35 Craft Time (Use one of the Extra Crafts)
- 9:45 Play with Toys /Check Diapers/Potty Break 2
- 9:55 Clean Up Toys
- 10:00 Snack Time
- 10:10 Memory Verse Time: Music, Movement & Memory; Bible Verse Review Game
- 10:20 Activity Centers (second set)
- 10:30 Clean Up Toys
- 10:45 Craft Time (one of the extra crafts)
- 10:55 Play with Toys /Check Diapers/Potty Break 2
- 11:00 Clean up Toys
- 11:05 Active Indoor/Outdoor Play
- 11:25 Closing Time Circle Time
- 11:15 Coloring Time/Take Home Sheet
- 11:30 Parents come

2 1/2 Hour Program (for 3-preK 5 year olds): (Hide 'n' Seek Kids or Deep Down Detectives)
- (8:45 Early Arriver Activity – a few puzzles or paper and crayons on a table)
- 9:00 Activity Centers (first set)
- 9:15 Clean Up Toys
- 9:20 Opening Circle Time (Add actions to songs to make this time more active)
- 9:40 Craft Time (Use one of the Extra Crafts)
- 9:55 Activity Centers (first set)
- 10:10 Clean Up Toys
- 10:15 Potty Break/Wash Hands
- 10:25 Snack Time
- 10:35 Active Indoor/Outdoor Play OR Activity Centers (second set)
- 10:50 Clean Up Toys
- 10:55 Memory Verse Time: Music, Movement & Memory; Bible Verse Review Game
- 11:10 Closing Time Circle Time
- 11:20 Coloring Time/Take Home Sheet
- 11:30 Parents come

2 1/2 Hour Program--elementary school (Praise Factory Investigators)
- 9:00 Opening Large Group Time: Welcome, Singing
- 9:15 Opening Large Group Time: Big Question, Bible Truth, Bible Verse and Bible Story
- 9:45 Small Group Activity 1: Discussion and Craft Activity
- 10:15 Active Outdoor/Indoor Play
- 10:30 Snack (Story-related snack) ACTS and Discussion Time (related to activity they are about to do 10:45 Small Group Activity 2: (Prepare this one for presentation to the rest of the children during Closing Large Group Time, if desired)
- 11:15: Closing Large Group Time: Small Group Presentations and/or Singing
- 11:30 Dismissal

VBS, Camps and other Programs: 6 Hour Schedule

6 Hour (Full Day) Program (for 3-preK 5 year olds): (Hide 'n' Seek Kids or Deep Down Detectives)
Use one Bible Truth and Bible story for the whole day's session. Afternoon provides an opportunity for reinforcement.

Morning Schedule

- 8:45 Early Arriver Activity – a few puzzles or paper and crayons on a table)
- 9:00 Activity Centers (first set)
- 9:15 Clean Up Toys
- 9:20 Opening Circle Time (Add actions to songs to make this time more active)
- 9:50 Active Indoor/Outdoor Play (Playground or organized games)
- 10:30 Potty Break/Wash Hands/Snack Time
- 10:45 Music, Movement & Memory Game and Singing
- 11:00 Craft Time (Use one of the Extra Crafts)
- 11:30 Activity Centers (second set)
- 12:00 - 1:00 Lunch and Play Time/Rest Time

Afternoon Schedule

- 1: 00 Bible Story Review & Bible Verse Review (repeat story and storyboard or use games to review)
- 1: 20 Craft Time (Use one of the take home sheet coloring activities of the Extra Crafts)
- 1:40 Activity Centers (second set)
- 2:00 Snack and Potty Break
- 2:30 Closing Circle Time Review/Singing
- 2:40 Free play, games, possibility outdoors
- 3:00 Dismissal

6 Hour (Full Day) Program--elementary school (Praise Factory Investigators)
Use two stories from same Bible Truth: one in the morning, one in the afternoon.

- 8:45 Greet children and parents as they arrive
- 9:00 Small Group Time: Introduce Big Question, Bible Truth, Bible Verse, etc.
- 9:15 Large Group Singing and Bible Story
- 9:45 Small Group Activity 1: Bible Truth Game
- 10:15 Small Group Activity 2: Craft
- 10:45 Snack and ACTS Prayer Time
- 11:00 Outdoor Fun - Active Game 1
- 12:00 Lunch and Free Play Time

Afternoon Schedule

- 1:00 Large Group Singing and Second Story (Other Bible Story or Story of the Saints)
- 1:30 Small Group Activity 1: Presentation Activity (Choose a different activity for each small group to work on during this time. They will present it to the rest of the children at the end of the session, if desired.)
- 2:15 Snack Time
- 2:30 Closing Large Group Time: Small Group Presentations and/or Singing
- 3:00 Dismissal

VBS, Camps and other Programs: Choosing Curriculum

You've figured out how many sessions your program will run and how long each session will last. Next, you need to figure out whichcurriculum you want to use. We suggest using Hide 'n' Seek Kids and/or Deep Down Detectives with your pre-schoolers and Praise Factory Investigators for your elementary school kids.

Find a unit you want to become the theme of your VBS. Choose the Bible Truths you want to teach. The charts of the following pages should help you see how the Bible Truths match up in the three curriculums. You've got tons of resources within each concept to fill up your schedule.

Here's a reminder of what you have in each:

Each Hide 'n' Seek Kids unit has:
* There is just one Bible Story and one Bible verse per unit.
* There are 5 lessons of curriculum in each unit.
* There is tons of music.
* The activities in each of the 5 lessons include:
    1 Bible Story Review Game
    1 Bible Verse Game
    1 Music, Movement & Memory Activity (especially good for Bible Memory)
    1 Coloring Sheet/Take Home Sheet
    There are also 3 extra crafts

Each Deep Down Detective unit has:
* There are multiple Bible truths within each unit.
* There are three lessons of curriculum, per Bible Truth, within each unit.
* There is one Bible story for each Bible Truth.
* There are 3 lessons of curriculum for each Bible Truth.
* There is tons of music
* The activities in each of the 3 lessons include:
    1 Bible Story Review Game
    1 Bible Verse Game
    1 Music, Movement & Memory Activity (especially good for Bible Memory)
    1 Coloring Sheet/Take Home Sheet
    There are also 3 extra crafts

Each Praise Factory Investigators unit has:
* Multiple Bible truths within it.
* There are three lessons of curriculum, per Bible Truth
* There are 3 stories for each Bible Truth: 1 Old Testament, 1 New Testament, and one Church History/missions.
* There are 3 lessons of curriculum for each Bible Truth--one for each of the three stories.
* There is tons of music.
* Each of the 3 lessons includes:
    1 Bible Story Review Game with Discussion Questions
    1 Bible Verse Game with Discussion Questions
    1 Bible Truth Game with Discussion Questions
    1 Craft with Discussion Questions
    1 Bible Verse Game with Discussion Questions
    1 Bible Verse Song with Discussion Questions, Sign Language and Song Game
    1 Hymn with Discussion Questions, Sign Language and Song Game
    1 Story-related Snack
    1 Take home sheet with the key concepts, the story and some discussion questions

Bible Truths that Match Up Across the Curriculums

Hide 'n' Seek Kids	Deep Down Detectives	Praise Factory Investigators
Unit 1: The God Who Reveals Himself Q: How Can I Know What God Is Like? A: He Shows Me What He's Like!	1. By the Heart He Gave Me to Know and Love Him	1. God Made Our Hearts to Know and Love Him
	2. In Everything I See All Around Me	2. God's Creations Tell Us about Him
	included in DDD Unit 1 Bible Truth 3, below	3. God Spoke to His People through Prophets Long Ago
	3. In the Bible, the Perfect Word of God	4. God Speaks through His Word, the Bible
	4. Through His Very Own Son, Jesus Christ	5. God Reveals Himself Most Completely through His Son, Jesus
Unit 2: God's Wonderful Word, the Bible Q: What's So Special about the Bible? A: It Alone Is God's Word!	1. God Made Sure It Was Written Down Just Right	1. God Inspired Many People to Write Down His Word Perfectly
	2. It Tells Us about God and His Plans	2. God's Word Tells God's Way and Plans for His People, Past, Present and Future
	3. God Uses It to Save His People	3. God Uses His Word to Save His People
	4. God Uses It to Change His People	4. God Uses His Word to Change His People
Unit 3: The Good News of God, the Gospel Q: What Is the Gospel? A: Salvation through Faith in Jesus Christ!	1. God Made Us and We Should Obey Him	1. God Is the Good Creator and King of the World
	2. We Have All Disobeyed God and Deserve His Punishment	2. All Have Rejected God and Deserve His Eternal Punishment
	3. God Sent Jesus to Pay for God's People's Sins	3. God Sent Jesus to Bear the Punishment for Sin
	4. God Saves All Who Repent of Their Sins and Trust in Jesus as Their Savior	4. God Saves Those Who Repent and Trust in Jesus
Unit 4: The God Like None Other Q: Can Anybody Tell Me What the LORD Is Like? A: He's Not Like Anyone Else!	1. He Is a Glorious Spirit	1. The LORD is a Glorious Spirit
	2. He Is the One, True God	2. The LORD is the Only True God
	3. He Is God the Father, Son and Holy Spirit: One God, But Three Persons	3. The LORD Is God the Father, Son and Holy Spirit: One God, But Three Persons
	4. He Is Everywhere, All the Time	4. The LORD Is Everywhere, All the Time
	5. He Knows Everything There Is to Know	5. The LORD Knows Everything There Is to Know
	6. He Is Perfectly Holy, Purely Good	6. The LORD is Holy
	7. He Can Do Anything He Wants to Do	7. The LORD is Omnipotent
	8. He Is Always Faithful, Through and Through	8. The LORD is Faithful
	included in DDD Unit 4 Bible Truth 2, above	9. The LORD's Names Tell Us About Him
Unit 5: God, the Good Creator Q: Can You Tell Me What God Made? A: God Made All Things Good!	1. He Made Everything Good in Heaven and Earth	1. God Created All Things Good in the Beginning
	2. God Made People in a Special Way	2. God Created People Good in the Beginning
	included in DDD Unit 5 Bible Truth 1, above	3. God Created the World to Praise and Glorify Him
	included in DDD Unit 5 Bible Truth 1, above	4. God's Plans For His Creation Are Good and Unfailing
Unit 6: God, the Just and Merciful Q: How Did Bad Things Come into God's Good World? A: Bad Things Came Through Sin!	1. When Adam and Eve Chose to Disobey God	1. Angels and People Rebelled against God in the Beginning
	included in DDD Unit 6 Bible Truth 1, above	2. God Treated the First Sinners with Justice and Mercy
	2. When It Spread to the Whole World	3. All People Are Born Sinful, All People Need God's Mercy
Unit 7: The Law-Giving God Q; What Are God's Laws Like? A: God's Laws Are Perfect!	1. They are Written in the Bible, God's Word	1. God's Laws Are Written in the Bible
	included in DDD Unit 7 Bible Truth 2, below	2. God Created Us Perfect Law Keepers, But We Are All Lawbreakers
	included in DDD Unit 7 Bible Truth 2, below	3. God Gave Us His Laws to Convict Us of Our Sin that We Might Be Saved
	2. They Show Us that We Need God to Save Us	4. Jesus Kept God's Law Perfectly to Save God's People by His Grace
	3. They Tell Us How to Love God and Others	5. The Heart of God's Law is Love

Bible Truths that Match Up Across the Curriculums

Hide 'n' Seek Kids	Deep Down Detectives	Praise Factory Investigators
Unit 8: The God Who Loves Q: What Is God's Love for His People Like? A: It's More than They Could Ever Deserve!	*included in DDD Unit 8, Bible Truth 1, below*	1. God Blesses All People with Many Good Gifts
	included in DDD Unit 8, Bible Truth 4, below	2. God Loved His People Before They Loved Him
	1. He Gave His Son, Jesus, to Save Them	3. God Showed the Depths of His Love by Giving His Son to Save His People
	2. He Always Takes Care of Them	4. God Loves His People by Caring for Their Needs
	3. He Uses Their Sadnesses for Good	5. God Uses Everything in His People's Lives for Their Good and His Glory
	4. He Will Never Stop Loving His People	6. God Will Never Stop Loving His People
Unit 9: Jesus Christ, Immanuel, God with Us Q: What Did Jesus Come to Do? A: Jesus Came to Bring Us to God!	1. He Left His Home in Heaven to Save Us	1. Jesus, the Servant King
	2. He Never, Ever Disobeyed God	2. Jesus, the Obedient Son
	3. He Taught about God and Did Amazing Things	3. Jesus, the Amazing Teacher
	included in DDD Unit Bible Truth 3, above	4. Jesus, the Ruler of All Creation
	included in DDD Unit 9, Bible Truth 5, above	5. Jesus, the Lord over Life and Death
	included in DDD Unit 9, Bible Truth 4, below	6. Jesus, the Forgiver of Sins
	included in DDD Unit 9, Bible Truth 2, above	7. Jesus, the Christ, the Son of the Living God
	included in DDD Unit 9, Bible Truth 1	8. Jesus, the Glory of God
	4. He Died on the Cross for God's People's Sins	9. Jesus, the Ransom for Sinners
	5. He Rose from the Dead	10. Jesus, the Conqueror of Death
	included in DDD Unit 9, Bible Truth 5, above	11. Jesus, the Firstborn of the Resurrection
	6. He Went Up to Rule in Heaven	12. Jesus, the Reigning Son in Heaven
Unit 10: The Holy Spirit: The Indwelling God Q: What Does the Holy Spirit Do in God's People? A: He Changes Their Hearts!	1. The Holy Spirit Lives in God's People	1. The Holy Spirit Lives in God's People
	2. The Holy Spirit Gives God's People Courage	2. The Holy Spirit Gives God's People Courage
	3. The Holy Spirit Gives God's People Wisdom	3. The Holy Spirit Gives God's People Wisdom
	4. The Holy Spirit Builds God's Church	4. The Holy Spirit Builds God's Church
Unit 11: The God Who Saves Q: How Can We Be Saved? A: It Is God's Free Gift!	1. When We Tell God Our Sins and Turn Away from Them	1. God Saves Sinners Who Confess Their Sins
	included in DDD Unit 11, Bible Truth 2, below	2. Jesus Is the Only Way to Be Saved
	2. When We Trust in Jesus As Our Own Savior	3. We Must Trust Jesus as Our Savior
	3. When the Holy Spirit Works in Our Hearts	4. The Holy Spirit Changes Our Hearts so We Can Be Saved
Unit 12: God's People Live for Him Q: How Should God's People Live? A: They Should Live Like Jesus!	1. By Asking God for His Help	1. God's People Grow to Be More Like Jesus
	2. By Loving Him Most of All	2. God's People Love Him with All Themselves
	3. By Loving Other People As God Has Loved Them	3. God's People Love Others
	4. By Trusting God and Being Happy With What He Wants	4. God's People Trust Him
	included in DDD Unit 12 Bible Truth 8, below	5. God's People Are Good Stewards of His Gifts
	included in DDD Unit 12 Bible Truth 5, below	6. God's People Obey Him
	included in DDD Unit 12 Bible Truth 5, below	7. God's People Do Good Works God Has Prepared for Them
	5. By Learning God's Word and Obeying It	8. God's People Read His Word, the Bible
	included in DDD Unit 12 Bible Truth 2, above	9. God's People Think about Him
	6. By Saying "No" to Disobeying God	10. God's People Say "No" to Temptation
	7. By Telling the Good News of Jesus	11. God's People Tell Others about Him
	included in DDD Unit 12 Bible Truth 4, above	12. God's People Suffer According to His Plan
	included in DDD Unit 12 Bible Truth 4, above	13. God's People Know Heaven Is Their Home
	8. By Making Much of God	14. God's People Delight in His Glory

Bible Truths that Match Up Across the Curriculums

Hide 'n' Seek Kids	Deep Down Detectives	Praise Factory Investigators
Unit 13: The Sustaining God Q: Why Do God's People Keep Believing in Him? A: It Is God's Sustaining Grace!	1. God, Alone, Sustains God's People	1. God, Alone, Sustains God's People
	2. God the Father Promises to Help God's People	2. God the Father Promises to Help God's People
	3. Jesus Provides God's People with Everything They Need	3. Jesus Provides God's People with Everything They Need
	4. The Holy Spirit Works in God's People	4. The Holy Spirit Works in God's People
	5. The Word of God Grows God's People	5. The Word of God Grows God's People
	6. God Uses His People to Strengthen and Comfort Each Other	6. God Uses His People to Strengthen and Comfort Each Other
Unit 14: The God Who Delights in Our Prayers Q: How Does God Want Us to Pray? A: Every Night and Day!	1. God Wants Us to Praise Him	1. God Delights in Our Adoration of Him
	2. God Wants Us to Confess Our Sins	2. God Delights in Our Humble Confession of Sin
	3. God Wants Us to Thank Him	3. God Delights in Our Thanksgiving to Him
	4. God Wants Us to Ask Him to Do Great Things	4. God Delights in Our Supplications to Him
	included in DDD Unit 14 Bible Truth 4, above	5. God Always Answers Prayers
	included in DDD Unit 14 Bible Truth 4, above	6. Jesus Is Why God Answers God's People's Prayers
Unit 15: God's People Gather Together Q: Why Do God's People Go to Church? A: To Worship God and Love One Another!	1. By Praising God for Jesus' Win over Death	1. God's People Gather Together for a Special, Weekly Worship Day
	included in DDD Unit 15 Bible Truth 2, below	2. God's People Are Led by Godly Leaders
	2. By Learning from God's Word, the Bible	3. God's People Gather to Hear God's Word
	included in DDD Unit 15 Bible Truth 3, below	4. God's People Are Called the Body of Christ
	3. By Caring for Each Other's Needs	5. God's People Love One Another with a Covenant Love
	included in DDD Unit 15 Bible Truth 3, above	6. God's People Gather to Give
	4. By Telling What God Has Done and Praying	7. God's People Gather for Fellowship
	included in DDD Unit 15 Bible Truth 4, above	8. God's People Invite Others to Gather with Them
	included in DDD Unit 15 Bible Truth 4, above	9. God's People Gather to Pray
	5. By Baptizing People Who Trust in and Live for Jesus	10. God's People Proclaim Their New Life in Christ through Baptism
	6. By Remembering Jesus Died to Save Them	11. God's People Celebrate Christ's Redeeming Sacrifice for Them
Unit 16: Jesus, the Returning King Q: What Will Happen When Jesus Comes Back? A: God Will Make Everything New!	1. Jesus Will Give Out Fair and Last Punishments for Sin	1. King Jesus Will Return to End the World
	included in DDD Unit 16 Bible Truth 1, above	2. King Jesus Will Return When God's Work on Earth is Done
	included in DDD Unit 16 Bible Truth 1, above	3. When King Jesus Returns, God's People Will Be Made Like Him
	included in DDD Unit 16 Bible Truth 1, above	4. King Jesus Will Return to Bring the Wicked to Just and Final Punishment
	included in DDD Unit 16 Bible Truth 1, above	5. King Jesus Will Return to Judge God's People, Too
	included in DDD Unit 16 Bible Truth 2, below	6. King Jesus Will Be United with His Bride, God's People, Forever
	2. God's People Will Live Happily with God Forever	7. King Jesus Will Reign Forever

Hide 'N' SEEK KIDS	DEEP DOWN DETECTIVES	PFI
Focus group: 2-3 year olds Adaptable use: 2-pre-K 5's	Focus group: 4-6 year olds Adaptable use: 3's -2nd grade	Focus group: K-5th grade Adaptable use: pre-K 5's to 6th grade
16 Big Questions/16 Bible truths	16 Big Questions/69 Bible truths	16 Big Questions/104 Bible truths
taught as 16 units consisting of a single truth per unit	taught as 16 units, consisting of 2-8 Bible truths per unit	taught as 16 units, consisting of 3-14 Bible truths per unit
1 Bible story per unit	1 Bible story per Bible truth (70 in all)	1 Old Testament story 1 New Testament story 1 Church History/Missions story per Bible truth (312 stories in all)
1 Bible verse per unit	1 Bible verse per Bible truth	1 Bible verse per Bible truth
5 lessons per unit same story, all 5 lessons can use 1-5 of the lessons	*3 lessons for each Bible truth same story, all 3 lessons can use 1-3 of the lessons	3 lessons for each Bible truth different story each of the 3 lessons can use 1-3 of the lessons (but will lose stories if you do)
16+ months of curriculum	4+ years of curriculum	6 years of curriculum
	*If desired, you can start out each of the 16 units of Deep Down Detectives with one session (or more) from Hide 'n' Seek Kids curriculum. This creates a nice introduction to the over-arching theme for each unit. It would also add 16 or more sessions to the curriculum.	

Hide 'n' Seek Kids

Unit 1
Curriculum:
The God Who
Reveals Himself

Session Prep (especially good for newbies!)

Pray! *NOTE: Most 2 & 3 year olds do best simply learning the Big Question & Answer, a simple version of the Bible story, and maybe the Bible Verse. Use other activities, as time and attention span allow. Your session prep need only include what you use.*

Pray for the Holy Spirit to be at work in your heart and the children's hearts.

Review

If new to the curriculum, look at the **Getting Started with Hide 'n' Seek Kids section of this book** (p.5) It will be especially helpful to read through the Hide 'n' Seek Kids section of **The Praise Factory Tour: Extended Version Book.** This is a visual way to understand what goes on in the classroom. (A pdf of the book is found in the samples section on the website.)

Look through and Learn the Lesson

Read over **lesson plan**. Practice any **songs or action rhymes** you are using. Choose/make up motions to go with these. Choose less with younger children and more with older preschoolers. **Practice the lesson with the visual aids** and using the Big Question Box/Briefcase.

Read and Rehearse the Bible Story with Pictures

Read the Bible story from the Bible. Read the curriculum version. Practice telling it with the storyboard pictures. (If you have not previously laminated the story pictures, do that now.) Or, rehearse it from the Simple Story Scenes, if you are using those.

Let There Be Music

Download the music and listen to the songs. Choose which of the songs you will use with the children. If using live musicians, make sure they have the sheet music (found in Appendix A).

Put the Props in Place

1. Prepare your Visual Aids. Put the Bible Verse, Listening Assignment, Bible Story in one side of the Bible folder. Keep out the Big Question sign.
2. Get out your storyboard. If using Simple Story Scenes, put these in your BIble Folder. Or, if using the individual storyboard figures, put all background pictures in place (they have a BG by the number). Put the rest of the storyboard pictures (these have a SB by the number) in order of use in the other side of the Bible folder.
3. Put the HSK Bible Folder as well as the Big Question sign in the Big Question Box/Briefcase and shut it. If your box/briefcase has locks and you want to use the unlocking the box as part of your session, lock it now....but make sure you have the key or know the code first.
4. Prepare the music CD or sheet music or mp3 device for use in your session.

Set Out Free Play Activities

Choose and set up free time activities you will use with the children. Choose a variety of different activities that will be enjoyed by different types of children. Rotate the activities you provide to keep them interesting and fresh to your children. (Suggestions in Appendix D, Core Curriculum books.)

Prepare Any Activities

Choose which (if any) of the unit games and crafts activities you want to use in the session. Bear in mind your time frame as well as the developmental abilities/attention span of your children as you decide what/how many to prepare. **Look over the Discussion Sheet** and choose a few questions you might use to spark discussion with the children as they do their activities (especially good for ages 3's+). Pray for God to give you opportunities to talk about these things with the children.

Let Them Take It with Them

Make copies of the craft/take home sheets, if you are not already using them as one of your activities. You may also want to make copies of the story (see take-home version of each story included in Appendix C with the other take home resources) to have for parents to use with their children at home. There's a link on each craft/take home sheet to the story, if you don't make hard copies.

Store It

After your session is over, collect the resources and store them for future use.
This curriculum can be used over and over for years to come.

Unit I Overview of Key Concepts

UNIT 1: The God Who Reveals Himself

Unit Big Question (and Answer): "How Can I Know What God Is Like? He Shows Me What He's Like!"

Meaning:

God made us. He wants us to know what He is like, so we can know Him, love Him, and praise Him.

God shows us what He is like by the heart He gave us to know and love Him; through all of His creations we see around us; through His Word, the Bible; and most of all, through His very own Son, Jesus Christ.

Unit 1 Bible Verse: Amos 4:13 ESV

"He who declares to man what is His thought...The LORD, the God of hosts, is His name."

Meaning:

God wants us to know what He is like, so we can know Him, love Him, and praise Him. We don't have to figure out what God is like by ourselves. God show us what He's like--He declares His thoughts to us.

God shows us what He's like through the spirit He put in our hearts; through His creations we see around us; through His Word, the Bible; and most of all, through His very own Son, Jesus Christ.

And what's the name of the one and only true, living God? It's the LORD! Yes, the LORD is His name!

Unit 1 ACTS Prayer

A We praise You, God. You show us what You are like!

C LORD, in our heart we know that You are God. We know we should obey You, but many times we don't want to. Please forgive us. We need a Savior!

T Thank You for wanting us to know You. Thank You for giving us a heart to know You; and, for making this world that shows us what You are like. Thank You for what we learn about You in Your Word, the Bible. And most of all, thank You for showing us what You are like in Your Son, Jesus.

S Work deep inside our hearts. Help us to turn away from our sins and trust in Jesus as our Savior. Help us to know You. Put in our hearts the special kind of happy that comes only from knowing You. Help us to go and tell others what we've learned. In Jesus' name we pray. Amen.

Unit 1 Story

The Case of the Old Man Who Looked for God
Luke 2:25-32

Songs Used in Unit 1   *listen to or download songs for free at https://praisefactory.org: Hide n Seek Kids Music page*

Big Q & A 1 Song
Big Question 1 Song
Big Question 1 Bible Verse Song: "The LORD Declares" Amos 4:13, ESV
Extra Bible Verse Song: "He Who Declares His Thought" Amos 4:13, ESV
Extra Bible Verse Song: "He Who Forms the Mountains" Amos 4:13, ESV
Extra Bible Verse Song: "For Behold" Amos 4:13, ESV
Extra Bible Verse Song: "Behold" Amos 4:13, ESV
Big Question 1 Hymn: Joyful, Joyful, We Adore Thee
Big Question 1 Praise Song: Oh! Oh! Oh! How Good is the Lord

Hide 'n' Seek Kids ESV Songs I Track Numbers

This is a listing of all songs mentioned in the unit curriculum. You may or may not choose to use all of the songs. They are listed in easy-reference order--NOT in the order used in the curriculum.

You may choose to simply burn a CD/load them onto an mp3 device in this order. Or, you may want to do what we do: choose the songs we want to use and create a play list of them in that order. Then, we burn a CD/upload the play list onto an mp3 device. A teacher only has to click forward to the next song, instead of hunting for the right track. The track number have been included as part of the title of each song, so teachers will still have a reference to the track number listed in the curriculum (same as those listed below), even if you change the order on your customized play list.

SONGS USED EVERY UNIT OF THE CURRICULUM
1 The Classroom Song v.1
2 The Classroom Song v.2
3 The Classroom Song v.3
4 The Classroom Song v.4
5 Hide 'n' Seek Kids Theme Song
6 The Classroom Rules Song
7 Let's Pray Song
8 The Big Question Box Song
9 The Bible Chant Song
10 ACTS Prayer Song (Short Version)
11 ACTS Prayer Song (Full Version)

> **Why the Extra Songs?**
> Hide 'n' Seek Kids is a curriculum used by children of different ages. Sometimes one of the other songs is a better fit for your kids. Or, you may simply want to teach them more songs on the same Bible Truth. Use as many or as few as you want.

UNIT 1: THE GOD WHO REVEALS HIMSELF
12 Big Q & A 1 Song
13 Big Question 1 Song: How Can I Know What God Is Like?
14,14T Big Question 1 Bible Verse Song: The LORD Declares   Amos 4:13, ESV
15 *Extra Big Question 1 Bible Verse Song: He Who Declares His Thought   Amos 4:13, ESV (different version)*
16 *Extra Big Question 1 Bible Verse Song: He Who Forms the Mountains Amos 4:13, ESV (different version)*
17 *Extra Big Question 1 Bible Verse Song: For Behold   Amos 4:23, ESV (different version)*
18 *Extra Big Question Bible Verse Song: Behold Amos 4:23, ESV (different version)*
19 Big Question 1 Hymn: Joyful, Joyful, We Adore Thee
20 Big Question 1 Praise Song: Oh, Oh, Oh, How Good Is the Lord!

T* Tidbit   Shortened version of the Bible Verse Song

listen to or download songs for free at https://praisefactory.org: Hide n Seek Kids Music page

Lesson Plan: Big Question I ⭐ = follow the stars for a short & simple lesson plan p.l

1. GETTING STARTED
NOTE: Most 2 & 3 year olds do best simply learning the Big Question & Answer, a simple version of the Bible story, and maybe the Bible Verse. Use other activities, as time and attention span allow.

Intake Activity Ideas

Choose one of these open-ended activities to include children as they join the class:

Free Play Time *suggestions in Appendix D*	⭐ (usually best for 2 year olds) Offer your own or some of the easy-to-make, free play activities suggested in Appendix D.

OR Sing-along Music Time
 	
 lyrics and sheet music, Appendix A
 	
 listen to or download songs for free at https:// praisefactory.org: Hide n Seek Kids Music page
	Music *from* Hide 'n' Seek Kids (HSK) ESV Songs 1:
	 Big Q & A 1 Song — *HSK ESV Songs 1, track 12*
	 Big Question 1 Song — *HSK ESV Songs 1, track 13*
	 Big Question 1 (Unit) Bible Verse Song:
	     The LORD Declares Amos 4:13, ESV — *HSK ESV Songs 1, track 14,14T*
	 Extra Big Question 1 (Unit) Bible Verse Song:
	     He Who Declares His Thought Amos 4:13, ESV — *HSK ESV Songs 1, track 15*
	 Extra Big Question 1 (Unit) Bible Verse Song:
	     He Who Forms the Mountains Amos 4:13, ESV (other version) — *HSK ESV Songs 1, track 16*
	 Extra Big Question 1 (Unit) Bible Verse Song:
	     Behold Amos 4:13, ESV (different version) — *HSK ESV Songs 1, track 17*
	 Extra Big Question 1 (Unit) Bible Verse Song:
	     Behold Amos 4:13, ESV (different version) — *HSK ESV Songs 1, track 18*
	 Big Question 1 Hymn:
	     Joyful, Joyful, We Adore Thee — *HSK ESV Songs 1, track 19*
	 Big Question 1 Praise Song:
	     Oh! Oh! Oh! How Good is the Lord — *HSK ESV Songs 1, track 20*
	 Add more fun to Sing-along Music TIme by adding a Music, Movement & Memory Activity. These activities are listed on p. 8 of this lesson plan with the Response Activities. Instructions found in Appendix B.

***OR* Bible Verse Memory Game** *instructions found in Appendix B*	Lesson 1 Game: Lily Pad Jump Lesson 2 Game: Animal Cube Lesson 3 Game: Simon Says How Lesson 4 Game: Bean Bag Catch Lesson 5 Game: Slap, Clap and Stack *These activities are also included on p.8 of this lesson plan with the Response Activities.*

2. OPENING CIRCLE TIME *(introduce the Bible Truth and tell the related Bible story)*

Gathering the Children *lyrics and sheet music, Appendix A*	*Sing verse 1 of The Classroom Song to gather the children for Circle Time.* **The Classroom Song, verse 1** — *HSK ESV Songs 1, track 1* Let's gather together to worship God, Let's gather together to worship God, Let's gather together to worship God, Come gather here with me!
Welcome to Hide 'n' Seek Kids!	⭐ "Welcome to Hide 'n' Seek Kids! We're so glad you've joined us! We're here to seek God and learn His Word and Hide it in our heart so that it will always be with us. And we're here to Hide His Word, the Bible, in our hearts. We ask big questions about God and dig deep down in the truths of God's Word to find them."

Lesson Plan: Big Question 1   use with all FIVE lessons   p.2

2. OPENING CIRCLE TIME, continued   ⭐ = short & simple lesson plan

Hide 'n' Seek Kids Theme Song *lyrics and sheet music, Appendix A*	"Let's sing our Hide 'n' Seek Kids theme song." ⭐**Hide 'n' Seek Kids Theme Song** *HSK ESV Songs 1, track 5* Come along, we're gonna Hide 'n' seek! Hide God's Word in our heart and Him, we'll seek, God loves to show us the truths of His Word, That we might know Him and live out what we've learned.
Classroom Rules Song *lyrics and sheet music, Appendix A*	There are two very important things that Hide 'n' Seek Kids do together: we worship God and we love one another. Our Classroom Rules Song reminds us how we should act. Let's sing it." **Classroom Rules Song** *HSK ESV Songs 1, track 6* Shh, be quiet while someone is talking, Raise your hand, if you have something to say, Don't touch your friend, sitting beside you, Obey your teachers, Be kind as you play. These are our classroom rules, These are our classroom rules, They help us worship God and love one another, These are our classroom rules.
Opening Prayer Time *lyrics and sheet music, Appendix A*	"Children, we need God's help to keep these rules. Let's ask Him to help us right now. Let's get ready and pray." **Let's Pray** *HSK ESV Songs 1, track 7* 1-2-3! Fold your hands, Bow your head, Close your eyes. Let's pray! *(repeat)* "Let's pray:" ⭐**Opening Prayer** Dear Lord, We're so glad to get to gather together to worship You! Please help us keep the classroom rules. Please help us to love You and learn about You today. In Jesus' name we pray. Amen.

| Lesson Plan: Big Question I | use with all FIVE lessons | p.3 |

2. OPENING CIRCLE TIME, continued    = *short & simple lesson plan*

Reveal the Big Question **Introduce the Big Question Box/Briefcase** *lyrics and sheet music, Appendix A*	"It's time to get down to business, Hide 'n' Seek kids! Let's see what our Big Question for today is. It's right inside our Big Question Box/ Briefcase." **The Big Question Box Song** *HSK ESV Songs 1, track 8* We've got a big box, All closed up and locked, Filled with the truths of God's Word. We've got a brief case, There's no time to waste, Come on, kids, let's open it up!
The Big Question under Investigation VISUAL take out AID of BQB *Big Question & Answer Sign, front side* *found in the HSK Volume 1 Visual Aids, ESV Book*	Ok, who would like to open it up for me and pull out the Big Question?" *Choose a child to open the box/briefcase, take out the Big Question and hand it to you, then hold up the Big Question sign for all the children to see, and say:* The Big Question we are investigating today is Big Question Number 1: **How Can I Know What God Is Like?** and the Answer is: **He Shows Me What He's Like!**
Big Question Meaning	God made us. He wants us to know what He is like, so we can know Him, love Him, and praise Him. God shows us what He is like by the heart He gave us to know and love Him; through all of His creations we see around us; through His Word, the Bible; and most of all, through His very own Son, Jesus Christ.
Big Question Songs **Big Q & A 1 Song** *lyrics and sheet music, Appendix A*	"Let's sing our Big Question Song: **Big Q & A 1 Song** *HSK ESV Songs 1, track 12* *(adapted version of "This Is the Way We Wash Our Clothes")* How can I know what God is like, God is like, God is like? How can I know what God is like? He shows me what He's like!

Lesson Plan: Big Question 1	use with all FIVE lessons	p.4

2. OPENING CIRCLE TIME, continued   ⭐ = short & simple lesson plan

Learning about the Big Question ⭐ *(use one or both)*

Repeat the Big Question and Answer again:
"How Can I Know What God Is Like? He Shows Me What He's Like!"

Say: "Hmmmm, I wonder what that means... Let's do our action rhyme (or sing our song) that explains it."

Then do the action rhyme or sing the song using any of the optional motions suggested, if desired.

Big Question Action Rhyme

Big Question 1 Action Rhyme

	(POSSIBLE ACTIONS)
My heart can know and love God,	*place hand over heart*
He made everything I see.	*cup hand over eye and look around*
Big, tall mountains, galloping horses,	*gallop in place*
Every bird and bee.	
God gave me the Bible to read,	*make open book with flat hands*
And hear of His mighty deeds!	*hold up flexed arm*
But best of all, best of all,	
He sent Jesus, His Son, to save me!	*point to self*

Big Question (Action Rhyme) Song

lyrics and sheet music, Appendix A

⭐ Big Question 1 (Action Rhyme) Song

HSK ESV Songs 1, track 13

	(POSSIBLE ACTIONS)
I have a very big question,	
a big question 'bout God,	
I have a very big question,	
It's Big Question Number One,	*hold up 1 finger*
I wanna know...	
Refrain:	
How can I know what God is like?	
How can I know what God is like?	
How can I know what God is like?	
He shows me what He's like!	
Verse 1:	
My heart can know and love God,	*place hand over heart*
He made everything I see.	*cup hand over eye and look around*
Big tall mountain, galloping horses,	*gallop in place*
Every little bird and bee. *Refrain*	
Verse 2:	
He gave us the Bible, His Word,	*make open book with flat hands*
To learn of His might deeds,	*hold up flexed arm*
But most of all, through Jesus, His Son,	
God shows Himself to me. *Refrain*	*point to self*

| **Lesson Plan: Big Question I** | use with all FIVE lessons | **p.5** |

2. OPENING CIRCLE TIME, continued = short & simple lesson plan

Learning the Bible Verse **The Bible Chant Song** *lyrics and sheet music, Appendix A*	⭐ "And how do I know this is true? God tells me so in His special book, the Bible." *Say or sing the Bible Chant Song.* **The Bible Chant Song** *HSK ESV Songs 1, track 9* The Bible, the Bible, Let's get out the Bible. Let's hear what God has to say. The Bible, the Bible, God's given us the Bible. It's His Word for us to learn and obey! Yay!
The Bible Verse in the HSK Bible Folder *HSK 1 Bible Verse-front side (in the HSK Bible folder)* VISUAL AID Place verse in take out HSK Bible Folder *found in the HSK Vol. 1 Visual Aids, ESV Book*	"Who would like to get our Bible folder out of the Big Question Briefcase for me?" *Choose a child to open the briefcase, take out the "Bible" folder and hand it to you. Remove the Bible Verse Picture from the "Bible" folder and hold it up for all the children to see, then say:* ⭐ **Amos 4:13, ESV** "He who declares to man what is His thought...The LORD, the God of hosts, is His name."
Bible Verse Meaning *HSK 1 Bible Verse-back side*	⭐ **What does that mean?** God wants us to know what He is like, so we can know Him, love Him, and praise Him. We don't have to figure out what God is like by ourselves. God show us what He's like-- He declares His thoughts to us. God shows us what He's like through the spirit He put in our hearts; through His creations we see around us; through His Word, the Bible; and most of all, through His very own Son, Jesus Christ. And what's the name of the one and only true, living God? It's the LORD! Yes, the LORD is His name!
Bible Verse Song *lyrics and sheet music, Appendix A*	"We've said our Bible verse, now let's sing it!" **The LORD Declares: Amos 4:13** *HSK ESV Songs 1, tracks 14, 14T* The LORD declares to man his thought, The LORD declares to man his thought, The LORD declares to man his thought, Amos Four, thirteen.	*You might also enjoy:* *He Who Declares His Thought, Amos 4:13, ESV* *HSK ESV Songs 1, track 15* *He Who Forms the Mountains, Amos 4:13, ESV* *HSK ESV Songs 1, track 16* *For Behold, Amos 4:13, ESV* *HSK ESV Songs 1, track 17* *Behold, Amos 4:13, ESV* *HSK ESV Songs 1, track 18* *lyrics and sheet music, Appendix A*

Lesson Plan: Big Question I	use with all FIVE lessons	p.6

2. OPENING CIRCLE TIME, continued   ⭐ = *short & simple lesson plan*

Getting into the Case	"Now it's time to do a bit more deep down investigating. Let's see what Detective Dan wants us to help him figure out. Would someone like to get it out for me?"
Listening Assignments *Place in* *take out* **HSK Bible Folder** **? ? Big Question Briefcase ?** *of BQB*	**NOTE: Listening assignments are most suitable for ages 3+. Skip straight to the Bible story (see bottom of this page), if working with 2 year olds.** "Let's open up our listening assignment and see what we are supposed to figure out today. *Choose a child to take out the Listening Assignment (from the HSK Bible Folder) and hand it to you. Read Detective Dan's letter to the children that includes the listening assignment. The listening assignments are summarized below:*
VISUAL AID **#3** *HSK Vol. 1 Visual Aids, ESV*	**Detective Dan's Lesson #1 Listening Assignment:** As you listen to the story, see if you can figure out: 1. Who was the old man who looked for God? 2. How did he find out what God was like?
VISUAL AID **#4** *HSK Vol. 1 Visual Aids, ESV*	**Detective Dan's Lesson #2 Listening Assignment:** Our Bible verse is Amos 4:13: "He who declares to man what is His thought...The LORD, the God of hosts, is His name." As you listen to the story, see if you can figure out: 1. Who did the LORD declare His thoughts to? 2. What book did the LORD use to declare His thoughts?
VISUAL AID **#5A,B,C** **Listening Assignment #3 includes the Assignment Sheet, plus 4 clue pictures** *HSK Vol. 1 Visual Aids, ESV*	**Detective Dan's Lesson #3 Listening Assignment:** I found four clues, but one of them is NOT in the story. They are: baby Jesus, a chair, God's Word (on a scroll, like in Bible times) and a heart. *Hold up each of the four pictures for the children to see as you identify them. Better yet, put them up on your flannelgraph board, off to one side.* I need to know: 1. Which three pictures belong in the story and which one does not? 2. What did God use three of these things to show Simeon?
VISUAL AID **#6** *HSK Vol. 1 Visual Aids, ESV*	**Detective Dan's Lesson #4 Listening Assignment:** As you listen to the story, see if you can figure out: 1. Who did Simeon want to know more and more? 2. What was something Simeon thanked God for?
VISUAL AID **#7** *HSK Vol. 1 Visual Aids, ESV*	**Detective Dan's Lesson #5 Listening Assignment:** As you listen to the story, see if you can figure out: 1. Why was Simeon so happy to see baby Jesus? 2. What did God send Jesus to do?
Tell the Bible Story *Place story & pics in* *take out* **HSK Bible Folder** **? ? Big Question Briefcase ?** *of BQB* *HSK Vol. 1 Visual Aids, ESV* **Bible Story included in this book, immediately after the Lesson Plan and with the Visual Aids**	⭐*Then say,* "Ok, Hide 'n' Seekers! Put on your best listening ears and see if you can find the answers to Detective Dan's questions. When I finish telling the story, we'll see what we come up with." ⭐ **Bible Story: The Case of the Old Man Who Looked for God** *Luke 2:25-32* *Read the Bible Truth story, putting up the storyboard pictures/Simple Story Scenes as you tell it. Then, have the children answer the listening assignment. Present the the gospel and lead in prayer.* **Answers to questions, the gospel and ACTS prayer are included with the story text.**

| **Lesson Plan: Big Question 1** | use with all FIVE lessons | **p.7** |

2. OPENING CIRCLE TIME, continued   *= short & simple lesson plan*

Story Response Song(s)	*As attention span and time allow, you might want to end with one of the following songs which also tie in with the unit. If desired, use the Music and Movement activity ideas while singing, listed with the Response Activities.*
Hymn *lyrics and sheet music, Appendix A*	**Joyful, Joyful We Adore Thee, part of vs.1,2** *HSK ESV Songs 1, track 19* **Verse 1** Joyful, joyful, we adore Thee, God of glory, Lord of love, Hearts unfold like flowers before Thee, Opening to the sun above. **Verse 2** All Thy works with joy surround Thee, Heaven an earth reflect Thy rays, Stars and angels sing around Thee, Center of unbroken praise. **Tie-in:** "Children, the Lord shows us what He is like. He opens our hearts and let's us see how wonderful He is. He fills us with joy and we want to adore Him. Let's adore God right now!"
Praise Song *lyrics and sheet music, Appendix A*	**Praise Song: Oh! Oh! Oh! How Good Is the Lord** *HSK ESV Songs 1, track 20* **Verse 1** Oh! Oh! Oh! How good is the Lord, Oh! Oh! Oh! How good is the Lord, Oh! Oh! Oh! How good is the Lord, I never will forget what He has done for me. **Verse 2** He shows Himself to me, How good is the Lord, He shows Himself to me, How good is the Lord, He shows Himself to me, How good is the Lord, I never will forget what He has done for me. **Tie-in:** "Children, How good the Lord is to show us what He's like! We would never know if He didn't show us. Let's praise Him right now!"

3. TAKING ACTION: Response Activities *(choose from among these activities)*

Transition to Activities	⭐Well, Hide 'n' Seek Kids, you've done a great job diggin' deep down for answers in the truths of God's Word. Now it's time to enjoy some activities." ⭐*Tell children what activity/s you are providing for them: either free play or some of the response activities listed below. When you are ready to dismiss them, use this song to help the children transition in an orderly fashion to their next activity.*
Classroom Song, verse 2 *lyrics and sheet music, Appendix A*	"Children, let's sing our Time to Play Song. When we are finished you may get up and walk over to our next activity." **Classroom Song, verse 2** *HSK ESV Songs 1, track 2* We've gathered together to worship God, We've gathered together to worship God, And now it's time to play. *Dismiss the children to whatever activities you have prepared for them to do.*

Lesson Plan: Big Question I   use with all FIVE lessons   p.8

3. TAKING ACTION: Response Activities *(choose from among these activities)* ★ = *short & simple lesson plan*

Response Activities	Choose one or more activities appropriate for your children, based on classroom time and developmental needs. **Add the Discussion Sheet to any activity for deeper learning.** ★
Bible Verse Memory Game *game directions, Appendix B*	Though listed with the opening activities, you may choose to use this Bible verse game here instead (or as a repeat). • Lesson 1 Game: Lily Pad Jump • Lesson 2 Game: Animal Cube • Lesson 3 Game: Simon Says How • Lesson 4 Game: Bean Bag Catch • Lesson 5 Game: Slap, Clap and Stack *Use the Discussion Sheet with these activities for even deeper learning*
Music, Movement & Memory Activity *game directions, Appendix B*	A music activity that uses the songs from the Bible Truth and Big Question unit. • HSK Songs for Unit, plus: • Lesson 1 Activity: Thumping Drums • Lesson 2 Activity: Say, Spring Up and Shout • Lesson 3 Activity: Freeze Frame • Lesson 4 Activity: Egg Shakers • Lesson 5 Activity: Jingle Bell Hands *Use the Discussion Sheet with these activities for even deeper learning*
Bible Story Review Game *game directions, Appendix B*	A game that uses the storyboard pictures from the story to review the story. • Lesson 1 Game: Who's in the Basket? • Lesson 2 Game: Run to the Grocery Store • Lesson 3 Game: Treasure Hunt • Lesson 4 Game: Take Me through the Tunnel • Lesson 5 Game: Missing in Action *Use the Discussion Sheet with these activities for even deeper learning*
Coloring Pages/ Take Home Sheets *in Appendix C*	A coloring page related to the lesson assignment questions is provided for each lesson. On the back of each are the key concepts, a few questions and a song for parents to use with their children. (If desired, include a copy of the Bible story with the Take Home Sheet.) NOTE: Upgrade your coloring sheet to a more interesting craft by offering simple embellishments, such as jiggly eyes, craft sand, glitter, glitter glue, colored paper dots (made with a hole punch), fabric scraps, etc. Make cut-to-size glued-on clothes, hair, etc for characters by using a copy of the coloring sheet, cutting out the selected portions and making them the patterns for whatever you want to cut out of fabric, paper, foil, etc. ★ • Lesson 1 Coloring Sheet Emphasis: Bible Truth • Lesson 2 Coloring Sheet Emphasis: Bible Verse • Lesson 3 Coloring Sheet Emphasis: Bible Truth • Lesson 4 Coloring Sheet Emphasis: ACTS Prayer • Lesson 5 Coloring Sheet Emphasis: The Gospel *Use the Discussion Sheet with these activities for even deeper learning*
Extra Crafts: **Big Question Craft** *in Appendix C*	**These crafts are slightly more complex than the coloring sheets:** **The Big Question Craft** is a color, glue and stick craft of the Big Question and Answer. *Use the Discussion Sheet with these activities for even deeper learning*
Bible Verse Craft *in Appendix C*	**The Bible Verse Craft** is a craft that gives the Bible verse and explains it, also involving gluing and sticking and a few other, simple craft supplies.
Bible Story Puzzle *in Appendix C*	The **Storyboard Picture Placement Page** has been made into a puzzle that can be cut out and re-assembled by the children. This provides a nice summary of the story.
Free Play Activities *ideas in Appendix D*	★ Offer your own or some of the easy-to-make, free play activities suggested in Appendix D.

Lesson Plan: Big Question 1	use with all FIVE lessons	p.9

4. CLOSING CIRCLE TIME *(End-of-session activities for the last 5-10 minutes of class time)*   ★ *= short & simple lesson plan*

Transition to Closing Circle **Classroom Song, verse 3** *lyrics and sheet music, Appendix A*	*Use this song to help the children transition in an orderly fashion. Sing the song, then ask the children to gather with you for Closing Circle Time.* **Classroom Song, verse 3** *HSK ESV Songs 1, track 3* It's time to get ready to go and tell, It's time to get ready to go and tell, Come gather here with me.
Closing Circle Time **Classroom Song, verse 4** *lyrics and sheet music, Appendix A*	*When children are settled in the circle, say:* "It is almost time for your parents to come pick you up. And do you know what that means? It means…. (draw this out to build anticipation and excitement)…that it's almost time to go home and….it's almost time to…Go and Tell! We have learned some big news about God today. God wants us to take and tell it to the whole world!" **Classroom Song, verse 4** *HSK ESV Songs 1, track 4* So what's our big news to go and tell, So what's our big news to go and tell, Can you tell me now?
Big News to Tell **Big Question 1** *VISUAL AID* **#1** **found in the HSK Vol. 1 Visual Aids, ESV Book* *lyrics and sheet music, Appendix A*	"Let's see….there's so much big news to tell! There's so much we've learned! Can you tell me the answer to our **Big Question: "How can I know what God is like?"** *(Show them the Big Question and Answer picture.)* Say the answer with me: **"He shows me what He's like!"** *(If desired, you can sing the Big Q & A Song.)* *HSK ESV Songs 1, track 12*
Big Question 1 Bible Verse *VISUAL AID* **#2** **found in the HSK Vol. 1 Visual Aids, ESV Book* *lyrics and sheet music, Appendix A*	"And how do I know this is true? Can you tell me? Say it with me: **"The Bible tells me so!"** That's right! We learned: **Amos 4:13** **"He who declares to man what is His thought…The LORD, the God of hosts, is His name."** *(Show them the Bible Verse picture.)* The Bible tells us that God, Himself, shows us what He is like." *(If desired, you can sing the Bible verse song.)* *HSK ESV Songs 1, track 14,14T*

| Lesson Plan: Big Question I | use with all FIVE lessons | p.10 |

4. CLOSING CIRCLE TIME, continued   ⭐ = *short & simple lesson plan*

Closing ACTS Prayer Time	*Let's ask God to help us to remember this and even tell others this good news. Let's get ready and pray our ACTS prayer.*
ACTS Prayer Chant	*And what does ACTS mean? Let's sing/say our ACTS Prayer Chant!*
lyrics and sheet music, Appendix A	**ACTS Prayer Chant Song** *HSK ESV Songs 1, tracks 10,11* A, Adoration: God, we praise You! C, Confession: Forgive us our sins. That's the ACTS prayer, my friend, T, Thanksgiving,: Thank You for Jesus, Bow head, Close your eyes, Shhh, S, Supplication: Help us to live like Him. Let's begin!
Closing ACTS Prayer	"Let's pray!" *Lead the children in the ACTS prayer for this unit.* **A** We praise You, God. You show us what You are like! **C** LORD, in our heart we know that You are God. We know we should obey You, but many times we don't want to. Please forgive us. We need a Savior! **T** Thank You for wanting us to know You. Thank You for giving us a heart to know You; and, for making this world that shows us what You are like. Thank You for what we learn about You in Your Word, the Bible. And most of all, thank You for showing us what You are like in Your Son, Jesus. **S** Work deep inside our hearts. Help us to turn away from our sins and trust in Jesus as our Savior. Help us to know You. Put in our hearts the special kind of happy that comes only from knowing You. Help us to go and tell others what we've learned. In Jesus' name we pray. Amen.

5. TAKING IT HOME *(Take Home Sheet)*

Clean up and Dismissal	⭐"Now it's time to work together and clean up." *Have the children join you in cleaning up the room.*
Coloring Pages/ Take Home Sheets *in Appendix C*	⭐ *Give out the craft/take home sheet and any other papers from the session, as you dismiss children from class.* *(Reminder: The back side of the coloring page is the take home sheet for each lesson.)*
Bible Story to Take-Home *in Appendix C*	You may also want to include a copy of the story along with the take home sheet. (However, each coloring sheet/take home sheet includes a note to parents telling them where they can download the story from the Parent Resources section on the website.

Big Question I Bible Story   use with all FIVE lessons

Place story in **HSK Bible Folder**   *take out* **? ? Big Question Briefcase** *of BQB*   **p.1**

The Case of the Old Man Who Looked for God
Luke 2:25-32

Story-telling Tips

Ahead of time:
1. Read the Bible verses and story. Pray!
2. Choose story action cues and/or prepare storyboard pictures, if using. (Included in Visual Aids book)
3. Practice telling story with the pictures, timing your presentation. Shorten, if necessary to fit your allotted time.

During your presentation:
1. Maintain as much eye contact as possible as you tell the story.
2. Put up storyboard figures/add story action cues as you tell the story. Allow the children to help you put them on the board, if desired.
3. Include the children in your story with a few questions about what they think will happen or words/concepts that might be new to them.
4. Watch the kids for signs that their attention span has been reached. Shorten, if necessary.

INTRODUCTION/ LISTENING ASSIGNMENTS

"Our story is called: The Case of the Old Man Who Looked for God. Here is your listening assignment... "

Read from Detective Dan's Listening Assignment signs, but questions are summarized below:

Detective Dan's Lesson #1 Listening Assignment:

I need to find out:
1. Who was the old man who looked for God?
2. How did he find out what God was like?

Detective Dan's Lesson #2 Listening Assignment:

Our Bible verse is Amos 4:13: "He who declares to man what is His thought...The LORD, the God of hosts, is His name."

I need to find out:
1. Who did the LORD declare His thoughts to?
2. What book did the LORD use to declare His thoughts?

Detective Dan's Lesson #3 Listening Assignment:

I found four clues, but one of them is NOT in the story.
They are: baby Jesus, a chair, God's Word (on a scroll, like in Bible times) and a heart.
Hold up each of the four pictures for the children to see as you identify them. Better yet, put them up on your flannelgraph storyboard, off to one side.

I need to figure out:
1. Which three pictures belong in the story and which one does not?
2. What did God use three of these things to show Simeon?

Detective Dan's Lesson #4 Listening Assignment:

I need to find out:
1. Who did Simeon want to know more and more?
2. What was something Simeon thanked God for?

Detective Dan's Lesson #5 Listening Assignment:

I need to find out:
1. Why was Simeon so happy to see baby Jesus?
2. What did God send Jesus to do?

Read the questions, THEN SAY,

"Ok, Hide 'n' Seekers! Put on your best listening ears and see if you can find the answers to Detective Dan's questions. When I finish telling the story, we'll see what we come up with."

"The Case of the Old Man Who Looked for God"   Luke 2:25-32

Story with lines separating paragraphs (text in bold, optional interaction cues in italics)

Simeon was a very, very old man.

Have you seen a very old man? They often have gray hair and sometimes even have a long, grey beard. Simeon looked like that!

Simeon knew and loved God in his heart.

Can you point to where your heart is?

But oh, how Simeon wanted to know more about God and what He is like!

Simeon knew God created the whole world. He could learn more about God, as he looked at all that God had made. There was so much to see!

The big, tall mountains,

Can you stretch up your arms really high like a tall mountain?

the galloping horses,

When horses gallop they run really, really fast and make lots of noise with their feet. Can you stomp your feet like you were a galloping horse?

the flying birds,

Let's flap our arms like birds!

the buzzing bees.

What sound does a buzzing bee make?

Simeon could see how wonderful God was in all the things He had made. But oh, how Simeon wanted to know more about God and what He is like!

Simeon read the Bible, God's Word.

Where's our Bible? Have children point to your Bible.

He learned that God is good and great, loving and wise.

But oh, how Simeon wanted to know more about God and what He is like!

| Big Question I Bible Story | use with all FIVE lessons | p.3 |

*Story with lines separating paragraphs (**text in bold,** optional interaction cues in italics)*

Then one day, something very good happened to Simeon. God gave Simeon a wonderful promise: "I am sending My Son, Jesus, here to earth. He will show people what I am like, and will make the way for them to know and love Me. He will bring My forgiveness to everyone who trusts in Him as their Savior! They will know Me in their heart. Then one day, they will come to live happily with Me forever!" God promised. "And Simeon, you will get to see My Son, Jesus, at my Temple-Church before you die!" God told Simeon.

Simeon gathered with other people to worship God at a special place called the Temple. Where do we gather together to worship God? Why, it's right here! We're in it now! It's a church!

How excited Simeon was! Oh, how wonderful it would be to see God's very own Son!

Simeon went to God's Temple-Church.

Walk! Walk! Walk! Here goes Simeon to God's Temple-Church. Can you make a walking noise with your feet?

And who did Simeon see when he got there? Mary and Joseph. And who were they carrying? Baby Jesus, God's Son!

Pretend to hold a baby in your arms.

Simeon was very happy to see baby Jesus, God's Son, just as God had promised!

Yes, there was Jesus, just a little baby! But Jesus wouldn't stay a baby. He would grow up, up, up. He would tell everyone about God. He would show them what God is like. And, He would die on the cross to save God's people. They would be forgiven by God for disobeying Him! Yay!

Let's cheer really loud! Yay!

Then on Day One, Two, Three, Jesus would rise up from the dead, showing He had really done it! Yes, God's people were forgiven! Jesus had beaten sin and death for them! Yay!

Let's cheer really loud again! Yay!

One day, old Simeon died. Was that a sad day for Simeon? No, it was not!

Shake your head "no."

That was the day when God brought Simeon to live with Him in heaven. That's what made that day, Simeon's happiest day ever.

Now Simeon would really get to know how wonderful God is... more and more, forever and ever!

Simeon is so happy in heaven where he lives happily with God forever. Let's cheer really loud! Yay!

| Big Question I Bible Story | | |

Big Question I Bible Story	use with all FIVE lessons	p.4

Cracking the Case: (story wrap-up for Listening Assignments)

It's time to see how we did with our Listening Assignment.

Detective Dan's Lesson #1 Listening Assignment:
1. Who was the old man who looked for God?
Simeon.
2. How did he find out what God was like?
He knew God in his heart; he saw what God was like as he looked around him at the things God had made; he learned about Him in the Bible, God's Word; and most of all, he knew what God was like through His Son, Jesus.

For You and Me:
Like Simeon, we can know what God is like. God has given us a heart to know and love Him. We can look around us and see what He's like in the things He has made. We can learn about Him in the Bible; and, we can know what He's like most of all when we learn about Jesus. We can ask God to show us what He's like and help us to know and love Him. He delights to do this!

Detective Dan's Lesson #2 Listening Assignment:
Our Bible Verse is: Amos 4:13:
"He who declares to man what is His thought...The LORD, the God of hosts, is His name."

1. Who did the LORD declare His thoughts to?
Simeon.
2. What book did the LORD use to declare His thoughts? The Bible, God's Word.

For You and Me:
The LORD can show us what He's like, through the special hearts He gave us, as we look around at all the amazing things He has made. He can declare His thoughts to us as we read the Bible, His Word and learn about His Son, Jesus Ask God to show Himself to you! He delights to do this!

Detective Dan's Lesson #3 Listening Assignment:
I found four clues, but one of them is NOT in the story. They are: baby Jesus, a chair, God's Word (on a scroll, like in Bible times) and a heart.

I need to know:
1. Which three pictures belong in the story and which one does not? The chair does not belong.
2. What did God use three of these things to show Simeon? God used baby Jesus, the Bible and the heart He gave Simeon to show Simeon what He is like.

For You and Me:
The LORD wants to show us what He's like, too. He can use the heart He's given us, the Bible, and Jesus to show us what He's like, too.

Detective Dan's Lesson #4 Listening Assignment:
1. Who did Simeon want to know more and more about? God.
2. What was something Simeon thanked God for? Simeon thanked God for keeping His promise to let him see Jesus before he died. He was so happy to know that the time had come for God to save His people through Jesus.

For You and Me:
Like Simeon, we can thank God for sending Jesus to save sinners, like you and me.

Detective Dan's Lesson #5 Listening Assignment:
1. Why was Simeon so happy to see baby Jesus? He knew that the time had come for God to save God's people from their sins through Jesus.
2. What did God send Jesus to do? God sent Jesus to show us what He's like. And, to take the punishment for the sins of God's people so they could know God and be His people forever.

For You and Me:
God can show us what He's like through His Son, Jesus. Jesus can save us from our sins and make us God's people, too, when we repent of our sins and trust in Him as our Savior.

| Big Question I Bible Story | use with all FIVE lessons | p.5 |

The Gospel (story wrap-up if NOT using Listening Assignments)

Our Bible Truth is:
How Can I Know What God Is Like?
He Shows Me What He's Like!

God showed Simeon what He is like, and He can show us, too! We can ask Him to work in our heart and help us to turn away from disobeying Him and trust in Jesus as our Savior. When we do, God will forgive our sins and save us! He will live in our heart, helping us to know Him right now. He will satisfy our heart, giving us a special kind of happiness that comes only from knowing Him. And one day, we will go to live with Him in heaven forever. That will be best of all!

Close in prayer.

Closing Unit 1 ACTS Prayer

A=Adoration C=Confession T=Thanksgiving S=Supplication

A We praise You, God. You show us what You are like!

C LORD, in our heart we know that You are God. We know we should obey You, but many times we don't want to. Please forgive us. We need a Savior!

T Thank You for wanting us to know You. Thank You for giving us a heart to know You; and, for making this world that shows us what You are like. Thank You for what we learn about You in Your Word, the Bible. And most of all, thank You for showing us what You are like in Your Son, Jesus.

S Work deep inside our hearts. Help us to turn away from our sins and trust in Jesus as our Savior. Help us to know You. Put in our hearts the special kind of happy that comes only from knowing You. Help us to go and tell others what we've learned.

In Jesus' name we pray. Amen.

Return to page 7 of the Lesson Plan
for the script of the rest of this lesson.

| Big Question I Bible Story | | |

Unit I Discussion Sheet

use with all FIVE lessons

Use with all response activities for deeper learning

☆ P. I

Questions to aid discussion of the key concepts and for use in games

Be familiar with these questions and answers. Look for opportunities to ask questions and talk about their answers, such as while the children work on their coloring pages, as part of their games, or during play time. Remember: your goal isn't to ask all these questions or to only talk to the children about these things. It is to be deliberate in having good conversations with them, as natural opportunities arise.

BIG QUESTION	How Can I Know What God Is Like? He Shows Me What He's Like!
Meaning	God made us. He wants us to know what He is like, so we can know Him, love Him, and praise Him.
	God shows us what He is like by the heart He gave us to know and love Him; through all of His creations we see around us; through His Word, the Bible; and most of all, through His very own Son, Jesus Christ.
Discussion Questions	*choose a few*
	1. How can I know what God is like? *He shows me what He's like.*
	2. Who made us? *God did.*
	3. What does God want us to know? *What He is like.*
	4. Why does God want us to know Him? *So we can know Him, love Him, and praise Him.*
	5. What did God put inside us so we could know Him? *A heart.*
	6. Where can I look around me and learn more about God? *Everything around me that He made in this world.*
	7. What book did the Lord give us to tell us about Himself? *The Bible, His Word.*
	8. Who shows us what God is like most of all? *Jesus, God's Son.*
	9. Who can we ask to help us know what God is like? *God! He delights to help us!*
THE GOSPEL	What is God's good news for you and me? *The gospel!*
	God gave each of us a heart to know and love Him, too. But sadly, we all have chosen to turn away from God and live life our own way. This sin separates us from God. Only with God's help, we can know Him or be His people. But God sent His Son, Jesus, to make the way for people to know and love God once more. Jesus lived a perfect life, then He offered it as full payment for sins, when He suffered and died on the cross. On Day Three, He rose from the dead. He had beaten sin and death for God's people! God invites us to become His people, by turning away from our sins and trusting in Jesus as our Savior. If we do, His Holy Spirit will come live in our hearts, so we can know and love God now. And one day, go to live with God in heaven forever. That will be best of all!

Unit I Discussion Sheet

use with all FIVE lessons

Questions to aid discussion of the key concepts and for use in games

BIBLE VERSE	"He who declares to man what is His thought...The LORD, the God of hosts, is His name." Amos 4:13, ESV
Meaning	God wants us to know what He is like, so we can know Him, love Him, and praise Him. We don't have to figure out what God is like by ourselves. God show us what He's like--He declares His thoughts to us.
	God shows us what He's like through the spirit He put in our hearts; through His creations we see around us; through His Word, the Bible; and most of all, through His very own Son, Jesus Christ.
	And what's the name of the one and only true, living God? It's the LORD! Yes, the LORD is His name!
Discussion Questions	*choose a few*
	1. Why does God want us to know what He's like? *So we can know Him, love Him and praise Him.*
	2. Why does God declare His thoughts to us? *He wants us to know Him.*
	3. Do we have to figure out what God is like by ourselves? *No, God shows us what He's like. He reveals His thoughts to us.*
	4. Who does the Lord declare His thought to? Who does He show what He's like? *To man--to people, like you and me.*
	5. What did God put inside us so we could know Him? *A heart.*
	6. Where can I look around me and learn more about God? *Everything around me that He made in this world.*
	7. What book did God give us to tell us about Himself? *The Bible, His Word.*
	8. Who shows us what God is like most of all? *Jesus, God's Son.*
	9. Who can help us know God? *God, Himself! He loves to help us when we ask Him!*
	10. What is the name of the one and only true, living God? *It's the LORD!*
BIBLE STORY	**The Case of the Old Man Who Looked for God**
Discussion Questions	*choose a few*
	1. Who was the old man who looked for God? *Simeon.*
	2. What did God put inside of Simeon that helped him know God? *A heart to know and love God.*
	3. What did Simeon see around him that helped him know what God is like? *He saw everything that God made. The things God makes tell us something about Him.*
	4, What book did Simeon read and learn that helped him know what God is like? *The Bible. It is God's Word written down.*
	5. Who did God promise Simeon would get to see before he died? *The Savior. Jesus!*
	6. What did Jesus grow up to do that was so important? *He grew up to be the Savior of all God's people when he died on the cross to pay for their sins.*
	7. What did Jesus do on Day One, Two, Three after He died? *He rose from the dead. He had beaten sin and death once and for all?*
	8. Why was Simeon happiest of all when he died? Where did he go? Who did he see then? *He went to heaven to live with God. He is there even now, enjoying getting to be with God and knowing Him more and more...forever!*
	9. Can we know God and go to live with Him like Simeon did? *Yes, we can, when we turn away from our sins and trust in Jesus as our Savior. God loves to answer this prayer!*
	10. Who can we talk to and trust to help us? *God.*

Hide 'n' Seek Kids

Unit 2
Curriculum:
God's Wonderful
World, the Bible

Session Prep (especially good for newbies!)

Pray! *NOTE: Most 2 & 3 year olds do best simply learning the Big Question & Answer, a simple version of the Bible story, and maybe the Bible Verse. Use other activities, as time and attention span allow. Your session prep need only include what you use.*

Pray for the Holy Spirit to be at work in your heart and the children's hearts.

Review

If new to the curriculum, look at the **Getting Started with Hide 'n' Seek Kids section of this book** (p.5) It will be especially helpful to read through the Hide 'n' Seek Kids section of **The Praise Factory Tour: Extended Version Book.** This is a visual way to understand what goes on in the classroom. (A pdf of the book is found in the samples section on the website.)

Look through and Learn the Lesson

Read over **lesson plan**. Practice any **songs or action rhymes** you are using. Choose/make up motions to go with these. Choose less with younger children and more with older preschoolers. **Practice the lesson with the visual aids** and using the Big Question Box/Briefcase.

Read and Rehearse the Bible Story with Pictures

Read the Bible story from the Bible. Read the curriculum version. Practice telling it with the storyboard pictures. (If you have not previously laminated the story pictures, do that now.) Or, rehearse it from the Simple Story Scenes, if you are using those.

Let There Be Music

Download the music and listen to the songs. Choose which of the songs you will use with the children. If using live musicians, make sure they have the sheet music (found in Appendix A).

Put the Props in Place

1. Prepare your Visual Aids. Put the Bible Verse, Listening Assignment, Bible Story in one side of the Bible folder. Keep out the Big Question sign.

2. Get out your storyboard. If using Simple Story Scenes, put these in your BIble Folder. Or, if using the individual storyboard figures, put all background pictures in place (they have a BG by the number). Put the rest of the storyboard pictures (these have a SB by the number) in order of use in the other side of the Bible folder.

3. Put the HSK Bible Folder as well as the Big Question sign in the Big Question Box/Briefcase and shut it. If your box/briefcase has locks and you want to use the unlocking the box as part of your session, lock it now....but make sure you have the key or know the code first.

4. Prepare the music CD or sheet music or mp3 device for use in your session.

Set Out Free Play Activities

Choose and set up free time activities you will use with the children. Choose a variety of different activities that will be enjoyed by different types of children. Rotate the activities you provide to keep them interesting and fresh to your children. (Suggestions in Appendix D, Core Curriculum books.)

Prepare Any Activities

Choose which (if any) of the unit games and crafts activities you want to use in the session. Bear in mind your time frame as well as the developmental abilities/attention span of your children as you decide what/how many to prepare. **Look over the Discussion Sheet** and choose a few questions you might use to spark discussion with the children as they do their activities (especially good for ages 3's+). Pray for God to give you opportunities to talk about these things with the children.

Let Them Take It with Them

Make copies of the craft/take home sheets, if you are not already using them as one of your activities. You may also want to make copies of the story (see take-home version of each story included in Appendix C with the other take home resources) to have for parents to use with their children at home. There's a link on each craft/take home sheet to the story, if you don't make hard copies.

Store It

After your session is over, collect the resources and store them for future use.
This curriculum can be used over and over for years to come.

Unit 2 Overview of Key Concepts

UNIT 2: God's Wonderful Word, the Bible

Unit Big Question (and Answer): "What's So Special about the Bible? It Alone Is God's Word!"

Meaning:

There are millions of books in the world, but none is like the Bible. It alone is God's perfect Word! God made sure it was written down just right. It tells us everything we need to know God and how to live for Him. It is powerful to do everything God wants it to do. Everything else in this world may come and go, but God's Word will last forever. It will always prove true.

Unit 2 Bible Verse: Psalm 18:30, 46 ESV

"This God--His ways are perfect. The word of the LORD proves true. The Lord lives, and blessed be my rock, and exalted be the God of my salvation."

Meaning:

The LORD is like no one else. He is the one, true God. Everything He does is absolutely perfect! Everything God says is perfect, too. It is flawless. Flawless is a big word that means perfect--without even a single mistake. No, not one! God always tells us what is right and true. His Word always proves true!

Where can we read God's Word? In the Bible! It alone is God's Word. That's why we take time each day to learn from the Bible. We want to hear from God--all the wonderful things about Him; what He has done for us through Jesus, His Son; and, what good things are in store for those who love Him and live for Him. Oh, how we want to praise the LORD when we read His Word! He is the living God. He is our Savior!

Unit 2 ACTS Prayer

A We praise You, God. You are perfect, and everything You tell us in Your Word, the Bible, always proves true.

C God, we know You are perfect and everything You say is true, but too many times we still don't trust You or obey Your Word. Please forgive us! We need Jesus to be our Savior!

T Thank You for giving us Your words, written down perfectly in the Bible. Thank You that we can always know what is right and true when we read Your Word, the Bible. And thank You for all the wonderful things You tell us in the Bible, especially the stories about Jesus.

S Work deep inside our hearts. Help us to turn away from our sins and trust in Jesus as our Savior. Help us to want to read Your Word. Help us to know You better as we learn. Help us to go and tell others how they can learn about You in Your wonderful Word, the Bible. In Jesus' name we pray. Amen.

Unit 2 Story

The Case of the Women's Best Gift
1 Timothy

Songs Used in Unit 2   *listen to or download songs for free at https://praisefactory.org: Hide n Seek Kids Music page*

Big Q & A 2 Song
Big Question 2 Song: What's So Special About God's Word?
Unit 2 Bible Verse Song: Proves True Psalm 18:30, 46 ESV
Extra Unit 2 Bible Verse Song: This God, His Way Is Perfect   Psalm 18:30,46, ESV (other version)
Extra Unit 2 Bible Verse Song: The Word of the Lord 1 Peter 1:24,25, ESV
Unit 2 Hymn: How Precious Is the Book Divine, v.1
Unit 2 Praise Song: The Best Book to Read Is the Bible

Hide 'n' Seek Kids ESV Songs 2 Track Numbers

This is a listing of all songs mentioned in the unit curriculum. You may or may not choose to use all of the songs. They are listed in easy-reference order--NOT in the order used in the curriculum.

You may choose to simply burn a CD/load them onto an mp3 device in this order. Or, you may want to do what we do: choose the songs we want to use and create a play list of them in that order. Then, we burn a CD/upload the play list onto an mp3 device. A teacher only has to click forward to the next song, instead of hunting for the right track. The track number have been included as part of the title of each song, so teachers will still have a reference to the track number listed in the curriculum (same as those listed below), even if you change the order on your customized play list.

SONGS USED EVERY UNIT OF THE CURRICULUM

1 The Classroom Song v.1
2 The Classroom Song v.2
3 The Classroom Song v.3
4 The Classroom Song v.4
5 Hide 'n' Seek Kids Theme Song
6 The Classroom Rules Song
7 Let's Pray Song
8 The Big Question Box Song
9 The Bible Chant Song
10 ACTS Prayer Song (Short Version)
11 ACTS Prayer Song (Full Version)

> **Why the Extra Songs?**
> Hide 'n' Seek Kids is a curriculum used by children of different ages. Sometimes one of the other songs is a better fit for your kids. Or, you may simply want to teach them more songs on the same Bible Truth. Use as many or as few as you want.

UNIT 2: GOD'S WONDERFUL WORD, THE BIBLE

12 Big Q & A 2 Song
13 Big Question 2 Song: What's So Special About God's Word?
14,14T Unit 2 Bible Verse Song: Proves True Psalm 18:30, ESV
15 *Extra Unit 2 Bible Verse Song: This God Psalm 18:30,46, ESV*
16 *Extra Unit 2 Bible Verse Song: This God, His Way Is Perfect   Psalm 18:30,46, ESV*
17 *Extra Unit 2 Bible Verse Song: The Word of the Lord 1 Peter 1:24,25, ESV*
18 Unit 2 Hymn: How Precious Is the Book Divine, v.1
19 Unit 2 Praise Song: The Best Book to Read Is the Bible

T* Tidbit   Shortened version of the Bible Verse Song

listen to or download songs for free at https://praisefactory.org: Hide n Seek Kids Music page

Lesson Plan: Big Question 2   ⭐ = follow the stars for a short & simple lesson plan   p.1

1. GETTING STARTED *NOTE: Most 2 & 3 year olds do best simply learning the Big Question & Answer, a simple version of the Bible story, and maybe the Bible Verse. Use other activities, as time and attention span allow.*

Intake Activity Ideas	*Choose one of these open-ended activities to include children as they join the class:*
Free Play Time *suggestions in Appendix D*	⭐(usually best for 2 year olds) Offer your own or some of the easy-to-make, free play activities suggested in Appendix D.

OR Sing-along Music Time
 	
lyrics and sheet music, Appendix A
 	
listen to or download songs for free at https:// praisefactory.org: Hide n Seek Kids Music page
	Music *from* Hide 'n' Seek Kids (HSK) ESV Songs 2:
	Big Q & A 2 Song *HSK ESV Songs 2, track 12*
	Big Question 2 Song *HSK ESV Songs 2, track 13*
	Unit 2 Bible Verse Song:
	  Proves True Psalm 18:30 *HSK ESV Songs 2, track 14,14T*
	Extra Unit 2 Bible Verse Song:
	  This God, His Way Is Perfect Psalm 18:30,46 *HSK ESV Songs 2, track 15*
	Extra Unit 2 Bible Verse Song:
	  The Word of the Lord 1 Peter 1:24,25, ESV *HSK ESV Songs 2, track 16*
	Unit 2 Hymn:
	  How Precious Is the Book Divine, v.1 *HSK ESV Songs 2, track 17*
	Unit 2 Praise Song:
	  The Best Book to Read Is the Bible *HSK ESV Songs 2, track 18*
	
	Add more fun to Sing-along Music TIme by adding a Music, Movement & Memory Activity. These activities are listed on p. 8 of this lesson plan with the Response Activities. Instructions found in Appendix B.

OR **Bible Verse Memory Game** *instructions found in Appendix B*	Lesson 1 Game: Freeze 'n' Say Lesson 2 Game: Fill 'er Up Lesson 3 Game: Loud and Soft, Big and Little Lesson 4 Game: Roll 'n' Toss Lesson 5 Game: Duck, Duck, Goose *These activities are also included on p.8 of this lesson plan with the Response Activities.*

2. OPENING CIRCLE TIME *(introduce the Bible Truth and tell the related Bible story)*

Gathering the Children *lyrics and sheet music, Appendix A*	*Sing verse 1 of The Classroom Song to gather the children for Circle Time.* **The Classroom Song, verse 1** *HSK ESV Songs 2, track 1* Let's gather together to worship God, Let's gather together to worship God, Let's gather together to worship God, Come gather here with me!
Welcome to Hide 'n' Seek Kids!	⭐"Welcome to Hide 'n' Seek Kids! We're so glad you've joined us! We're here to seek God and learn His Word and Hide it in our heart so that it will always be with us. And we're here to Hide His Word, the Bible, in our hearts. We ask big questions about God and dig deep down in the truths of God's Word to find them."

| **Lesson Plan: Big Question 2** | use with all FIVE lessons | **p.2** |

2. OPENING CIRCLE TIME, continued   ⭐ = short & simple lesson plan

Hide 'n' Seek Kids Theme Song *lyrics and sheet music, Appendix A*	"Let's sing our Hide 'n' Seek Kids theme song." ⭐**Hide 'n' Seek Kids Theme Song**　　　　　　*HSK ESV Songs 2, track 5* Come along, we're gonna Hide 'n' seek! Hide God's Word in our heart and Him, we'll seek, God loves to show us the truths of His Word, That we might know Him and live out what we've learned.
Classroom Rules Song *lyrics and sheet music, Appendix A*	There are two very important things that Hide 'n' Seek Kids do together: we worship God and we love one another. Our Classroom Rules Song reminds us how we should act. Let's sing it." **Classroom Rules Song**　　　　　　*HSK ESV Songs 2, track 6* Shh, be quiet while someone is talking, Raise your hand, if you have something to say, Don't touch your friend, sitting beside you, Obey your teachers, Be kind as you play. These are our classroom rules, These are our classroom rules, They help us worship God and love one another, These are our classroom rules.
Opening Prayer Time *lyrics and sheet music, Appendix A*	"Children, we need God's help to keep these rules. Let's ask Him to help us right now. Let's get ready and pray." **Let's Pray**　　　　　　*HSK ESV Songs 2, track 7* 1-2-3! Fold your hands, Bow your head, Close your eyes. Let's pray! *(repeat)* "Let's pray:" ⭐**Opening Prayer** Dear Lord, We're so glad to get to gather together to worship You! Please help us keep the classroom rules. Please help us to love You and learn about You today. In Jesus' name we pray. Amen.

Lesson Plan: Big Question 2   use with all FIVE lessons   p.3

2. OPENING CIRCLE TIME, continued   = *short & simple lesson plan*

Reveal the Big Question **Introduce the Big Question Box/Briefcase** *lyrics and sheet music, Appendix A*	"It's time to get down to business, Hide 'n' Seek kids! Let's see what our Big Question for today is. It's right inside our Big Question Box/ Briefcase." **The Big Question Box Song** *HSK ESV Songs 2, track 8* We've got a big box, All closed up and locked, Filled with the truths of God's Word. We've got a brief case, There's no time to waste, Come on, kids, let's open it up!
The Big Question under Investigation VISUAL take out AID of BQB *Big Question & Answer Sign, front side* *found in the HSK Vol. 1 Visual Aids, ESV Book*	Ok, who would like to open it up for me and pull out the Big Question?" *Choose a child to open the box/briefcase, take out the Big Question and hand it to you, then hold up the Big Question sign for all the children to see, and say:* The Big Question we are investigating today is Big Question Number 2: **What's So Special about the Bible?** and the Answer is: **It Alone Is God's Word!**
Big Question Meaning	There are millions of books in the world, but none is like the Bible. It alone is God's perfect Word! God made sure it was written down just right. It tells us everything we need to know God and how to live for Him. It is powerful to do everything God wants it to do. Everything else in this world may come and go, but God's Word will last forever. It will always prove true.
Big Question Songs **Big Q & A 2 Song** *lyrics and sheet music, Appendix A*	"Let's sing our Big Question Song: **Big Q & A 2 Song** *HSK ESV Songs 2, track 12* *(adapted version of "Three, Blind Mice")* What's so special about the Bible? It alone is God's Word! It alone is God's Word! It's always true, It can make you wise, It can work pow'rf'ly in your life. It alone is God's Word! It alone is God's Word!

Lesson Plan: Big Question 2   use with all FIVE lessons   p.4

2. OPENING CIRCLE TIME, continued   ⭐ = *short & simple lesson plan*

Learning about the Big Question ⭐

Repeat the Big Question and Answer again:
"What's So Special about the Bible? It Alone Is God's Word!"

Say: "Hmmmm, I wonder what that means... Let's do our action rhyme/sing our song that explains it."

Then do the action rhyme /sing song using any of the optional motions suggested, if desired.

Big Question (Action Rhyme) Song

lyrics and sheet music, Appendix A

⭐ **Big Question 2 Action Rhyme/ Song**   *HSK ESV Songs 2, track 13*

Lyrics	(POSSIBLE ACTIONS)
Refrain: What's so special about the Bible? It alone is God's Word, What's so special about the Bible? It alone is God's Word.	*hold up a Bible and point to it Point up to God hold up a Bible and point to it Point up to God*

There are millions and millions of books
  in the world,
But only the Bible is God's perfect Word,
There are millions and millions of books
  in the world,
But only the Bible is God's perfect Word.
	make "book" with your hands by placing your flat palms next to each other like an open book
	
	*hold up a Bible and point to it
	Point up to God*

Verse 1 God's Word was written down perfectly, By godly men long ago, The Holy Spirit worked through them, Inspiring every word they wrote.	*use index of one hand to pretend to write on open palm of the other hand* *hold open hands up to God, then bring them down and place on your head*
Verse 2 God's Word is powerful and living, It changes us, deep inside, The Holy Spirit uses it To make God's people like Christ.	*flex arms touch heart hold open hands up to God, then bring them down and place over your heart*

| Lesson Plan: Big Question 2 | use with all FIVE lessons | p.5 |

2. OPENING CIRCLE TIME, continued ⭐ = short & simple lesson plan

Learning the Bible Verse

The Bible Chant Song

lyrics and sheet music, Appendix A

⭐"And how do I know this is true? God tells me so in His special book, the Bible."

Say or sing the Bible Chant Song.

The Bible Chant Song   *HSK ESV Songs 2, track 9*
The Bible, the Bible,
Let's get out the Bible.
Let's hear what God has to say.
The Bible, the Bible,
God's given us the Bible.
It's His Word for us to learn and obey! Yay!

The Bible Verse in the HSK Bible Folder
HSK 2 Bible Verse-front side
(in the HSK Bible folder)

VISUAL AID   Place verse in   take out

HSK Bible Folder   of BQB

found in the HSK Vol. 1 Visual Aids, ESV Book

"Who would like to get our Bible folder out of the Big Question Briefcase for me?"

Choose a child to open the briefcase, take out the "Bible" folder and hand it to you. Remove the Bible Verse Picture from the "Bible" folder and hold it up for all the children to see, then say:

⭐**Psalm 18:30, 46, ESV**
"This God--His ways are perfect. The word of the LORD proves true. The Lord lives, and blessed be my rock, and exalted be the God of my salvation."

Bible Verse Meaning

HSK 2 Bible Verse-back side

⭐**What does that mean?**
The LORD is like no one else. He is the one, true God. Everything He does is absolutely perfect! Everything God says is perfect, too. It is flawless. Flawless is a big word that means perfect--without even a single mistake. No, not one! God always tells us what is right and true. His Word always proves true!

Where can we read God's Word? In the Bible! It alone is God's Word. That's why we take time each day to learn from the Bible. We want to hear from God--all the wonderful things about Him; what He has done for us through Jesus, His Son; and, what good things are in store for those who love Him and live for Him. Oh, how we want to praise the LORD when we read His Word! He is the living God. He is our Savior!

Bible Verse Song

lyrics and sheet music, Appendix A

"We've said our Bible verse, now let's sing it!"

Proves True: Psalm 18:30   *HSK ESV Songs 2, track 14,14T*

This God, His ways are perfect,
The word of the LORD proves true,
This God, His ways are perfect,
The word of the LORD proves true.

This God, His ways are perfect,
The word of the LORD proves true,
This God, His ways are perfect,
The word of the LORD proves true.

Psalm Eighteen, thirty.

You might also enjoy:

This God: Psalm 18:30,46, ESV
HSK ESV Songs 2, track 15

This God, His Way Is Perfect: Psalm 18:30,46, ESV
HSK ESV Songs 2, track 16

The Word of the LORD: 1 Peter 1:24,25, ESV
HSK ESV Songs 2, track 17

lyrics and sheet music, Appendix A

Lesson Plan: Big Question 2   use with all FIVE lessons   p.6

2. OPENING CIRCLE TIME, continued   ⭐ = short & simple lesson plan

Getting into the Case	"Now it's time to do a bit more deep down investigating. Let's see what Detective Dan wants us to help him figure out. Would someone like to get it out for me?"
Listening Assignments *Place in* *take out* HSK Bible Folder ❓Big Questions Briefcase❓ *of BQB*	**NOTE: Listening assignments are most suitable for ages 3+. Skip straight to the Bible story (see bottom of this page), if working with 2 year olds.** "Let's open up our listening assignment and see what we are supposed to figure out today. *Choose a child to take out the Listening Assignment (from the HSK Bible Folder) and hand it to you. Read Detective Dan's letter to the children that includes the listening assignment. The listening assignments are summarized below:*
VISUAL AID **#3** *HSK Vol. 1 Visual Aids, ESV*	**Detective Dan's Lesson #1 Listening Assignment:** As you listen to the story, see if you can figure out: 1. Who are the women in our story? 2. What was their best gift and who did they give it to?
VISUAL AID **#4** *HSK Vol. 1 Visual Aids, ESV*	**Detective Dan's Lesson #2 Listening Assignment:** Our Bible verse is Psalm 18:30,46: "This God--His ways are perfect. The word of the LORD proves true. The Lord lives, and blessed be my rock, and exalted be the God of my salvation." As you listen to the story, see if you can figure out: 1. Who in our story knew that God and His Word were perfect? 2. Who did they teach God's Word to?
VISUAL AID **#5A,B,C** **Listening Assignment #3 includes the Assignment Sheet, plus 4 clue pictures** *HSK Vol. 1 Visual Aids, ESV*	**Detective Dan's Lesson #3 Listening Assignment:** I found four clues, but one of them is NOT in the story. They are: Food, a zebra, God's Word (on a scroll, like in Bible times) and some clothes. *Hold up each of the four pictures for the children to see as you identify them. Better yet, put them up on your flannelgraph board, off to one side.* I need to know: 1. Which of these things did Grandma Lois and Mother Eunice NOT give to Timothy? 2. Which of these things did they think was most important of all?
VISUAL AID **#6** *HSK Vol. 1 Visual Aids, ESV*	**Detective Dan's Lesson #4 Listening Assignment:** As you listen to the story, see if you can figure out: 1. Who did Grandma Lois and Mother Eunice want Timothy to know and love most of all? 2. What book did they thank God for giving to them?
VISUAL AID **#7** *HSK Vol. 1 Visual Aids, ESV*	**Detective Dan's Lesson #5 Listening Assignment:** As you listen to the story, see if you can figure out: 1. What happened in Timothy's heart as he listened to God's Word, the Bible? 2. What good news from the Bible did Timothy preach about when he grew up?
Tell the Bible Story *Place story & pics in* *take out* HSK Bible Folder ❓Big Question Briefcase❓ *of BQB* *HSK Vol. 1 Visual Aids, ESV* **Bible Story included in this book, immediately after the Lesson Plan and with the Visual Aids**	⭐***Then say,*** "Ok, Hide 'n' Seekers! Put on your best listening ears and see if you can find the answers to Detective Dan's questions. When I finish telling the story, we'll see what we come up with." ⭐**Bible Story: The Case of the Women's Best Gift** *1 Timothy* *Read the Bible Truth story, putting up the storyboard pictures/Simple Story Scenes as you tell it. Then, have the children answer the listening assignment. Present the the gospel and lead in prayer.* **Answers to questions, the gospel and ACTS prayer are included with the story text.**

Lesson Plan: Big Question 2   use with all FIVE lessons   p.7

2. OPENING CIRCLE TIME, continued   = short & simple lesson plan

Story Response Song(s)	*As attention span and time allow, you might want to end with one of the following songs which also tie in with the unit. If desired, use the Music and Movement activity ideas while singing, listed with the Response Activities.*

Hymn

lyrics and sheet music, Appendix A

How Precious Is the Book Divine   *HSK ESV Songs 2, track 18*

Verse 1
How precious is the book divine,
By inspiration given;
Bright as a lamp its doctrines shine,
To guide our souls to heaven.

Tie-in: "The Bible is precious. It is no regular book. It is the only book divine, inspired by God. That means that God's Holy Spirit helped godly people write it down just right. Yes, the Bible is God's Word. In it, God tells us about Himself and how He sent Jesus to save us from our sins. He tells us how He wants us to live for Him."

Praise Song

lyrics and sheet music, Appendix A

Praise Song: The Best Book to Read Is the Bible   *HSK ESV Songs 2, track 19*

Verse 1
The best book to read is the Bible,
The best book to read is the Bible,
It alone is God's true Word,
With the best news ever heard!
Yes! The best book to read is the Bible.

Verse 2
The best book to read is the Bible,
The best book to read is the Bible,
If you read it ev'ry day,
God will teach you His ways.
Yes! The best book to read is the Bible.

Tie-in: "The Bible is the best book to read, because it alone is God's true word! In it, God tells us about Himself and the good news that He sent Jesus to save us from our sins. In it, He tells us how He wants us to live for Him. How God will bless us when we read His book, the Bible, every day!"

3. TAKING ACTION: Response Activities *(choose from among these activities)*

Transition to Activities

★Well, Hide 'n' Seek Kids, you've done a great job diggin' deep down for answers in the truths of God's Word. Now it's time to enjoy some activities."

★*Tell children what activity/s you are providing for them: either free play or some of the response activities listed below. When you are ready to dismiss them, use this song to help the children transition in an orderly fashion to their next activity.*

Classroom Song, verse 2

lyrics and sheet music, Appendix A

"Children, let's sing our Time to Play Song. When we are finished you may get up and walk over to our next activity."

Classroom Song, verse 2   *HSK ESV Songs 2, track 2*
We've gathered together to worship God,
We've gathered together to worship God,
And now it's time to play.

Dismiss the children to whatever activities you have prepared for them to do.

Lesson Plan: Big Question 2   use with all FIVE lessons   **p.8**

3. TAKING ACTION: Response Activities *(choose from among these activities)* ⭐ = *short & simple lesson plan*

Response Activities	*Choose one or more activities appropriate for your children, based on classroom time and developmental needs.* **Add the Discussion Sheet to any activity for deeper learning.** ⭐
Bible Verse Memory Game *game directions, Appendix B*	Though listed with the opening activities, you may choose to use this Bible verse game here instead (or as a repeat). • Lesson 1 Game: Freeze 'n' Say • Lesson 2 Game: Fill 'er Up • Lesson 3 Game: Loud and Soft, Big and Little • Lesson 4 Game: Roll 'n' Toss • Lesson 5 Game: Duck, Duck, Goose *Use the Discussion Sheet with these activities for even deeper learning* Unit Discussion Questions
Music, Movement & Memory Activity *game directions, Appendix B*	A music activity that uses the songs from the Bible Truth and Big Question unit. • HSK Songs for Unit, plus: • Lesson 1 Activity: Big Voice, Little Voice • Lesson 2 Activity: Sing, Dance and Fall Down • Lesson 3 Activity: Bottle Shakers • Lesson 4 Activity: March 'n' Say • Lesson 5 Activity: Clap, Tap and Say *Use the Discussion Sheet with these activities for even deeper learning* Unit Discussion Questions
Bible Story Review Game *game directions, Appendix B*	A game that uses the storyboard pictures from the story to review the story. • Lesson 1 Game: Hide 'n' Seek Kids Clue Hunt • Lesson 2 Game: Who's Inside? • Lesson 3 Game: Look Who's Coming Down the Tracks • Lesson 4 Game: Going Fishing • Lesson 5 Game: Pony Express *Use the Discussion Sheet with these activities for even deeper learning* Unit Discussion Questions
Coloring Pages/ Take Home Sheets *in Appendix C*	A coloring page related to the lesson assignment questions is provided for each lesson. On the back of each are the key concepts, a few questions and a song for parents to use with their children. (If desired, include a copy of the Bible story with the Take Home Sheet.) NOTE: Upgrade your coloring sheet to a more interesting craft by offering simple embellishments, such as jiggly eyes, craft sand, glitter, glitter glue, colored paper dots (made with a hole punch), fabric scraps, etc. Make cut-to-size glued-on clothes, hair, etc for characters by using a copy of the coloring sheet, cutting out the selected portions and making them the patterns for whatever you want to cut out of fabric, paper, foil, etc. ⭐ • Lesson 1 Coloring Sheet Emphasis: Bible Truth • Lesson 2 Coloring Sheet Emphasis: Bible Verse • Lesson 3 Coloring Sheet Emphasis: Bible Truth • Lesson 4 Coloring Sheet Emphasis: ACTS Prayer • Lesson 5 Coloring Sheet Emphasis: The Gospel *Use the Discussion Sheet with these activities for even deeper learning* Unit Discussion Questions
Extra Crafts: **Big Question Craft** *in Appendix C* **Bible Verse Craft** *in Appendix C* **Bible Story Puzzle** *in Appendix C*	**These crafts are slightly more complex than the coloring sheets:** **The Big Question Craft** is a color, glue and stick craft of the Big Question and Answer. **The Bible Verse Craft** is a craft that gives the Bible verse and explains it, also involving gluing and sticking and a few other, simple craft supplies. The **Storyboard Picture Placement Page** has been made into a puzzle that can be cut out and re-assembled by the children. This provides a nice summary of the story. *Use the Discussion Sheet with these activities for even deeper learning* Unit Discussion Questions
Free Play Activities *ideas in Appendix D*	⭐ Offer your own or some of the easy-to-make, free play activities suggested in Appendix D.

Lesson Plan: Big Question 2   use with all FIVE lessons   p.9

4. CLOSING CIRCLE TIME *(End-of-session activities for the last 5-10 minutes of class time)*   ⭐ = *short & simple lesson plan*

Transition to Closing Circle **Classroom Song, verse 3** *lyrics and sheet music, Appendix A*	*Use this song to help the children transition in an orderly fashion. Sing the song, then ask the children to gather with you for Closing Circle Time.* **Classroom Song, verse 3** *HSK ESV Songs 2, track 3* It's time to get ready to go and tell, It's time to get ready to go and tell, Come gather here with me.
Closing Circle Time **Classroom Song, verse 4** *lyrics and sheet music, Appendix A*	*When children are settled in the circle, say:* "It is almost time for your parents to come pick you up. And do you know what that means? It means…. (draw this out to build anticipation and excitement)…that it's almost time to go home and….it's almost time to…Go and Tell! We have learned some big news about God today. God wants us to take and tell it to the whole world!" **Classroom Song, verse 4** *HSK ESV Songs 2, track 4* So what's our big news to go and tell, So what's our big news to go and tell, Can you tell me now?
Big News to Tell **Big Question 2** *VISUAL AID* **#1** **found in the HSK Vol. 1 Visual Aids, ESV Book* *lyrics and sheet music, Appendix A*	"Let's see….there's so much big news to tell! There's so much we've learned! Can you tell me the answer to our **Big Question: "What's So Special about the Bible?"** *(Show them the Big Question and Answer picture.)* Say the answer with me: **"It Alone Is God's Word!"** *(If desired, you can sing the Big Q & A Song.)* *HSK ESV Songs 2, track 12*
Big Question 2 Bible Verse *VISUAL AID* **#2** **found in the HSK Vol. 1 Visual Aids, ESV Book* *lyrics and sheet music, Appendix A*	"And how do I know this is true? Can you tell me? Say it with me: **"The Bible tells me so!"** That's right! We learned: **Psalm 18:30,46, ESV** **"This God--His ways are perfect. The word of the LORD proves true. The Lord lives, and blessed be my rock, and exalted be the God of my salvation."** *(Show them the Bible Verse picture.)* The Bible tells us that it is God's Word; and, it tells us that it is perfect, just like God. That's why it's so special!" *(If desired, you can sing the Bible verse song.)* *HSK ESV Songs 2, track 14,14T*

| **Lesson Plan: Big Question 2** | use with all FIVE lessons | **p.10** |

4. CLOSING CIRCLE TIME, continued   ⭐ = *short & simple lesson plan*

Closing ACTS Prayer Time	*Let's ask God to help us to remember this and even tell others this good news. Let's get ready and pray our ACTS prayer.*
ACTS Prayer Chant *lyrics and sheet music, Appendix A*	*And what does ACTS mean? Let's sing/say our ACTS Prayer Chant!* **ACTS Prayer Chant Song** *HSK ESV Songs 2, tracks 10,11* A, Adoration: God, we praise You! C, Confession: Forgive us our sins. That's the ACTS prayer, my friend, T, Thanksgiving,: Thank You for Jesus, Bow head, Close your eyes, Shhh, S, Supplication: Help us to live like Him. Let's begin!
Closing ACTS Prayer	"Let's pray!" *Lead the children in the ACTS prayer for this unit.* **A** We praise You, God. You are perfect, and everything You tell us in Your Word, the Bible, always proves true. **C** God, we know You are perfect and everything You say is true, but too many times we still don't trust You or obey Your Word. Please forgive us! We need Jesus to be our Savior! **T** Thank You for giving us Your words, written down perfectly in the Bible. Thank You that we can always know what is right and true when we read Your Word, the Bible. And thank You for all the wonderful things You tell us in the Bible, especially the stories about Jesus. **S** Work deep inside our hearts. Help us to turn away from our sins and trust in Jesus as our Savior. Help us to want to read Your Word. Help us to know You better as we learn. Help us to go and tell others how they can learn about You in Your wonderful Word, the Bible. In Jesus' name we pray. Amen.

5. TAKING IT HOME *(Take Home Sheet)*

Clean up and Dismissal	⭐"Now it's time to work together and clean up." *Have the children join you in cleaning up the room.*
Coloring Pages/ Take Home Sheets *in Appendix C*	⭐ *Give out the craft/take home sheet and any other papers from the session, as you dismiss children from class.* *(Reminder: The back side of the coloring page is the take home sheet for each lesson.)*
Bible Story to Take-Home *in Appendix C*	You may also want to include a copy of the story along with the take home sheet. (However, each coloring sheet/take home sheet includes a note to parents telling them where they can download the story from the Parent Resources section on the website.)

Big Question 2 Bible Story

use with all FIVE lessons

Place story in **HSK Bible Folder**

take out [? Big Question Briefcase ?] of BQB

p.1

The Case of the Women's Best Gift

I Timothy

Story-telling Tips

Ahead of time:
1. Read the Bible verses and story. Pray!
2. Choose story action cues and/or prepare storyboard pictures, if using. (Included in Visual Aids book)
3. Practice telling story with the pictures, timing your presentation. Shorten, if necessary to fit your allotted time.

During your presentation:
1. Maintain as much eye contact as possible as you tell the story.
2. Put up storyboard figures/add story action cues as you tell the story. Allow the children to help you put them on the board, if desired.
3. Include the children in your story with a few questions about what they think will happen or words/concepts that might be new to them.
4. Watch the kids for signs that their attention span has been reached. Shorten, if necessary.

INTRODUCTION/ LISTENING ASSIGNMENTS

"Our story is called: The Case of the Women's Best Gift. Here is your listening assignment... "

Read from Detective Dan's Listening Assignment signs, but questions are summarized below:

Detective Dan's Lesson #1 Listening Assignment:

I need to find out:
1. Who are the women in our story?
2. What was their best gift and who did they give it to?

Detective Dan's Lesson #2 Listening Assignment:

Our Bible verse is Psalm 18:30,46: "This God--His ways are perfect. The word of the LORD proves true. The Lord lives, and blessed be my rock, and exalted be the God of my salvation."

As you listen to the story, see if you can figure out:
1. Who in our story knew that God and His Word were perfect?
2. Who did they teach God's Word to?

Detective Dan's Lesson #3 Listening Assignment:

I found four clues, but one of them is NOT in the story.
They are: Food, a zebra, God's Word (on a scroll, like in Bible times) and some clothes.
Hold up each of the four pictures for the children to see as you identify them. Better yet, put them up on your flannelgraph board, off to one side.

I need to know:
1. Which of these things did Grandma Lois and Mother Eunice NOT give to Timothy?
2. Which of these things did they think was most important of all?

Detective Dan's Lesson #4 Listening Assignment:

As you listen to the story, see if you can figure out:
1. Who did Grandma Lois and Mother Eunice want Timothy to know and love most of all?
2. What book did they thank God for giving to them?

Detective Dan's Lesson #5 Listening Assignment:

As you listen to the story, see if you can figure out:
1. What happened in Timothy's heart as he listened to God's Word, the Bible?
2. What good news from the Bible did Timothy preach about when he grew up?

Read the questions, THEN SAY,

"Ok, Hide 'n' Seekers! Put on your best listening ears and see if you can find the answers to Detective Dan's questions. When I finish telling the story, we'll see what we come up with."

"The Case of the Women's Best Gift" I Timothy

Story with lines separating paragraphs (text in bold, optional interaction cues in italics)

Grandma Lois and Mother Eunice loved the Bible. They loved what the Bible told them about God and His Son, Jesus. They loved how it worked in their heart and helped them know God and live for Him! If Grandma Lois and Mother Eunice knew one thing, it was that there was NO BOOK like the Bible! It alone was God's Word! It was always true. They could count on it.

Do you see a Bible in this room? Point to it.

Now, Mother Eunice had a little boy named Timothy. She and Grandma Lois loved Timothy very, very much. And because they loved him, they hugged him…and they fed him good food…and they gave him clothes to wear…and a good place to sleep at night. They taught good manners and how to do his chores and all sorts of things that would help him grow up to be a fine, young man one day.

Do you have a mother or a grandmother? What kinds of things do they do for you because they love you?

But most of all, because Grandma Lois and Mother Eunice loved Timothy so much, they wanted him to know and love God. And oh, how they wanted Timothy to turn away from his sins and trust in Jesus as his Savior!

So, Grandma Lois and Mother Eunice taught Timothy every day from the only book in the whole, wide world where the truths about God are written down just right. Can you guess what that book is?

Can you guess what that book is called? (I bet you can!) Let's say its name all together—The Bible!

The Bible, yes, the Bible was that one, special book. It alone is God's Word and Grandma Lois and Mother Eunice knew it.

The Bible is a very BIG book filled with so many good stories and so many important truths about God. There was so, so much to teach Timothy!

Hold up your Bible and show the children how big it is. Open it up and show them all the words on the pages.

But of everything in the whole Bible, Grandma Lois and Mother Eunice most wanted Timothy to know one thing.

Can you guess what it is?

They wanted him to know the gospel—the good news of Jesus. They wanted him to know how he could become one of God's people.

"Long ago, God created the whole world, Timothy," they told him. "He gave us His good laws to live by, but we all choose to disobey them, Timothy. "We need a Savior to save us from our sins and God sent that Savior to us! It's Jesus!" Grandma Lois and Mother Eunice taught Timothy. "We hope one day you will ask Jesus to forgive your sins and trust in Him as your Savior like we have, Timothy," they told him. "There's nothing better than knowing God and living for Him."

| Big Question 2 Bible Story | use with all FIVE lessons | p.3 |

Story with lines separating paragraphs (text in bold, optional interaction cues in italics)

At first, Timothy just listened and learned as Grandma Lois and Mother Eunice taught him from the Bible. But after a while, something wonderful happened: God's Word began to work powerfully in Timothy's heart and mind, helping him to believe.

"God, I believe what is written in Your Word, the Bible. I believe in Your Son, Jesus, and trust in Him as my Savior. Please forgive me for disobeying You. I want to live my life for you. Please save me!" Timothy prayed.

God was happy to answer Timothy's prayers. And Timothy was happy to be one of God's people!

Did you know that we can become God's people, too, when we pray like Timothy did, for God to forgive our sins and help us to trust in Jesus as our Savior? It's true!

But that was only the beginning. Now Timothy wanted to learn from the Bible more than ever! He wanted to know more about God and love Him more, too. too. He wanted God's Word to go on working inside his heart, changing him more and more, too.

And that's just what happened! As Timothy kept learning from the Bible, God's Word, it kept on working inside him. And Timothy, the little boy, grew up and up and up to be Timothy, the man with a heart full of love for God, His Word, and His people.

A grown-up man needs a grown up man's job. And what job do you think God gave Timothy to do?

What job do you think Timothy did?

God called Timothy to be a pastor—a man who teaches God's Word to God's people and loves them as they gather together as a church.

Now others gathered around Timothy as he preached to them the same truths from the God's Word that Grandma Lois and Mother Eunice had taught him long ago as a little boy!

How happy Grandma Lois and Mother Eunice must have been! What a great work God had done in Timothy through His Word, the Bible! And now God was even using Timothy to do a great work in the hearts of others, too!

Let's clap and say, "Yay!" for all the good things God did in Timothy through His Word, the Bible!

Big Question 2 Bible Story
use with all FIVE lessons

Cracking the Case: (story wrap-up for Listening Assignments)

It's time to see how we did with our Listening Assignment.

Detective Dan's Lesson #1 Listening Assignment:
1. Who are the women in our story? Grandma Lois and Mother Eunice.
2. What was their best gift and who did they give it to? Their best gift was teaching God's Word and the good news of Jesus. They taught it to Timothy, Mother Eunice's son.

For You and Me:
Timothy learned God's truths in the Bible and so are you...right now! God used His Word, the Bible, to work in Timothy's heart and help him trust in Jesus as His Savior. God can use His Word to work inside of us, too.

Detective Dan's Lesson #3 Listening Assignment:
I found four clues, but one of them is NOT in the story. They are: Food, a zebra, God's Word (on a scroll, like in Bible times) and some clothes.

1. Which of these things did Grandma Lois and Mother Eunice NOT give to Timothy? The zebra.
2. Which of these things did they think was most important of all? God's Word, the Bible.

For You and Me:
Like Timothy, we have people who love us and who give us many good things. But of everything we can ever have, learning God's Word, the Bible is the most important of all. Ask them to help you learn God's Word.

Detective Dan's Lesson #2 Listening Assignment:
Our Bible verse is Psalm 18:30,46:
"This God--His ways are perfect. The word of the LORD proves true. The Lord lives, and blessed be my rock, and exalted be the God of my salvation."

1. Who in our story knew that God and His Word were perfect? Grandma Lois and Mother Eunice.
2. Who did they teach God's Word to? Timothy.

For You and Me:
God is the living God! He and His Word, the Bible, are still perfect! God's Word will always prove true. We can trust in God and His Word, just like Grandma Lois, Mother Eunice and Timothy did!

Detective Dan's Lesson #4 Listening Assignment:
1. Who did Grandma Lois and Mother Eunice want Timothy to know and love most of all? God.
2. What book did they thank God for giving to them?
The Bible, God's Word.

For You and Me:
God is the person best person we can know and love, too. God can use His Word to do wonderful things in our hearts, too. Grandma Lois, Mother Eunice and Timothy knew this. Let's thank God for His Word, the Bible. Let's ask Him to use it to do wonderful things in our hearts, too.

Detective Dan's Lesson #5 Listening Assignment:
1. What happened in Timothy's heart as he listened to God's Word, the Bible? God worked in his heart. He turned away from his sins and trust in Jesus as his Savior. Then God kept working in his heart, changing him in wonderful ways, more and more.
2. What good news from the Bible did Timothy preach about when he grew up? God will forgive us our sins and make us His people when we repent and trust in Jesus as our Savior.

For You and Me:
God can use His perfect Word, the Bible, to help us know Him and to change us in wonderful ways. Jesus can save us from our sins and make us God's people, too, when we repent of our sins and trust in Him as our Savior.

Big Question 2 Bible Story   use with all FIVE lessons   p.5

The Gospel (story wrap-up if NOT using Listening Assignments)

Our Bible Truth is:
What's So Special about the Bible?
It Alone Is God's Word!

God used His Word, the Bible, to work inside Timothy in wonderful ways. He can work in our hearts, too. We can ask Him to work in our heart and help us to turn away from disobeying Him and trust in Jesus as our Savior. When we do, God will forgive our sins and save us! He will live in our heart, helping us to know Him right now. He will satisfy our heart, giving us a special kind of happiness that comes only from knowing Him. And one day, we will go to live with Him in heaven forever. That will be best of all!

Close in prayer.

Closing Unit 2 ACTS Prayer

A=Adoration C=Confession T=Thanksgiving S=Supplication

A   We praise You, God. You are perfect, and everything You tell us always proves true.

C   God, we know You are perfect and everything You say is true, but too many times we still don't trust You or obey Your Word. Please forgive us! We need Jesus to be our Savior!

T   Thank You for giving us Your words, written down perfectly in the Bible. Thank You that we can always know what is right and true when we read Your Word, the Bible. And thank You for all the wonderful things You tell us in the Bible, especially the stories about Jesus.

S   Work deep inside our hearts. Help us to turn away from our sins and trust in Jesus as our Savior. Help us to want to read Your Word. Help us to know You better as we learn. Help us to go and tell others how they can learn about You in Your wonderful Word, the Bible.

In Jesus' name we pray. Amen.

Unit 2 Discussion Sheet
use with all FIVE lessons

Questions to aid discussion of the key concepts and for use in games

Be familiar with these questions and answers. Look for opportunities to ask questions and talk about their answers, such as while the children work on their coloring pages, as part of their games, or during play time. Remember: your goal isn't to ask all these questions or to only talk to the children about these things. It is to be deliberate in having good conversations with them, as natural opportunities arise.

BIG QUESTION	What's So Special about the Bible? It Alone Is God's Word!
Meaning	There are millions of books in the world, but none is like the Bible. It alone is God's perfect Word! God made sure it was written down just right. It tells us everything we need to know God and how to live for Him. It is powerful to do everything God wants it to do. Everything else in this world may come and go, but God's Word will last forever. It will always prove true.
Discussion Questions	*choose a few* 1. What's so special about the Bible? *It alone is God's Word!* 2. How many books are there in the world? *Millions!* 3. How many books are like the Bible? *None!* 4. Why is the Bible different from all the other books in the world? *It alone is God's Word.* 5. What does the Bible tell us about God? *Everything we need to know.* 6. What does the Bible tell us about how we should live? *Everything we need to know.* 7. What is the Bible powerful to do? *Everything God wants it to do.* 8. WIll the things in this world last forever? *No, they won't. They will come and go.* 9. How long will God's Word last? *Forever!* 10. What will always prove true? *The Bible! It is God's perfect Word.* 11. Who can help me to understand God's Word, the Bible? *God can.* 12. What does the Bible tell me to do if I want to know God? *It tells me to ask God to forgive my sins and to ask Jesus to be my Savior. God will help us do this, if we ask Him. He loves to answer this prayer!*
THE GOSPEL	What is God's good news for you and me that God gives us in His Word, the Bible? *The gospel!* *The Bible tells us so many good and important things. But the very best thing the Bible tells us, is how we can be saved from our sins. The Bible tells us that, even though we are sinners who deserve God's punishment for our sins, God sent His Son, Jesus, to save us. Jesus lived a perfect life. Then, He offered it up to God as full payment for the sins of God's people, as He suffered and died on the cross. On Day Three, Jesus rose up from the dead. He had really beaten sin and death for God's people! We can become God's people, too, when we turn away from disobeying God (repent) and trust in Jesus as our Savior. Ask God to help you do this. He loves to answer this prayer!*

Unit 2 Discussion Sheet

Questions to aid discussion of the key concepts and for use in games

BIBLE VERSE	"This God--His ways are perfect. The word of the LORD proves true. The Lord lives, and blessed be my rock, and exalted be the God of my salvation." Psalm 18:30,46
Meaning	The LORD is like no one else. He is the one, true God. Everything He does is absolutely perfect! Everything God says is perfect, too. It is flawless. Flawless is a big word that means perfect-- without even a single mistake. No, not one! God always tells us what is right and true. His Word always proves true! Where can we read God's Word? In the Bible! It alone is God's Word. That's why we take time each day to learn from the Bible. We want to hear from God--all the wonderful things about Him; what He has done for us through Jesus, His Son; and, what good things are in store for those who love Him and live for Him. Oh, how we want to praise the LORD when we read His Word! He is the living God. He is our Savior!

Discussion Questions

choose a few

1. What is God and His ways like? *Perfect.*
2. What does perfect mean? *God never, ever makes a mistake!*
3. Flawless is another word for perfect. Whose word is flawless? *The LORD's!*
4. Who is the living God? *The LORD!*
5. A rock is something strong and dependable. Who is the god who is always strong and dependable? *The LORD!*
6. Who do we praise for being our Savior? *The LORD.*
7. How many mistakes are there is God's Word, the Bible? *None!*
8. Whose words will always, always, always prove true? *The LORD's!*
9. What book can we go to that will always tell us what is true about God? *The Bible!*
10. Who can help us understand God's Word? *God! He loves to help us when we ask.*

BIBLE STORY

The Case of the Women's Best Gift

Discussion Questions

choose a few

1. Who were the women in our story today? *Grandma Lois and Mother Eunice.*
2. Who did Grandma Lois and Mother Eunice take care of? *Timothy, Eunice's son.*
3. What kinds of things did they do because they loved him? *They made sure he had good food to eat, a good place to sleep; they taught him good things.*
4. What was their best gift and who did they give it to? *Their best gift was teaching God's Word. They taught it to Timothy, Mother Eunice's son.*
5. What truth from the Bible did they want Timothy to know most of all? *The good news of Jesus.*
6. What happened in Timothy's heart as he learned God's Word? *God worked in his heart and helped him turn from his sins and trust in Jesus as his Savior.*
7. How did God's Word keep on changing Timothy? *As Timothy learned God's Word, God helped him to love God and people more and more.*
8. What did Timothy do when he grew up? *He became a pastor.*
9. What does a pastor do? *He preaches God's Word and cares for God's people.*
10. What can work in our hearts and change us? *God's Word.*
11. Who can we ask to help change our hearts? *God! He loves to answer this prayer.*

Hide 'n' Seek Kids

Unit 3
Curriculum:
The Good News of God, the Gospel

Session Prep (especially good for newbies!)

Pray! *NOTE: Most 2 & 3 year olds do best simply learning the Big Question & Answer, a simple version of the Bible story, and maybe the Bible Verse. Use other activities, as time and attention span allow. Your session prep need only include what you use.*

Pray for the Holy Spirit to be at work in your heart and the children's hearts.

Review

If new to the curriculum, look at the **Getting Started with Hide 'n' Seek Kids section of this book** (p.5) It will be especially helpful to read through the Hide 'n' Seek Kids section of **The Praise Factory Tour: Extended Version Book.** This is a visual way to understand what goes on in the classroom. (A pdf of the book is found in the samples section on the website.)

Look through and Learn the Lesson

Read over **lesson plan**. Practice any **songs or action rhymes** you are using. Choose/make up motions to go with these. Choose less with younger children and more with older preschoolers. **Practice the lesson with the visual aids** and using the Big Question Box/Briefcase.

Read and Rehearse the Bible Story with Pictures

Read the Bible story from the Bible. Read the curriculum version. Practice telling it with the storyboard pictures. (If you have not previously laminated the story pictures, do that now.) Or, rehearse it from the Simple Story Scenes, if you are using those.

Let There Be Music

Download the music and listen to the songs. Choose which of the songs you will use with the children. If using live musicians, make sure they have the sheet music (found in Appendix A).

Put the Props in Place

1. Prepare your Visual Aids. Put the Bible Verse, Listening Assignment, Bible Story in one side of the Bible folder. Keep out the Big Question sign.
2. Get out your storyboard. If using Simple Story Scenes, put these in your BIble Folder. Or, if using the individual storyboard figures, put all background pictures in place (they have a BG by the number). Put the rest of the storyboard pictures (these have a SB by the number) in order of use in the other side of the Bible folder.
3. Put the HSK Bible Folder as well as the Big Question sign in the Big Question Box/Briefcase and shut it. If your box/briefcase has locks and you want to use the unlocking the box as part of your session, lock it now....but make sure you have the key or know the code first.
4. Prepare the music CD or sheet music or mp3 device for use in your session.

Set Out Free Play Activities

Choose and set up free time activities you will use with the children. Choose a variety of different activities that will be enjoyed by different types of children. Rotate the activities you provide to keep them interesting and fresh to your children. (Suggestions in Appendix D, Core Curriculum books.)

Prepare Any Activities

Choose which (if any) of the unit games and crafts activities you want to use in the session. Bear in mind your time frame as well as the developmental abilities/attention span of your children as you decide what/how many to prepare. **Look over the Discussion Sheet** and choose a few questions you might use to spark discussion with the children as they do their activities (especially good for ages 3's+). Pray for God to give you opportunities to talk about these things with the children.

Let Them Take It with Them

Make copies of the craft/take home sheets, if you are not already using them as one of your activities. You may also want to make copies of the story (see take-home version of each story included in Appendix C with the other take home resources) to have for parents to use with their children at home. There's a link on each craft/take home sheet to the story, if you don't make hard copies.

Store It

After your session is over, collect the resources and store them for future use. This curriculum can be used over and over for years to come.

Unit 3 Overview of Key Concepts

UNIT 3: The Good News of God, the Gosepl

Unit Big Question (and Answer): "What's the Gospel? It's Salvation through Faith in Jesus Christ!"

Meaning:

Gospel means "good news." In the Bible, the gospel is the good news that God sent His Son, Jesus, to save sinners like you and me from the punishment we deserve for our sins. Jesus did this when He suffered and died on the cross, giving His perfect life as the full payment for our sins. This salvation is for all who turn away from their sins and trust in Jesus as their Savior. It is a gift God offers to us, too. Now that is good news, indeed!

Unit 3 Bible Verse: John 3:16 ESV

"For God so loved the world, that he gave his only Son, that whoever believes in him should not perish but have eternal life."

Meaning:

How great is God's love for sinners like you and me, that He would send His own Son, Jesus, to suffer and die for us! Now, all who turn from their sins and trust in Jesus as their Savior will not perish. They will not receive the punishment they deserve for their sins. Jesus has already paid for their sins when He died on the cross. Because of what Jesus has done for them, these people will enjoy eternal life with God. Here on earth, they will know God in their hearts and His care in their lives. And when they die, they will go to be with Him forever! God offers us eternal life, too, when we turn away from our sins and trust in Jesus as our Savior.

Unit 3 ACTS Prayer

A We praise You, God. You love us so much! You, Yourself, have chosen to send a Savior to save us!

C God, in our heart, we know that You are God and that we should obey You, but many times we don't. We are all sinners who deserve Your punishment for disobeying You. Oh, how we need a Savior!

T Thank You for sending Your dear Son, Jesus to be that Savior. Thank You for making the way for our sins to be forgiven.

S Work deep inside our hearts. Help us to turn away from our sins and trust in Jesus as our Savior. Help us to know You and live for You. Help us to go and tell others the good news of the gospel, too.

In Jesus' name we pray. Amen.

Unit 3 Story

The Case of the Stranger's Very Good News
Acts 8:1-8

Songs Used in Unit 3   *listen to or download songs for free at https://praisefactory.org: Hide n Seek Kids Music page*

Big Q & A 3 Song
Big Question 3 Song: What's the Gospel?
Unit 3 Bible Verse Song: For God So Loved the World   John 3:16 ESV
Extra Unit 3 Bible Verse Song: For God So Loved the World John 3:16 ESV (other version)
Extra Unit 3 Bible Verse Song: For God So Loved the World John 3:16 ESV (other version)
Unit 3 Hymn: And Can It Be, v.1 Refrain
Unit 3 Praise Song: I Have Decided to Follow Jesus

Hide 'n' Seek Kids ESV Songs 3 Track Numbers

This is a listing of all songs mentioned in the unit curriculum. You may or may not choose to use all of the songs. They are listed in easy-reference order--NOT in the order used in the curriculum.

You may choose to simply burn a CD/load them onto an mp3 device in this order. Or, you may want to do what we do: choose the songs we want to use and create a play list of them in that order. Then, we burn a CD/upload the play list onto an mp3 device. A teacher only has to click forward to the next song, instead of hunting for the right track. The track number have been included as part of the title of each song, so teachers will still have a reference to the track number listed in the curriculum (same as those listed below), even if you change the order on your customized play list.

SONGS USED EVERY UNIT OF THE CURRICULUM

1 The Classroom Song v.1
2 The Classroom Song v.2
3 The Classroom Song v.3
4 The Classroom Song v.4
5 Hide 'n' Seek Kids Theme Song
6 The Classroom Rules Song
7 Let's Pray Song
8 The Big Question Box Song
9 The Bible Chant Song
10 ACTS Prayer Song (Short Version)
11 ACTS Prayer Song (Full Version)

> **Why the Extra Songs?**
> Hide 'n' Seek Kids is a curriculum used by children of different ages. Sometimes one of the other songs is a better fit for your kids. Or, you may simply want to teach them more songs on the same Bible Truth. Use as many or as few as you want.

UNIT 3: GOD'S GOOD NEWS, THE GOSPEL

12 Big Q & A 3 Song
13 Big Question 3 Song: What's the Gospel?
14,14T Unit 3 Bible Verse Song: For God So Loved the World   John 3:16 ESV
15 *Extra Unit 3 Bible Verse Song: For God So Loved the World John 3:16 ESV (other version)*
16 *Extra Unit 3 Bible Verse Song: For God So Loved the World John 3:16 ESV (other version)*
17 Unit 3 Hymn: And Can It Be, v.1 Refrain
18 Unit 3 Praise Song: I Have Decided to Follow Jesus

T* Tidbit   Shortened version of the Bible Verse Song

listen to or download songs for free at https://praisefactory.org: Hide n Seek Kids Music page

Lesson Plan: Big Question 3   ⭐ = follow the stars for a short & simple lesson plan   p.1

1. GETTING STARTED   NOTE: Most 2 & 3 year olds do best simply learning the Big Question & Answer, a simple version of the Bible story, and maybe the Bible Verse. Use other activities, as time and attention span allow.

Intake Activity Ideas   *Choose one of these open-ended activities to include children as they join the class:*

Free Play Time *suggestions in Appendix D*	⭐(usually best for 2 year olds) Offer your own or some of the easy-to-make, free play activities suggested in Appendix D.

OR   Sing-along Music Time
 	
lyrics and sheet music, Appendix A
 	
listen to or download songs for free at https:// praisefactory.org: Hide n Seek Kids Music page
	Music *from* Hide 'n' Seek Kids (HSK) ESV Songs 3:
	Big Q & A 3 Song *HSK ESV Songs 3, track 12*
	Big Question 3 Song *HSK ESV Songs 3, track 13*
	Unit 3 Bible Verse Song:
	   For God So Loved the World John 3:16, ESV *HSK ESV Songs 3, track 14,14T*
	Extra Unit 3 Bible Verse Song:
	   For God So Loved the World John 3:16, ESV (other version) *HSK ESV Songs 3, track 15*
	Extra Unit 3 Bible Verse Song:
	   For God So Loved the World John 3:16, ESV (other version) *HSK ESV Songs 3, track 15*
	Unit 3 Hymn:
	   And Can It Be, v.1 Refrain *HSK ESV Songs 3, track 18*
	Unit 3 Praise Song:
	   I Have Decided to Follow Jesus *HSK ESV Songs 3, track 19*
	
	Add more fun to Sing-along Music TIme by adding a Music, Movement & Memory Activity. These activities are listed on p. 8 of this lesson plan with the Response Activities. Instructions found in Appendix B.

OR Bible Verse Memory Game *instructions found in Appendix B*	Lesson 1 Game: Detective Mission Madness Practice Lesson 2 Game: Block Clapping Lesson 3 Game: Meet, Greet and Keep It Up Lesson 4 Game: Lily Pad Jump Lesson 5 Game: Animal Cube *These activities are also included on p.8 of this lesson plan with the Response Activities.*

2. OPENING CIRCLE TIME *(introduce the Bible Truth and tell the related Bible story)*

Gathering the Children *lyrics and sheet music, Appendix A*	*Sing verse 1 of The Classroom Song to gather the children for Circle Time.* **The Classroom Song, verse 1** *HSK ESV Songs 3, track 1* Let's gather together to worship God, Let's gather together to worship God, Let's gather together to worship God, Come gather here with me!
Welcome to Hide 'n' Seek Kids!	⭐"Welcome to Hide 'n' Seek Kids! We're so glad you've joined us! We're here to seek God and learn His Word and Hide it in our heart so that it will always be with us. And we're here to Hide His Word, the Bible, in our hearts. We ask big questions about God and dig deep down in the truths of God's Word to find them."

Lesson Plan: Big Question 3   use with all FIVE lessons   **p.2**

2. OPENING CIRCLE TIME, continued   ⭐ = *short & simple lesson plan*

Hide 'n' Seek Kids Theme Song *lyrics and sheet music, Appendix A*	"Let's sing our Hide 'n' Seek Kids theme song." ⭐**Hide 'n' Seek Kids Theme Song** *HSK ESV Songs 3, track 5* Come along, we're gonna Hide 'n' seek! Hide God's Word in our heart and Him, we'll seek, God loves to show us the truths of His Word, That we might know Him and live out what we've learned.
Classroom Rules Song *lyrics and sheet music, Appendix A*	There are two very important things that Hide 'n' Seek Kids do together: we worship God and we love one another. Our Classroom Rules Song reminds us how we should act. Let's sing it." **Classroom Rules Song** *HSK ESV Songs 3, track 6* Shh, be quiet while someone is talking, Raise your hand, if you have something to say, Don't touch your friend, sitting beside you, Obey your teachers, Be kind as you play. These are our classroom rules, These are our classroom rules, They help us worship God and love one another, These are our classroom rules.
Opening Prayer Time *lyrics and sheet music, Appendix A*	"Children, we need God's help to keep these rules. Let's ask Him to help us right now. Let's get ready and pray." **Let's Pray** *HSK ESV Songs 3, track 7* 1-2-3! Fold your hands, Bow your head, Close your eyes. Let's pray! *(repeat)* "Let's pray:" ⭐**Opening Prayer** Dear Lord, We're so glad to get to gather together to worship You! Please help us keep the classroom rules. Please help us to love You and learn about You today. In Jesus' name we pray. Amen.

Lesson Plan: Big Question 3   use with all FIVE lessons   p.3

2. OPENING CIRCLE TIME, continued   = short & simple lesson plan

Reveal the Big Question	"It's time to get down to business, Hide 'n' Seek kids! Let's see what our Big Question for today is. It's right inside our Big Question Box/ Briefcase."
Introduce the Big Question Box/Briefcase *lyrics and sheet music, Appendix A*	**The Big Question Box Song** *HSK ESV Songs 3, track 8* We've got a big box, All closed up and locked, Filled with the truths of God's Word. We've got a brief case, There's no time to waste, Come on, kids, let's open it up!

The Big Question under Investigation

VISUAL   take out
AID

#1   of BQB
Big Question & Answer Sign, front side
*found in the HSK Vol. 1 Visual Aids, ESV Book

Ok, who would like to open it up for me and pull out the Big Question?"

Choose a child to open the box/briefcase, take out the Big Question and hand it to you, then hold up the Big Question sign for all the children to see, and say:

The Big Question we are investigating today is Big Question Number 3:
    What Is the Gospel?
and the Answer is:
    It's Salvation through Faith in Jesus Christ!

Big Question Meaning

Gospel means "good news." In the Bible, the gospel is the good news that God sent His Son, Jesus, to save sinners like you and me from the punishment we deserve for our sins. Jesus did this when He suffered and died on the cross, giving His perfect life as the full payment for our sins. This salvation is for all who turn away from their sins and trust in Jesus as their Savior. It is a gift God offers to us, too. Now that is good news, indeed!

Big Question Songs

Big Q & A 3 Song

lyrics and sheet music, Appendix A

"Let's sing our Big Question Song:

Big Q & A 3 Song   *HSK ESV Songs 3, track 12*
(adapted version of "Oh, My Darlin' Clementine")

What's the gospel?
What's the gospel?
Can you tell me what it is?
It's salvation through faith in Jesus,
That's what the gospel is. (repeat)

Lesson Plan: Big Question 3   use with all FIVE lessons   p.4

2. OPENING CIRCLE TIME, continued   ⭐ = short & simple lesson plan

Learning about the Big Question ⭐	*Repeat the Big Question and Answer again:* "What Is the Gospel? It's Salvation through Faith in Jesus Christ" *Say:* "Hmmmm, I wonder what that means… Let's do our action rhyme/sing our song that explains it." *Then do the action rhyme /sing song using any of the optional motions suggested, if desired.*

Big Question ⭐ **(Action Rhyme) Song** *lyrics and sheet music, Appendix A*	**Big Question 3 Action Rhyme/ Song** *HSK ESV Songs 3, track 13*

Big Question 3 Action Rhyme/ Song   *HSK ESV Songs 3, track 13*

	(POSSIBLE ACTIONS)
Refrain: What is the gospel? G-O-S-P-E-L? What is the gospel? Can anybody tell me? What is the gospel? Yes, I know what it is! Salvation through faith in Christ, That's what the gospel is.	*Make question gesture with your arms (arms bent and palms facing upward)* *Point out to others in a arc movement*
"G" is for God, our good King and Creator, O, we should obey Him, but instead we're disobeyers, So S, we need a Savior to save us from our sins, That Savior is Jesus, who "P" took the punishment.	*Point up to God* *Make a grumpy face* *Use your index fingers to make a cross*
Yes, Jesus died upon the cross, the perfect sacrifice, Then on day three, He rose again To prove He'd won the fight,	*Use your index fingers to make a cross* *Hold up three fingers, then straighten arm up and point up with one finger*

And now "E"everyone who repents
  and believes in Him,
He gives "E-L" eternal life:
  forever life with Him. Refrain
	Make prayer hands
	
	Raise hands and waggle them back and forth (celebrating)

| Lesson Plan: Big Question 3 | use with all FIVE lessons | p.5 |

2. OPENING CIRCLE TIME, continued   ⭐ = short & simple lesson plan

Learning the Bible Verse **The Bible Chant Song** lyrics and sheet music, Appendix A	⭐"And how do I know this is true? God tells me so in His special book, the Bible." *Say or sing the Bible Chant Song.* **The Bible Chant Song** *HSK ESV Songs 3, track 9* The Bible, the Bible, Let's get out the Bible. Let's hear what God has to say. The Bible, the Bible, God's given us the Bible. It's His Word for us to learn and obey! Yay!
The Bible Verse in the HSK Bible Folder HSK 3 Bible Verse-front side (in the HSK Bible folder) VISUAL Place take out AID verse in #2 HSK Bible Folder of BQB HSK Bible Folder *found in the HSK Vol. 1 Visual Aids, ESV Book*	"Who would like to get our Bible folder out of the Big Question Briefcase for me?" *Choose a child to open the briefcase, take out the "Bible" folder and hand it to you. Remove the Bible Verse Picture from the "Bible" folder and hold it up for all the children to see, then say:* ⭐**John 3:16, ESV** "For God so loved the world, that he gave his only Son, that whoever believes in him should not perish but have eternal life."
Bible Verse Meaning HSK 3 Bible Verse-back side	⭐**What does that mean?** How great is God's love for sinners like you and me, that He would send His own Son, Jesus, to suffer and die for us! Now, all who turn from their sins and trust in Jesus as their Savior will not perish. They will not receive the punishment they deserve for their sins. Jesus has already paid for their sins when He died on the cross. Because of what Jesus has done for them, these people will enjoy eternal life with God. Here on earth, they will know God in their hearts and His care in their lives. And when they die, they will go to be with Him forever! God offers us eternal life, too, when we turn away from our sins and trust in Jesus as our Savior.
Bible Verse Song lyrics and sheet music, Appendix A	"We've said our Bible verse, now let's sing it!" **For God So Loved the World: John 3:16** *HSK ESV Songs 3, track 14,14T* For God so loved the world, That He gave His only Son, That whoever believes in Him shouldn't perish, But have eternal life. For God so loved the world, That He gave His only Son, That whoever believes in Him shouldn't perish, But have eternal life. John Three, sixteen. *You might also enjoy:* *For God So Loved the World: John 3:16, ESV (2nd version) HSK ESV Songs 3, track 15* *For God So Loved the World: John 3:16, ESV (3rd version) HSK ESV Songs 3, track 16* *lyrics and sheet music, Appendix A*

| **Lesson Plan: Big Question 3** | use with all FIVE lessons | **p.6** |

2. OPENING CIRCLE TIME, continued   ⭐ = short & simple lesson plan

Getting into the Case	"Now it's time to do a bit more deep down investigating. Let's see what Detective Dan wants us to help him figure out. Would someone like to get it out for me?"
Listening Assignments *Place in* *take out* HSK Bible Folder ?❓? *Big Question Briefcase* *of BQB*	**NOTE: Listening assignments are most suitable for ages 3+. Skip straight to the Bible story (see bottom of this page), if working with 2 year olds.** "Let's open up our listening assignment and see what we are supposed to figure out today. *Choose a child to take out the Listening Assignment (from the HSK Bible Folder) and hand it to you. Read Detective Dan's letter to the children that includes the listening assignment. The listening assignments are summarized below:*
VISUAL AID **#3** *HSK Vol. 1 Visual Aids, ESV*	**Detective Dan's Lesson #1 Listening Assignment:** As you listen to the story, see if you can figure out: 1. Who ran away from Jerusalem went to Samaria? 2. What was the good news he brought with him and shared?
VISUAL AID **#4** *HSK Vol. 1 Visual Aids, ESV*	**Detective Dan's Lesson #2 Listening Assignment:** Our Bible verse is John 3:16: "For God so loved the world, that he gave his only Son, that whoever believes in him should not perish but have eternal life." As you listen to the story, see if you can figure out: 1. Who did God use to tell the world the good news about His Son, Jesus? 2. What happened when they shared the good news?
VISUAL AID **#5A,B,C** *Listening Assignment #3 includes the Assignment Sheet, plus 4 clue pictures* *HSK Vol. 1 Visual Aids, ESV*	**Detective Dan's Lesson #3 Listening Assignment:** I found four clues, but one of them is NOT in the story. They are: Some enemies; some bags; some sick people; and a horse. *Hold up each of the four pictures for the children to see as you identify them. Better yet, put them up on your flannelgraph board, off to one side.* I need to know: 1. Which three pictures belong in the story and which one does not? 2. How did God use the other three things to spread the good news of Jesus?
VISUAL AID **#6** *HSK Vol. 1 Visual Aids, ESV*	**Detective Dan's Lesson #4 Listening Assignment:** As you listen to the story, see if you can figure out: 1. Philip tell the good news of Jesus to the people of what city? 2. What did they confess to God when they heard the gospel?
VISUAL AID **#7** *HSK Vol. 1 Visual Aids, ESV*	**Detective Dan's Lesson #5 Listening Assignment:** As you listen to the story, see if you can figure out: 1. Why was it bad news that the Christians had to leave Jerusalem? 2. What good news did they share with others as they ran away to other places?
Tell the Bible Story⭐ *Place story & pics in* *take out* HSK Bible Folder ?❓? *Big Question Briefcase* *of BQB* *HSK Vol. 1 Visual Aids, ESV* **Bible Story included in this book, immediately after the Lesson Plan and with the Visual Aids**	*Then say,* "Ok, Hide 'n' Seekers! Put on your best listening ears and see if you can find the answers to Detective Dan's questions. When I finish telling the story, we'll see what we come up with." ⭐ **Bible Story: The Case of the Stranger's Very Good News** *Acts 8:1-8* *Read the Bible Truth story, putting up the storyboard pictures/Simple Story Scenes as you tell it. Then, have the children answer the listening assignment. Present the the gospel and lead in prayer.* *Answers to questions, the gospel and ACTS prayer are included with the story text.*

Lesson Plan: Big Question 3   use with all FIVE lessons   p.7

2. OPENING CIRCLE TIME, continued

 = short & simple lesson plan

Story Response Song(s)	*As attention span and time allow, you might want to end with one of the following songs which also tie in with the unit. If desired, use the Music and Movement activity ideas while singing, listed with the Response Activities.*

Hymn

lyrics and sheet music, Appendix A

And Can It Be   *HSK ESV Songs 3, track 17*

Refrain
Amazing love, how can it be?
That thou, my God, should die for me?
Amazing love, how can it be?
That thou, my God, should die for me?

Tie-in: "God's love is amazing! How He loves His people! They deserved the full punishment for their sins. They deserved to die and be separated from God forever. But Jesus came to die for the sins of all who would ever turn from their sins and trust in Him as their Savior. He died in their place. He took their sins. So that they could be forgiven and live as God's people forever. When we turn from our sins and trust in Jesus as our Savior, then His death pays for our sins, too. We, too, can know God now in our hearts, and one day, go to live with Him forever."

Praise Song

lyrics and sheet music, Appendix A

Praise Song: I Have Decided to Follow Jesus   *HSK ESV Songs 3, track 18*

I have decided to follow Jesus,
I have decided to follow Jesus,
I have decided to follow Jesus,
No turning back, no turning back.

Tie-in: "God offers to forgive our sins when we turn away from sinning and trust in Jesus as our Savior. He gives us eternal life and makes us His people. God's people love God and want to please Him. Every day, they ask God to help them to follow Jesus by how they live. They want to love God and others the way Jesus did. God loves to answer this prayer. He promises to send the Holy Spirit to help them do this."

3. TAKING ACTION: Response Activities *(choose from among these activities)*

Transition to Activities

⭐ Well, Hide 'n' Seek Kids, you've done a great job diggin' deep down for answers in the truths of God's Word. Now it's time to enjoy some activities."

⭐ *Tell children what activity/s you are providing for them: either free play or some of the response activities listed below. When you are ready to dismiss them, use this song to help the children transition in an orderly fashion to their next activity.*

Classroom Song, verse 2

lyrics and sheet music, Appendix A

"Children, let's sing our Time to Play Song. When we are finished you may get up and walk over to our next activity."

Classroom Song, verse 2   *HSK ESV Songs 3, track 2*
We've gathered together to worship God,
We've gathered together to worship God,
And now it's time to play.

Dismiss the children to whatever activities you have prepared for them to do.

Lesson Plan: Big Question 3	use with all FIVE lessons	p.8

3. TAKING ACTION: Response Activities *(choose from among these activities)* ⭐ *= short & simple lesson plan*

Response Activities	*Choose one or more activities appropriate for your children, based on classroom time and developmental needs.* **Add the Discussion Sheet to any activity for deeper learning.** ⭐
Bible Verse Memory Game *game directions, Appendix B*	Though listed with the opening activities, you may choose to use this Bible verse game here instead (or as a repeat). • Lesson 1 Game: Detective Mission Madness Practice • Lesson 2 Game: Block Clapping • Lesson 3 Game: Meet, Greet and Keep It Up • Lesson 4 Game: Lily Pad Jump • Lesson 5 Game: Animal Cube *Use the Discussion Sheet with these activities for even deeper learning* — Unit Discussion Questions for Activities / Discussion Questions
Music, Movement & Memory Activity *game directions, Appendix B*	A music activity that uses the songs from the Bible Truth and Big Question unit. • HSK Songs for Unit, plus: • Lesson 1 Activity: Block Clappers • Lesson 2 Activity: Musical Squares • Lesson 3 Activity: Lullabies, Bells and Lions • Lesson 4 Activity: Thumping Drums • Lesson 5 Activity: Say, Spring Up and Shout *Use the Discussion Sheet with these activities for even deeper learning* — Unit Discussion Questions for Activities / Discussion Questions
Bible Story Review Game *game directions, Appendix B*	A game that uses the storyboard pictures from the story to review the story. • Lesson 1 Game: Clothespin Line Up and Drop • Lesson 2 Game: Fix Up the Mix Up • Lesson 3 Game: Who's in the Basket? • Lesson 4 Game: Run to the Grocery Store • Lesson 5 Game: Treasure Hunt *Use the Discussion Sheet with these activities for even deeper learning* — Unit Discussion Questions for Activities / Discussion Questions
Coloring Pages/ Take Home Sheets *in Appendix C*	A coloring page related to the lesson assignment questions is provided for each lesson. On the back of each are the key concepts, a few questions and a song for parents to use with their children. (If desired, include a copy of the Bible story with the Take Home Sheet.) NOTE: Upgrade your coloring sheet to a more interesting craft by offering simple embellishments, such as jiggly eyes, craft sand, glitter, glitter glue, colored paper dots (made with a hole punch), fabric scraps, etc. Make cut-to-size glued-on clothes, hair, etc for characters by using a copy of the coloring sheet, cutting out the selected portions and making them the patterns for whatever you want to cut out of fabric, paper, foil, etc. ⭐ • Lesson 1 Coloring Sheet Emphasis: Bible Truth • Lesson 2 Coloring Sheet Emphasis: Bible Verse • Lesson 3 Coloring Sheet Emphasis: Bible Truth • Lesson 4 Coloring Sheet Emphasis: ACTS Prayer • Lesson 5 Coloring Sheet Emphasis: The Gospel *Use the Discussion Sheet with these activities for even deeper learning* — Unit Discussion Questions for Activities / Discussion Questions
Extra Crafts: **Big Question Craft** *in Appendix C*	**These crafts are slightly more complex than the coloring sheets:** **The Big Question Craft** is a color, glue and stick craft of the Big Question and Answer. *Use the Discussion Sheet with these activities for even deeper learning* — Unit Discussion Questions for Activities
Bible Verse Craft *in Appendix C*	**The Bible Verse Craft** is a craft that gives the Bible verse and explains it, also involving gluing and sticking and a few other, simple craft supplies. Discussion Questions
Bible Story Puzzle *in Appendix C*	The **Storyboard Picture Placement Page** has been made into a puzzle that can be cut out and re-assembled by the children. This provides a nice summary of the story.
Free Play Activities *ideas in Appendix D*	⭐ Offer your own or some of the easy-to-make, free play activities suggested in Appendix D.

Lesson Plan: Big Question 3   use with all FIVE lessons   p.9

4. CLOSING CIRCLE TIME *(End-of-session activities for the last 5-10 minutes of class time)*   ⭐ *= short & simple lesson plan*

Transition to Closing Circle **Classroom Song, verse 3** *lyrics and sheet music, Appendix A*	*Use this song to help the children transition in an orderly fashion. Sing the song, then ask the children to gather with you for Closing Circle Time.* **Classroom Song, verse 3** *HSK ESV Songs 3, track 3* It's time to get ready to go and tell, It's time to get ready to go and tell, Come gather here with me.
Closing Circle Time **Classroom Song, verse 4** *lyrics and sheet music, Appendix A*	*When children are settled in the circle, say:* "It is almost time for your parents to come pick you up. And do you know what that means? It means…. (draw this out to build anticipation and excitement)…that it's almost time to go home and….it's almost time to…Go and Tell! We have learned some big news about God today. God wants us to take and tell it to the whole world!" **Classroom Song, verse 4** *HSK ESV Songs 3, track 4* So what's our big news to go and tell, So what's our big news to go and tell, Can you tell me now?
Big News to Tell **Big Question 3** *VISUAL AID* **#1** **found in the HSK Vol. 1 Visual Aids, ESV Book* *lyrics and sheet music, Appendix A*	"Let's see….there's so much big news to tell! There's so much we've learned! Can you tell me the answer to our **Big Question: "What Is the gospel?"** *(Show them the Big Question and Answer picture.)* Say the answer with me: **"It's Salvation through Faith in Jesus Christ!"** *(If desired, you can sing the Big Q & A Song.)* *HSK ESV Songs 3, track 12*
Big Question 3 Bible Verse *VISUAL AID* **#2** **found in the HSK Vol. 1 Visual Aids, ESV Book* *lyrics and sheet music, Appendix A*	"And how do I know this is true? Can you tell me? Say it with me: **"The Bible tells me so!"** That's right! We learned: **John 3:16, ESV** **"For God so loved the world, that he gave his only Son, that whoever believes in him should not perish but have eternal life."** *(Show them the Bible Verse picture.)* The Bible tells us that God saves all who trust in Jesus as their Savior." *(If desired, you can sing the Bible verse song.)* *HSK ESV Songs 3, track 14,14T*

Lesson Plan: Big Question 3   use with all FIVE lessons   p.10

4. CLOSING CIRCLE TIME, continued   ⭐ = short & simple lesson plan

Closing ACTS Prayer Time	*Let's ask God to help us to remember this and even tell others this good news. Let's get ready and pray our ACTS prayer.*
ACTS Prayer Chant *lyrics and sheet music, Appendix A*	*And what does ACTS mean? Let's sing/say our ACTS Prayer Chant!* **ACTS Prayer Chant Song** *HSK ESV Songs 3, tracks 10,11* A, Adoration: God, we praise You! C, Confession: Forgive us our sins. That's the ACTS prayer, my friend, T, Thanksgiving,: Thank You for Jesus, Bow head, Close your eyes, Shhh, S, Supplication: Help us to live like Him. Let's begin!

Closing ACTS Prayer	"Let's pray!" *Lead the children in the ACTS prayer for this unit.* **A** We praise You, God. You love us so much! You, Yourself, have chosen to send a Savior to save us! **C** God, in our heart, we know that You are God and that we should obey You, but many times we don't. We are all sinners who deserve Your punishment for disobeying You. Oh, how we need a Savior! **T** Thank You for sending Your dear Son, Jesus to be that Savior. Thank You for making the way for our sins to be forgiven. **S** Work deep inside our hearts. Help us to turn away from our sins and trust in Jesus as our Savior. Help us to know You and live for You. Help us to go and tell others the good news of the gospel, too. In Jesus' name we pray. Amen.

5. TAKING IT HOME *(Take Home Sheet)*

Clean up and Dismissal	⭐"Now it's time to work together and clean up." *Have the children join you in cleaning up the room.*
Coloring Pages/ Take Home Sheets *in Appendix C*	⭐ *Give out the craft/take home sheet and any other papers from the session, as you dismiss children from class.* *(Reminder: The back side of the coloring page is the take home sheet for each lesson.)*
Bible Story to Take-Home *in Appendix C*	You may also want to include a copy of the story along with the take home sheet. (However, each coloring sheet/take home sheet includes a note to parents telling them where they can download the story from the Parent Resources section on the website.

Big Question 3 Bible Story   use with all FIVE lessons

Place story in / take out   p.l

HSK Bible Folder   of BQB

The Case of the Stranger's Very Good News
Acts 8:1-8

Story-telling Tips

Ahead of time:
1. Read the Bible verses and story. Pray!
2. Choose story action cues and/or prepare storyboard pictures, if using. (Included in Visual Aids book)
3. Practice telling story with the pictures, timing your presentation. Shorten, if necessary to fit your allotted time.

During your presentation:
1. Maintain as much eye contact as possible as you tell the story.
2. Put up storyboard figures/add story action cues as you tell the story. Allow the children to help you put them on the board, if desired.
3. Include the children in your story with a few questions about what they think will happen or words/concepts that might be new to them.
4. Watch the kids for signs that their attention span has been reached. Shorten, if necessary.

INTRODUCTION/ LISTENING ASSIGNMENTS

"Our story is called: The Case of the Stranger's Very Good News. Here is your listening assignment... "

Read from Detective Dan's Listening Assignment signs, but questions are summarized below:

Detective Dan's Lesson #1 Listening Assignment:

As you listen to the story, see if you can figure out:
1. Who ran away from Jerusalem went to Samaria?
2. What was the good news he brought with him and shared?

Detective Dan's Lesson #2 Listening Assignment:

Our Bible verse is John 3:16: "For God so loved the world, that he gave his only Son, that whoever believes in him should not perish but have eternal life."

As you listen to the story, see if you can figure out:
1. Who did God use to tell the world the good news about His Son, Jesus?
2. What happened when they shared the good news?

Detective Dan's Lesson #3 Listening Assignment:

I found four clues, but one of them is NOT in the story.
They are: Some enemies; some bags; some sick people; and a horse.
Hold up each of the four pictures for the children to see as you identify them. Better yet, put them up on your flannelgraph board, off to one side.

I need to know:
1. Which three pictures belong in the story and which one does not?
2. How did God use the other three things to spread the good news of Jesus?

Detective Dan's Lesson #4 Listening Assignment:

As you listen to the story, see if you can figure out:
1. Philip told the good news of Jesus to the people of what city?
2. What did they confess to God when they heard the gospel?

Detective Dan's Lesson #5 Listening Assignment:

As you listen to the story, see if you can figure out:
1. Why was it bad news that the Christians had to leave Jerusalem?
2. What good news did they share with people as they ran away to live in new places?

Read the questions, THEN SAY,

"Ok, Hide 'n' Seekers! Put on your best listening ears and see if you can find the answers to Detective Dan's questions. When I finish telling the story, we'll see what we come up with."

"The Case of the Stranger's Very Good News"   Acts 8:1-8

Story with lines separating paragraphs (text in bold, optional interaction cues in italics)

"Run! Pack your bags! Get out of town!" The church leaders told the other Christians. "Jerusalem isn't safe anymore! The enemies of Jesus are after you! They will hurt you and put you in jail if they catch you!" the leaders warned. "So get out of town…NOW!"

How fast would you run if you had enemies trying to get you? Run in place and show me!

That's exactly what most of the Christians did. They packed their bags and ran, ran, ran out of town!

Oh, what bad news this was! Or was it? Yes, it was BAD news that these Christians had to leave their homes and their friends and everything they knew in Jerusalem. And, it was BAD news that they had enemies who wanted to hurt them. But…. it was GOOD news for the people of the world.

Why? Because when those Christians ran away, they took the gospel with them--that wonderful, marvelous, amazing good news about Jesus--and they shared it with everyone they met.

Some of the Christians went down the sea and made their home there. And what good news did they tell the people they met there? The gospel--the good news of Jesus!

Some went out to dry, deserty lands and made their home there. And what did they tell the people they met there? The gospel--the good news of Jesus!

Some went up to the tall mountains and made their home there.

Can you pretend to climb up a mountain…carrying your bags with you???

And what did they tell the people they met there? The gospel--the good news of Jesus!

Some even went far away to other countries. One of these people was a godly man named Philip. Philip went to the land of Samaria to live. And what did he tell the people he met there?

Can you tell me…the good news of who? Jesus!

You guessed it! The gospel--the good news of Jesus!

As Philip told the good news of Jesus, crowds of people gathered around and listened. There were poor people and rich people; sick people and well people; old people and young people. And to all of these people, Philip told the gospel, good news of Jesus. This is what he told them:

"God is the good King and Creator of the whole world. He created us and we should obey Him. But instead, we've all chosen to disobey Him. Disobeying God is what God calls "sin"; and, we deserve His punishment for our sins against Him. We need a Savior!" Philip told them.

"God sent Jesus to be that Savior. Jesus is God's perfect Son who came to earth to suffer and die on the cross to pay for our sins. Then, on the third day, Jesus rose from the dead, showing that He had beaten sin and death," Philip shared.

*Story with lines separating paragraphs (**text in bold,** optional interaction cues in italics)*

"Now, everyone who turns away from sinning and trusts in Jesus as their Savior will be saved. God makes them His people. And they will get to know God and live with Him forever! This is the gospel—God's good news to you. Come, turn from your sins and trust in Jesus as your Savior today!" Philip told them.

Have you heard this good news before? It is very good news, isn't it?

"What amazing things this stranger is saying," the Samaritans thought! "We haven't heard anything like this before. Could it really be true?" they wondered.

Then God did something marvelous to help them know this good news really was true. Philip prayed for God to heal the sick people listening to him preach. And right then and there, without any medicine, or doctor, or hospital, God made them well. By His great power alone!

The people of Samaria were even more amazed! God Holy Spirit worked in the hearts of many people as they heard the good news of Jesus and saw God's mighty power to heal the sick. "Surely this good news is true!" they exclaimed. They turned away from their sins and trusted in Jesus as their Savior. They were saved from their sins! God had made them His people!

Let's clap our hands and say, "Yay" for the good things God did in those people!

So, yes, maybe it had been bad news that made Philip run away from Jerusalem. But God had turned that bad news into good news for the people of Samaria. And that made Philip --and them --very, very happy!

Big Question 3 Bible Story
use with all FIVE lessons

Cracking the Case: (story wrap-up for Listening Assignments)

It's time to see how we did with our Listening Assignment.

Detective Dan's Lesson #1 Listening Assignment:
As you listen to the story, see if you can figure out:
1. Who ran away from Jerusalem and went to Samaria? Philip.
2. What was the good news he brought with him and shared? God forgives our sins and makes us His people when we turn away from our sins and trust in Jesus as our Savior..

For You and Me:
The good news Philip shared wasn't just for the people of Samaria. It's for us, too! God will forgive our sins and make us His people when we turn away from our sins and trust in Jesus as our Savior.. God will help us do this, if we ask Him to. What good news that is!

Detective Dan's Lesson #2 Listening Assignment:
Our Bible verse is John 3:16: "For God so loved the world, that he gave his only Son, that whoever believes in him should not perish but have eternal life."

As you listen to the story, see if you can figure out:
1. Who did God use to tell the world the good news about His Son, Jesus? His people--Philip and the other Christians.
2. What happened when they shared the good news? God worked in the hearts of many. They turned from their sins and trusted in Jesus as their Savior.

For You and Me:
God still uses His people today to tell others the good news about His Son, Jesus. God has even used them to tell us the good news of Jesus today! We can ask God to work in our hearts and help us to believe the good news of Jesus. We can ask Him to help us to turn away from our sins and trust in Jesus as our Savior.

Detective Dan's Lesson #3 Listening Assignment:
I found four clues, but one of them is NOT in the story. They are: Some enemies; some bags; another country; and a horse.

1. Which of the three pictures belong in the story and which one does not? The horse does not belong.
2. How did God use the other three things to spread the good news of Jesus? The Christians packed their bags and left Jerusalem to get away from their enemies who wanted to hurt them. They went to live in many places, even other countries, and told the people there the good news of Jesus.

For You and Me:
God has a wonderful plan to tell the whole world the good news of Jesus. He wants everyone to know how their sins can be forgiven and they can become one of His people. And God will use everything as part of this great plan--even very sad things like those believers having to leave them homes. How great is our God! How good and great are His plans!

Detective Dan's Lesson #4 Listening Assignment:
As you listen to the story, see if you can figure out:
1. Philip told the good news of Jesus to the people of what city? The city of Samaria.
2. What did many people confess to God when they heard the gospel? They confessed their sins and asked God to forgive their sins....and He did!

For You and Me:
Like the people of Samaria, we are sinners who need to confess our sins to God. Like them, we can ask Him to forgive our sins... and He can!

Detective Dan's Lesson #5 Listening Assignment:
As you listen to the story, see if you can figure out:
1. Why was it bad news that the Christians had to leave Jerusalem? They had to leave their homes and their friends.
2. What good news did they share with people as they ran away to live in new places? They told them the gospel--how they could become God's people by turning away from their sins and trusting in Jesus as their Savior.

For You and Me:
This good news is for us, too. Jesus can save us from our sins and make us God's people, too, when we repent of our sins and trust in Him as our Savior.

Big Question 3 Bible Story   use with all FIVE lessons   p.5

The Gospel (story wrap-up if NOT using Listening Assignments)

Our Bible Truth is:
What Is the Gospel?
It's Salvation through Faith in Jesus Christ!

Philip was so happy when the people of Samaria heard the good news of Jesus and believed. That good news is for us, too! We can ask God to work in our heart and help us to turn away from disobeying Him and trust in Jesus as our Savior. When we do, God will forgive our sins and save us! He will live in our heart, helping us to know Him right now. And one day, we will go to live with Him in heaven forever. That will be best of all!

Close in prayer.

Closing Unit 3 ACTS Prayer

A=Adoration C=Confession T=Thanksgiving S=Supplication

A   We praise You, God. You love us so much! You, Yourself, have chosen to send a Savior to save us!

C   God, in our heart, we know that You are God and that we should obey You, but many times we don't. We are all sinners who deserve Your punishment for disobeying You. Oh, how we need a Savior!

T   Thank You for sending Your dear Son, Jesus to be that Savior. Thank You for making the way for our sins to be forgiven.

S   Work deep inside our hearts. Help us to turn away from our sins and trust in Jesus as our Savior. Help us to know You and live for You. Help us to go and tell others the good news of the gospel, too. In Jesus' name we pray.

  In Jesus' name we pray. Amen.

Unit 3 Discussion Sheet

use with all FIVE lessons

Use with all response activities for deeper learning

P. 1

Questions to aid discussion of the key concepts and for use in games

Be familiar with these questions and answers. Look for opportunities to ask questions and talk about their answers, such as while the children work on their coloring pages, as part of their games, or during play time. Remember: your goal isn't to ask all these questions or to only talk to the children about these things. It is to be deliberate in having good conversations with them, as natural opportunities arise.

BIG QUESTION	What is the Gospel? It's salvation through Faith in Jesus Christ!
Meaning	Gospel means "good news." In the Bible, the gospel is the good news that God sent His Son, Jesus, to save sinners like you and me from the punishment we deserve for our sins. Jesus did this when He suffered and died on the cross, giving His perfect life as the full payment for our sins. This salvation is for all who turn away from their sins and trust in Jesus as their Savior. It is a gift God offers to us, too. Now that is good news, indeed!
Discussion Questions	*choose a few* 1. What is the gospel? *It's salvation through Faith in Jesus Christ!* 2. What does the word "gospel" mean? *It means "good news."* 3. Why is the gospel such good news? *It tells us how can forgive our sins and make us His people forever!* 4. Who do we need to have faith in? *Jesus.* 5. What did Jesus do so we can be saved? *He took the punishment for sin when He died on the cross.* 6. What does God want us to turn away from? *Our sins.* 7. What does it mean to turn away from our sins? *To say "no" to disobeying God and to want to obey Him, instead.* 8. Who can we ask to help us turn away from our sins and trust in Jesus? *God! He loves to help us when we ask Him.*
THE GOSPEL	What is God's good news for you and me? *The gospel!* *God made all people--including you and me! And He made us to know Him, love Him, and obey Him. He's our good King. But like the people in our story today, we have all disobeyed God. We want to live life our own way, not His. We all deserve His punishment. How sad! But God is so merciful that He sent a Savior--His Son, Jesus! Jesus suffered and died on the cross. Jesus offered up His perfect life to God to completely pay for the sins of God's people, then He rose from the dead in victory on the third day. We can be God's people, too, when we turn away from our sins and trust in Jesus as our Savior. He loves to help us do this. Ask Him! How good is God to us!*

Unit 3 Discussion Sheet

Questions to aid discussion of the key concepts and for use in games

BIBLE VERSE

"For God so loved the world, that he gave his only Son, that whoever believes in him should not perish but have eternal life." John 3:16, ESV

Meaning

How great is God's love for sinners like you and me, that He would send His own Son, Jesus, to suffer and die for us! Now, all who turn from their sins and trust in Jesus as their Savior will not perish. They will not receive the punishment they deserve for their sins. Jesus has already paid for their sins when He died on the cross. Because of what Jesus has done for them, these people will enjoy eternal life with God. Here on earth, they will know God in their hearts and His care in their lives. And when they die, they will go to be with Him forever! God offers us eternal life, too, when we turn away from our sins and trust in Jesus as our Savior.

Discussion Questions

choose a few

1. Who loved the world? *God did.*
2. What did God do because He loved the world so much? *He gave his only Son to suffer and die for sinful people, like you and me.*
3. What is the name of God's One and Only Son? *Jesus.*
4. What does God give all who believe in Jesus? *Eternal life--life that never ever ends.*
5. What do we each deserve for disobeying God? *We deserve to perish--to die and be separate from God and all His goodness forever.*
6. What can we have instead of punishment for our sins? *We can have eternal life!*
7. How can we have eternal life? *By trusting in Jesus as our Savior and living our lives for Him.*

BIBLE STORY

The Case of the Stranger's Very Good News

Discussion Questions

choose a few

1. Why did the Christians have to leave their home in Jerusalem? *Enemies wanted to hurt them and put them in jail for believing in Jesus.*
2. Where did the Christians go when they left Jerusalem? *They went many places-- to dry, deserty places, to places by the sea, to places in the mountains, and even to other countries.*
3. What did the Christians tell people when they went to these new places? *The good news of Jesus.*
4. Where did Philip go when he left Jerusalem? *He went to Samaria.*
5. What did Philip tell the people of Samaria when he went there? *The good news of Jesus.*
6. What marvelous thing did God do to help the people of Samaria believe when Philip shared the gospel with them? *God healed many sick people by His mighty power alone, helping them believe Philip's good news.*
7. What happened in the hearts of the people of Samaria? *God worked in their hearts as they heard the good news of Jesus and saw how God healed the sick people. Many turned away from their sins and trusted in Jesus as their Savior.*
8. What was the good news that Philip and the others told? *God will forgive our sins when we turn away from our sins and trust in Jesus as our Savior.*
9. Who can help us believe the good news of Jesus? *God can! He loves to help us when we ask Him.*

Hide 'n' Seek Kids

Unit 4
Curriculum:
The God Like None Other

Session Prep (especially good for newbies!)

Pray! *NOTE: Most 2 & 3 year olds do best simply learning the Big Question & Answer, a simple version of the Bible story, and maybe the Bible Verse. Use other activities, as time and attention span allow. Your session prep need only include what you use.*

Pray for the Holy Spirit to be at work in your heart and the children's hearts.

Review

If new to the curriculum, look at the **Getting Started with Hide 'n' Seek Kids section of this book** (p.5) It will be especially helpful to read through the Hide 'n' Seek Kids section of **The Praise Factory Tour: Extended Version Book.** This is a visual way to understand what goes on in the classroom. (A pdf of the book is found in the samples section on the website.)

Look through and Learn the Lesson

Read over **lesson plan**. Practice any **songs or action rhymes** you are using. Choose/make up motions to go with these. Choose less with younger children and more with older preschoolers. **Practice the lesson with the visual aids** and using the Big Question Box/Briefcase.

Read and Rehearse the Bible Story with Pictures

Read the Bible story from the Bible. Read the curriculum version. Practice telling it with the storyboard pictures. (If you have not previously laminated the story pictures, do that now.) Or, rehearse it from the Simple Story Scenes, if you are using those.

Let There Be Music

Download the music and listen to the songs. Choose which of the songs you will use with the children. If using live musicians, make sure they have the sheet music (found in Appendix A).

Put the Props in Place

1. Prepare your Visual Aids. Put the Bible Verse, Listening Assignment, Bible Story in one side of the Bible folder. Keep out the Big Question sign.
2. Get out your storyboard. If using Simple Story Scenes, put these in your BIble Folder. Or, if using the individual storyboard figures, put all background pictures in place (they have a BG by the number). Put the rest of the storyboard pictures (these have a SB by the number) in order of use in the other side of the Bible folder.
3. Put the HSK Bible Folder as well as the Big Question sign in the Big Question Box/Briefcase and shut it. If your box/briefcase has locks and you want to use the unlocking the box as part of your session, lock it now....but make sure you have the key or know the code first.
4. Prepare the music CD or sheet music or mp3 device for use in your session.

Set Out Free Play Activities

Choose and set up free time activities you will use with the children. Choose a variety of different activities that will be enjoyed by different types of children. Rotate the activities you provide to keep them interesting and fresh to your children. (Suggestions in Appendix D, Core Curriculum books.)

Prepare Any Activities

Choose which (if any) of the unit games and crafts activities you want to use in the session. Bear in mind your time frame as well as the developmental abilities/attention span of your children as you decide what/how many to prepare. **Look over the Discussion Sheet** and choose a few questions you might use to spark discussion with the children as they do their activities (especially good for ages 3's+). Pray for God to give you opportunities to talk about these things with the children.

Let Them Take It with Them

Make copies of the craft/take home sheets, if you are not already using them as one of your activities. You may also want to make copies of the story (see take-home version of each story included in Appendix C with the other take home resources) to have for parents to use with their children at home. There's a link on each craft/take home sheet to the story, if you don't make hard copies.

Store It

After your session is over, collect the resources and store them for future use.
This curriculum can be used over and over for years to come.

Unit 4 Overview of Key Concepts

UNIT 4: The God Like None Other

Unit Big Question (and Answer): "Can Anybody Tell Me What the LORD Is Like? He's Not Like Anyone Else!"

Meaning:

There are many gods that people worship, but none is like the LORD. He is the one, true God. He's not like anyone else! He's always been alive--and He will never die. He's completely good and loving. He's all-powerful and all-wise. And that's just the beginning of what the LORD is like. He is so great! There will always be more of Him to know.

Unit 4 Bible Verse: 1 Kings 8:23

"O LORD...there is no God like you, in heaven above or on earth beneath."

Meaning:

The LORD is God's name. He is the one, true God. There is no one like Him, in heaven or earth. Let's praise Him!

Unit 4 ACTS Prayer

A We praise You, God. You are the one, true God in heaven above and here on earth.

C God, in our heart, we know that You are God and that we should obey You, but many times we don't want to. Please forgive us. We need a Savior!

T Thank You for not just being good and great, but being so good and so great to people like us! Thank You for caring about us so much and for wanting us to know You. And thank You for sending Jesus to be our Savior.

S Work deep inside our hearts. Help us to turn away from our sins and trust in Jesus as our Savior. Help us to know You and live for You. Help us to go and tell others what we've learned about You, the one, true God. In Jesus' name we pray. Amen.

Unit 4 Story
The Case of the Big Showdown
Exodus 1-12

Songs Used in Unit 4   *listen to or download songs for free at https://praisefactory.org: Hide n Seek Kids Music page*

Big Q & A 4 Song
Big Question 4 Song: Can Anybody Tell Me What the LORD Is Like?
Inspector Graff's Rap: The ABC's of God
Unit 4 Bible Verse Song: O, O, Lord 1 Kings 8:23, ESV
Extra Unit 4 Bible Verse Song: In Heaven Above Kings 8:23, *ESV (short version)*
Extra Unit 4 Bible Verse Song: In Heaven Above Kings 8:23, *ESV (full version)*
Extra Unit 4 Bible Verse Song: In Heaven Above or Earth Beneath Kings 8:23, *ESV (other version)*
Unit 4 Hymn: Praise Him, Praise Him, All Ye Little Children
Unit 4 Praise Song: God Is So Good

Hide 'n' Seek Kids ESV Songs 4 Track Numbers

This is a listing of all songs mentioned in the unit curriculum. You may or may not choose to use all of the songs. They are listed in easy-reference order--NOT in the order used in the curriculum. You may choose to simply burn a CD/load them onto an mp3 device in this order. Or, you may want to do what we do: choose the songs we want to use and create a play list of them in that order. Then, we burn a CD/upload the play list onto an mp3 device. A teacher only has to click forward to the next song, instead of hunting for the right track. The track number have been included as part of the title of each song, so teachers will still have a reference to the track number listed in the curriculum (same as those listed below), even if you change the order on your customized play list.

SONGS USED EVERY UNIT OF THE CURRICULUM

1 The Classroom Song v.1
2 The Classroom Song v.2
3 The Classroom Song v.3
4 The Classroom Song v.4
5 Hide 'n' Seek Kids Theme Song
6 The Classroom Rules Song
7 Let's Pray Song
8 The Big Question Box Song
9 The Bible Chant Song
10 ACTS Prayer Song (Short Version)
11 ACTS Prayer Song (Full Version)

Why the Extra Songs?
Hide 'n' Seek Kids is a curriculum used by children of different ages. Sometimes one of the other songs is a better fit for your kids. Or, you may simply want to teach them more songs on the same Bible Truth. Use as many or as few as you want.

UNIT 4: THE GOD LIKE NONE OTHER

12 Big Q & A 4 Song
13 Big Question 4 Song: Can Anybody Tell Me What the LORD Is Like?
14 Inspector Graff's Rap: The ABC's of God
15,15T Unit 4 Bible Verse Song: O, O, LORD 1 Kings 8:23, ESV
16 *Extra Unit 4 Bible Verse Song: In Heaven Above* Kings 8:23, *ESV (short version)*
17 *Extra Unit 4 Bible Verse Song: In Heaven Above* Kings 8:23, *ESV (full version)*
18 *Extra Unit 4 Bible Verse Song: In Heaven Above or Earth Beneath* Kings 8:23, *ESV (other version)*
19 Unit 4 Hymn: Praise Him, Praise Him, All Ye Little Children
20 Unit 4 Praise Song: God Is So Good

T* Tidbit   Shortened version of the Bible Verse Song

listen to or download songs for free at https://praisefactory.org: Hide n Seek Kids Music page

Lesson Plan: Big Question 4   ⭐ = follow the stars for a short & simple lesson plan   p.1

1. GETTING STARTED   NOTE: Most 2 & 3 year olds do best simply learning the Big Question & Answer, a simple version of the Bible story, and maybe the Bible Verse. Use other activities, as time and attention span allow.

Intake Activity Ideas

Choose one of these open-ended activities to include children as they join the class:

Free Play Time *suggestions in Appendix D*	⭐(usually best for 2 year olds) Offer your own or some of the easy-to-make, free play activities suggested in Appendix D.

OR Sing-along Music Time *lyrics and sheet music, Appendix A* *listen to or download songs for free at https:// praisefactory.org: Hide n Seek Kids Music page*	Music *from* Hide 'n' Seek Kids (HSK) ESV Songs 4:

Big Q & A 4 Song	*HSK ESV Songs 4, track 12*
Big Question 4 Song	*HSK ESV Songs 4, track 13*
Extra Big Question 4 Song:	
Inspector Graff's Rap: The ABC's of God	*HSK ESV Songs 4, track 14*
Unit 4 Bible Verse Song:	
O, O, Lord 1 Kings 8:23, ESV	*HSK ESV Songs 4, track 15,15T*
Extra Unit 4 Bible Verse Song:	
In Heaven Above Kings 8:23, *ESV (short version)*	*HSK ESV Songs 4, track 16*
Extra Unit 4 Bible Verse Song:	
In Heaven Above Kings 8:23, *ESV (full version)*	*HSK ESV Songs 4, track 17*
Extra Unit 4 Bible Verse Song:	
In Heaven Above or Earth Beneath Kings 8:23, *ESV*	*HSK ESV Songs 4, track 18*
Big Question 1 Hymn:	
Praise Him, Praise Him, All Ye Little Children	*HSK ESV Songs 4, track 19*
Big Question 1 Praise Song:	
God Is So Good	*HSK ESV Songs 4, track 20*

Add more fun to Sing-along Music TIme by adding a Music, Movement & Memory Activity. These activities are listed on p. 8 of this lesson plan with the Response Activities. Instructions found in Appendix B.

***OR* Bible Verse Memory Game** *instructions found in Appendix B*	Lesson 1 Game: Simon Says How Lesson 2 Game: Bean Bag Catch Lesson 3 Game: Slap, Clap and Stack Lesson 4 Game: Freeze 'n' Say Lesson 5 Fill 'er Up *These activities are also included on p.8 of this lesson plan with the Response Activities.*

2. OPENING CIRCLE TIME *(introduce the Bible Truth and tell the related Bible story)*

Gathering the Children *lyrics and sheet music, Appendix A*	*Sing verse 1 of The Classroom Song to gather the children for Circle Time.*

The Classroom Song, verse 1	*HSK ESV Songs 4, track 1*
Let's gather together to worship God,	
Let's gather together to worship God,	
Let's gather together to worship God,	
Come gather here with me!	

Welcome to Hide 'n' Seek Kids!	⭐"Welcome to Hide 'n' Seek Kids! We're so glad you've joined us! We're here to seek God and learn His Word and Hide it in our heart so that it will always be with us. And we're here to Hide His Word, the Bible, in our hearts. We ask big questions about God and dig deep down in the truths of God's Word to find them."

| Lesson Plan: Big Question 4 | use with all FIVE lessons | p.2 |

2. OPENING CIRCLE TIME, continued ⭐ = *short & simple lesson plan*

Hide 'n' Seek Kids Theme Song *lyrics and sheet music, Appendix A*	"Let's sing our Hide 'n' Seek Kids theme song." ⭐**Hide 'n' Seek Kids Theme Song**　　　　*HSK ESV Songs 4, track 5* Come along, we're gonna Hide 'n' seek! Hide God's Word in our heart and Him, we'll seek, God loves to show us the truths of His Word, That we might know Him and live out what we've learned.
Classroom Rules Song *lyrics and sheet music, Appendix A*	There are two very important things that Hide 'n' Seek Kids do together: we worship God and we love one another. Our Classroom Rules Song reminds us how we should act. Let's sing it." **Classroom Rules Song**　　　　*HSK ESV Songs 4, track 6* Shh, be quiet while someone is talking, Raise your hand, if you have something to say, Don't touch your friend, sitting beside you, Obey your teachers, Be kind as you play. These are our classroom rules, These are our classroom rules, They help us worship God and love one another, These are our classroom rules.
Opening Prayer Time *lyrics and sheet music, Appendix A*	"Children, we need God's help to keep these rules. Let's ask Him to help us right now. Let's get ready and pray." **Let's Pray**　　　　*HSK ESV Songs 4, track 7* 1-2-3! Fold your hands, Bow your head, Close your eyes. Let's pray! *(repeat)* "Let's pray:" ⭐**Opening Prayer** Dear Lord, We're so glad to get to gather together to worship You! Please help us keep the classroom rules. Please help us to love You and learn about You today. In Jesus' name we pray. Amen.

Lesson Plan: Big Question 4   use with all FIVE lessons   p.3

2. OPENING CIRCLE TIME, continued   = short & simple lesson plan

Reveal the Big Question **Introduce the Big Question Box/Briefcase** *lyrics and sheet music, Appendix A*	"It's time to get down to business, Hide 'n' Seek kids! Let's see what our Big Question for today is. It's right inside our Big Question Box/ Briefcase." **The Big Question Box Song** *HSK ESV Songs 4, track 8* We've got a big box, All closed up and locked, Filled with the truths of God's Word. We've got a brief case, There's no time to waste, Come on, kids, let's open it up!
The Big Question under Investigation VISUAL take out AID of BQB *Big Question & Answer Sign, front side* *found in the HSK Vol. 1 Visual Aids, ESV Book*	Ok, who would like to open it up for me and pull out the Big Question?" *Choose a child to open the box/briefcase, take out the Big Question and hand it to you, then hold up the Big Question sign for all the children to see, and say:* The Big Question we are investigating today is Big Question Number 4: **Can Anybody Tell Me What the LORD Is Like?** and the Answer is: **He's Not Like Anyone Else!**
Big Question Meaning	There are many gods that people worship, but none is like the LORD. He is the one, true God. He's not like anyone else! He's always been alive--and He will never die. He's completely good and loving. He's all-powerful and all-wise. And that's just the beginning of what the LORD is like. He is so great! There will always be more of Him to know.
Big Question Songs **Big Q & A 4 Song** *lyrics and sheet music, Appendix A*	"Let's sing our Big Question Song: **Big Q & A 4 Song** *HSK ESV Songs 4, track 12* *(adapted version of "Have You Ever Seen a Lassie")* Can anybody tell me, Tell me, tell me, Can anybody tell me, What the LORD is like? He's not like anyone else, Anyone else, anyone else, He's not like anyone else, That's what the LORD is like.

Lesson Plan: Big Question 4 use with all FIVE lessons **p.4**

2. OPENING CIRCLE TIME, continued ⭐ = short & simple lesson plan

Learning about the Big Question ⭐ *(use one or both)*

Repeat the Big Question and Answer again:
"Can Anybody Tell Me What the LORD Is Like? He's Not Like Anyone Else!"

Say: "Hmmmm, I wonder what that means… Let's do our action rhyme/sing our song that explains it."

Then do the action rhyme or sing the song using any of the optional motions suggested, if desired.

Big Question Action Rhyme ⭐

Big Question 4 Action Rhyme

	(POSSIBLE ACTIONS)
The LORD is not like anyone else.	*Shake your head side to side in a "no"*
He's not like you or me.	*point out to someone else, then to self*
He is a glorious spirit	
I cannot touch or see.	*close eyes*
He's very, very, VERY strong.	*flex arm muscle*
He knows everything,	*Touch head*
He never does any wrong!	*Shake your head side to side in a "no"*
And He is with us all the time.	*Stretch your hands out wide*
No matter where we may be.	

Big Question (Action Rhyme) Song

lyrics and sheet music, Appendix A

You might also enjoy:

Inspector Graff's Rap: The ABC's of God HSK ESV Songs 4, track 14

lyrics and sheet music, Appendix A

Big Question 4 (Action Rhyme) Song

HSK ESV Songs 4, track 13

	(POSSIBLE ACTIONS)
Refrain:	
Tell me, can anybody tell me,	*Point out to others in a arc movement*
Tell me, what the LORD is like?	
Tell me, can anybody tell me,	*Point up to God*
Tell me, what the LORD is like?	
He's not like anyone else,	*Shake head "no"*
He's not like anyone else,	
He's not like anyone else,	
He's not like anyone else,	
Verse 1	*Touch head*
He's Omniscient! *(He knows all things)*	*Point out to others in a arc movement*
Omnipresent! *(He's everywhere you can be)*	
Omni-benevolent! *(He's always good!)*	*hold up flexed arm*
and Omnipotent! *(He can do all things!)* Refrain	
Verse 2	*fold arms over chest and shake head "no"*
He's Immutable! *(He never changes!)*	
He's Infallible! *(He makes no mistakes!)*	*extend out arms to each side*
He's Infinite! *(There's always more of Him to know!)*	
And purely Righteous!	*hand gesture for tiny, by place index and*
(He has no sin! Not even a teeny, tiny speck!) Refrain	*thumb of same hand a little space apart*

| Lesson Plan: Big Question 4 | use with all FIVE lessons | p.5 |

2. OPENING CIRCLE TIME, continued   ⭐ = short & simple lesson plan

Learning the Bible Verse **The Bible Chant Song** *lyrics and sheet music, Appendix A*	⭐ "And how do I know this is true? God tells me so in His special book, the Bible." *Say or sing the Bible Chant Song.* **The Bible Chant Song** *HSK ESV Songs 4, track 9* The Bible, the Bible, Let's get out the Bible. Let's hear what God has to say. The Bible, the Bible, God's given us the Bible. It's His Word for us to learn and obey! Yay!
The Bible Verse in the HSK Bible Folder *HSK 4 Bible Verse-front side (in the HSK Bible folder)* VISUAL AID Place verse in take out 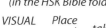 #2 *HSK Bible Folder* of BQB *found in the HSK Vol. 1 Visual Aids, ESV Book*	"Who would like to get our Bible folder out of the Big Question Briefcase for me?" *Choose a child to open the briefcase, take out the "Bible" folder and hand it to you. Remove the Bible Verse Picture from the "Bible" folder and hold it up for all the children to see, then say:* ⭐ **1 Kings 8:23, ESV** "O LORD...there is no God like you, in heaven above or on earth beneath."
Bible Verse Meaning *HSK 4 Bible Verse-back side*	⭐ **What does that mean?** The LORD is the one, true God. There is no one like Him, in heaven or earth. Let's praise Him!

Bible Verse Song
 	
lyrics and sheet music, Appendix A
	"We've said our Bible verse, now let's sing it!"
	O, O, LORD: 1 Kings 8:23, ESV *HSK ESV Songs 4, tracks 15, 15T*
	
	You might also enjoy:
	O, O, LORD,
	There is no, no God like You, *In Heaven Above,*
	O, O, LORD, *1 Kings 8:23, ESV (2nd version)*
	There is no God like You. *HSK ESV Songs 4, track 16*
	O, O, LORD,
	There is no, no God like You, *In Heaven Above or Earth Beneath,*
	First Kings Eight, twenty-three. *1 Kings 8:23, ESV (3rd version)*
	  HSK ESV Songs 4, track 17
	
	  lyrics and sheet music, Appendix A

Lesson Plan: Big Question 4   use with all FIVE lessons   p.6

2. OPENING CIRCLE TIME, continued   ⭐ = *short & simple lesson plan*

Getting into the Case	"Now it's time to do a bit more deep down investigating. Let's see what Detective Dan wants us to help him figure out. Would someone like to get it out for me?"
Listening Assignments *Place in* *take out* [HSK Bible Folder] [?Big Question Briefcase?] *of BQB*	**NOTE: Listening assignments are most suitable for ages 3+. Skip straight to the Bible story (see bottom of this page), if working with 2 year olds.** "Let's open up our listening assignment and see what we are supposed to figure out today. *Choose a child to take out the Listening Assignment (from the HSK Bible Folder) and hand it to you. Read Detective Dan's letter to the children that includes the listening assignment. The listening assignments are summarized below:*
VISUAL AID **#3** *HSK Vol. 1 Visual Aids, ESV*	**Detective Dan's Lesson #1 Listening Assignment:** As you listen to the story, see if you can figure out: 1. A showdown is like a fight to see who's the best. Who won the showdown in this story? 2. What did He prove when He won?
VISUAL AID **#4** *HSK Vol. 1 Visual Aids, ESV*	**Detective Dan's Lesson #2 Listening Assignment:** Our Bible verse is 1 Kings 8:23: "O LORD... there is no God like you in heaven above or on earth beneath." As you listen to the story, see if you can figure out: 1. Who didn't believe the LORD was the one, true God in our story? 2. How did the LORD show that He really was the one, true God?
VISUAL AID **#5A,B,C** **Listening Assignment #3 includes the Assignment Sheet, plus 4 clue pictures** *HSK Vol. 1 Visual Aids, ESV*	**Detective Dan's Lesson #3 Listening Assignment:** I found four clues, but one of them is NOT in the story. They are: A rug; A frog; A king (Pharaoh); and Moses. *Hold up each of the four pictures for the children to see as you identify them. Better yet, put them up on your flannelgraph board, off to one side.* I need to know: 1. Which three pictures belong in the story and which one does not? 2. How did the LORD use three things to show He was the one, true God?
VISUAL AID **#6** *HSK Vol. 1 Visual Aids, ESV*	**Detective Dan's Lesson #4 Listening Assignment:** As you listen to the story, see if you can figure out: 1. Who did the LORD prove He was in our story? 2. What was something God's people asked the LORD for and He answered their prayers?
VISUAL AID **#7** *HSK Vol. 1 Visual Aids, ESV*	**Detective Dan's Lesson #5 Listening Assignment:** As you listen to the story, see if you can figure out: 1. Who did the LORD save His people from in our story? 2. What would He send Jesus to save His people from one day?
Tell the Bible Story ⭐ *Place story & pics in* *take out* [HSK Bible Folder] [?Big Question Briefcase?] *of BQB* *HSK Vol. 1 Visual Aids, ESV* **Bible Story included in this book, immediately after the Lesson Plan and with the Visual Aids**	***Then say,*** "Ok, Hide 'n' Seekers! Put on your best listening ears and see if you can find the answers to Detective Dan's questions. When I finish telling the story, we'll see what we come up with." ⭐ **Bible Story: The Case of the Big Showdown** *Exodus 1-12* *Read the Bible Truth story, putting up the storyboard pictures/Simple Story Scenes as you tell it. Then, have the children answer the listening assignment. Present the the gospel and lead in prayer.* **Answers to questions, the gospel and ACTS prayer are included with the story text.**

Lesson Plan: Big Question 4	use with all FIVE lessons	p.7

2. OPENING CIRCLE TIME, continued   = *short & simple lesson plan*

Story Response Song(s)	*As attention span and time allow, you might want to end with one of the following songs which also tie in with the unit. If desired, use the Music and Movement activity ideas while singing, listed with the Response Activities.*
Hymn *lyrics and sheet music, Appendix A*	**Praise Him, Praise Him, All Ye Little Children** *HSK ESV Songs 4, track 19* Praise Him, praise Him, All ye little children, God is love (powerful, holy), God is love (powerful, holy), Praise Him, praise Him, All ye little children, God is love (powerful, holy), Praise Him, praise Him, All ye little children, God is love (powerful, holy). **Tie-in:** "Children God is so good, so powerful and so holy! Let's praise Him!"
Praise Song *lyrics and sheet music, Appendix A*	**Praise Song: God Is So Good** *HSK ESV Songs 4, track 20* God is so good (powerful, holy), God is so good (powerful, holy), God is so good (powerful, holy), He's so good (powerful, holy) to me. **Tie-in:** "Children God is so good, so powerful and so holy! Let's praise Him!"

3. TAKING ACTION: Response Activities *(choose from among these activities)*

Transition to Activities	Well, Hide 'n' Seek Kids, you've done a great job diggin' deep down for answers in the truths of God's Word. Now it's time to enjoy some activities." *Tell children what activity/s you are providing for them: either free play or some of the response activities listed below. When you are ready to dismiss them, use this song to help the children transition in an orderly fashion to their next activity.*
Classroom Song, verse 2 *lyrics and sheet music, Appendix A*	"Children, let's sing our Time to Play Song. When we are finished you may get up and walk over to our next activity." **Classroom Song, verse 2** *HSK ESV Songs 4, track 2* We've gathered together to worship God, We've gathered together to worship God, And now it's time to play. *Dismiss the children to whatever activities you have prepared for them to do.*

Lesson Plan: Big Question 4	use with all FIVE lessons	p.8

3. TAKING ACTION: Response Activities *(choose from among these activities)* ⭐ = *short & simple lesson plan*

Response Activities	*Choose one or more activities appropriate for your children, based on classroom time and developmental needs.* **Add the Discussion Sheet to any activity for deeper learning.** ⭐
Bible Verse Memory Game *game directions, Appendix B*	Though listed with the opening activities, you may choose to use this Bible verse game here instead (or as a repeat). • Lesson 1 Game: Simon Says How • Lesson 2 Game: Bean Bag Catch • Lesson 3 Game: Slap, Clap and Stack • Lesson 4 Game: Freeze 'n' Say • Lesson 5 Game: Fill 'er Up
Music, Movement & Memory Activity *game directions, Appendix B*	A music activity that uses the songs from the Bible Truth and Big Question unit. • HSK Songs for Unit, plus: • Lesson 1 Activity: Freeze Frame • Lesson 2 Activity: Egg Shakers • Lesson 3 Activity: Jingle Bell Hands • Lesson 4 Activity: Big Voice, Little Voice • Lesson 5 Activity: Sing, Dance and Fall Down
Bible Story Review Game *game directions, Appendix B*	A game that uses the storyboard pictures from the story to review the story. • Lesson 1 Game: Take Me through the Tunnel • Lesson 2 Game: Missing in Action • Lesson 3 Game: Hide 'n' Seek Kids Clue Hunt • Lesson 4 Game: Who's Inside? • Lesson 5 Game: Look Who's Coming Down the Tracks
Coloring Pages/ Take Home Sheets *in Appendix C*	A coloring page related to the lesson assignment questions is provided for each lesson. On the back of each are the key concepts, a few questions and a song for parents to use with their children. (If desired, include a copy of the Bible story with the Take Home Sheet.) NOTE: Upgrade your coloring sheet to a more interesting craft by offering simple embellishments, such as jiggly eyes, craft sand, glitter, glitter glue, colored paper dots (made with a hole punch), fabric scraps, etc. Make cut-to-size glued-on clothes, hair, etc for characters by using a copy of the coloring sheet, cutting out the selected portions and making them the patterns for whatever you want to cut out of fabric, paper, foil, etc. ⭐ • Lesson 1 Coloring Sheet Emphasis: Bible Truth • Lesson 2 Coloring Sheet Emphasis: Bible Verse • Lesson 3 Coloring Sheet Emphasis: Bible Truth • Lesson 4 Coloring Sheet Emphasis: ACTS Prayer • Lesson 5 Coloring Sheet Emphasis: The Gospel
Extra Crafts: **Big Question Craft** *in Appendix C* **Bible Verse Craft** *in Appendix C* **Bible Story Puzzle** *in Appendix C*	**These crafts are slightly more complex than the coloring sheets:** **The Big Question Craft** is a color, glue and stick craft of the Big Question and Answer. **The Bible Verse Craft** is a craft that gives the Bible verse and explains it, also involving gluing and sticking and a few other, simple craft supplies. The **Storyboard Picture Placement Page** has been made into a puzzle that can be cut out and re-assembled by the children. This provides a nice summary of the story.
Free Play Activities *ideas in Appendix D*	⭐Offer your own or some of the easy-to-make, free play activities suggested in Appendix D.

Lesson Plan: Big Question 4   use with all FIVE lessons   **p.9**

4. CLOSING CIRCLE TIME *(End-of-session activities for the last 5-10 minutes of class time)*   ★ = *short & simple lesson plan*

Transition to Closing Circle **Classroom Song, verse 3** *lyrics and sheet music, Appendix A*	*Use this song to help the children transition in an orderly fashion. Sing the song, then ask the children to gather with you for Closing Circle Time.* **Classroom Song, verse 3** *HSK ESV Songs 1, track 3* It's time to get ready to go and tell, It's time to get ready to go and tell, Come gather here with me.
Closing Circle Time **Classroom Song, verse 4** *lyrics and sheet music, Appendix A*	*When children are settled in the circle, say:* "It is almost time for your parents to come pick you up. And do you know what that means? It means…. (draw this out to build anticipation and excitement)…that it's almost time to go home and….it's almost time to…Go and Tell! We have learned some big news about God today. God wants us to take and tell it to the whole world!" **Classroom Song, verse 4** *HSK ESV Songs 4, track 4* So what's our big news to go and tell, So what's our big news to go and tell, Can you tell me now?
Big News to Tell **Big Question 4** *VISUAL AID* **#1** **found in the HSK Vol. 1 Visual Aids, ESV Book* *lyrics and sheet music, Appendix A*	"Let's see….there's so much big news to tell! There's so much we've learned! Can you tell me the answer to our **Big Question: "Can Anybody Tell Me What the LORD Is Like?"** *(Show them the Big Question and Answer picture.)* Say the answer with me: **"He's Not Like Anyone Else!"** *(If desired, you can sing the Big Q & A Song.)* *HSK ESV Songs 4, track 12*
Big Question 4 Bible Verse *VISUAL AID* **#2** **found in the HSK Vol. 1 Visual Aids, ESV Book* *lyrics and sheet music, Appendix A*	"And how do I know this is true? Can you tell me? Say it with me: **"The Bible tells me so!"** That's right! We learned: **1 Kings 8:23** **"O LORD… there is no God like you in heaven above or on earth below."** *(Show them the Bible Verse picture.)* The Bible tells us that God is not like anyone else." *(If desired, you can sing the Bible verse song.)* *HSK ESV Songs 4, tracks 15, 15T*

| Lesson Plan: Big Question 4 | use with all FIVE lessons | p.10 |

4. CLOSING CIRCLE TIME, continued   ⭐ = short & simple lesson plan

Closing ACTS Prayer Time

Let's ask God to help us to remember this and even tell others this good news. Let's get ready and pray our ACTS prayer.

ACTS Prayer Chant

lyrics and sheet music, Appendix A

And what does ACTS mean? Let's sing/say our ACTS Prayer Chant!

ACTS Prayer Chant Song   *HSK ESV Songs 4, tracks 10,11*

A, Adoration: God, we praise You!
C, Confession: Forgive us our sins.   That's the ACTS prayer, my friend,
T, Thanksgiving,: Thank You for Jesus,   Bow head, Close your eyes, Shhh,
S, Supplication: Help us to live like Him.   Let's begin!

Closing ACTS Prayer

"Let's pray!"

Lead the children in the ACTS prayer for this unit.

A   We praise You, God. You are the one, true God in heaven above and here on earth.

C   God, in our heart, we know that You are God and that we should obey You, but many times we don't want to. Please forgive us. We need a Savior!

T   Thank You for not just being good and great, but being so good and so great to people like us! Thank You for caring about us so much and for wanting us to know You. And thank You for sending Jesus to be our Savior.

S   Work deep inside our hearts. Help us to turn away from our sins and trust in Jesus as our Savior. Help us to know You and live for You. Help us to go and tell others what we've learned about You, the one, true God.

In Jesus' name we pray. Amen.

---

5. TAKING IT HOME *(Take Home Sheet)*

Clean up and Dismissal

⭐ *"Now it's time to work together and clean up."*
Have the children join you in cleaning up the room.

Coloring Pages/ Take Home Sheets

in Appendix C

⭐ *Give out the craft/take home sheet and any other papers from the session, as you dismiss children from class.*

(Reminder: The back side of the coloring page is the take home sheet for each lesson.)

Bible Story to Take-Home

in Appendix C

You may also want to include a copy of the story along with the take home sheet. (However, each coloring sheet/take home sheet includes a note to parents telling them where they can download the story from the Parent Resources section on the website.

Big Question 4 Bible Story   use with all FIVE lessons

Place story in
take out
HSK Bible Folder
of BQB
p.1

The Case of the Big Showdown
Exodus 1-12

> **Story-telling Tips**
>
> Ahead of time:
> 1. Read the Bible verses and story. Pray!
> 2. Choose story action cues and/or prepare storyboard pictures, if using. (Included in Visual Aids book)
> 3. Practice telling story with the pictures, timing your presentation. Shorten, if necessary to fit your allotted time.
>
> During your presentation:
> 1. Maintain as much eye contact as possible as you tell the story.
> 2. Put up storyboard figures/add story action cues as you tell the story. Allow the children to help you put them on the board, if desired.
> 3. Include the children in your story with a few questions about what they think will happen or words/concepts that might be new to them.
> 4. Watch the kids for signs that their attention span has been reached. Shorten, if necessary.

INTRODUCTION/ LISTENING ASSIGNMENTS

"Our story is called: The Case of the Big Showdown. Here is your listening assignment… "

Read from Detective Dan's Listening Assignment signs, but questions are summarized below:

Detective Dan's Lesson #1 Listening Assignment:

As you listen to the story, see if you can figure out:
1. A showdown is like a fight to see who's the best. Who won the showdown in this story?
2. What did He prove when He won?

Detective Dan's Lesson #2 Listening Assignment:

Our Bible verse is 1 Kings 8:23: "O LORD… there is no God like you in heaven above or on earth beneath."

As you listen to the story, see if you can figure out:
1. Who didn't believe the LORD was the one, true God in our story?
2. How did the LORD show that He really was the one, true God?

Detective Dan's Lesson #3 Listening Assignment:

I found four clues, but one of them is NOT in the story.
They are: A rug; A frog; A king (Pharaoh); and Moses.
Hold up each of the four pictures for the children to see as you identify them. Better yet, put them up on your flannelgraph board, off to one side.

I need to know:
1. Which three pictures belong in the story and which one does not?
2. How did the LORD use three things to show He was the one, true God?

Detective Dan's Lesson #4 Listening Assignment:

As you listen to the story, see if you can figure out:
1. Who did the LORD prove He was in our story?
2. What was something God's people asked the LORD for and He answered their prayers?

Detective Dan's Lesson #5 Listening Assignment:

As you listen to the story, see if you can figure out:
1. Who did the LORD save His people from in our story?
2. What would He send Jesus to save His people from one day?

Read the questions, THEN SAY,

"Ok, Hide 'n' Seekers! Put on your best listening ears and see if you can find the answers to Detective Dan's questions. When I finish telling the story, we'll see what we come up with."

Big Question 4 Bible Story	use with all FIVE lessons	p.2

"The Case of the Big Showdown"   Exodus 1-12

Story with lines separating paragraphs (text in bold, optional interaction cues in italics)

God's people were very sad.

What do you look like when you are sad? Can you show me?

A mighty, mean king was hurting them. He made them work too hard. He didn't take care of them. He wouldn't let them go home.

"Help us, LORD! Help us! DO SOMETHING!" God's people cried out.

Can you help God's people cry out? Say, "Help, us, LORD! Help us! DO SOMETHING!"

The LORD heard the people. He saw what the mighty, mean king did. He knew how sad His people were and He DID something! He sent Moses and Aaron to rescue them.

"What do you think the LORD did?"

The LORD told Moses and Aaron to talk to the king. "The LORD says: 'Let My people go!' they told the king.

Can you tell the mean king the LORD's message? Say: "Let My people go!"

But the mighty, mean king did NOT think the LORD was any god at all. He said, "No!" to Moses. "I will not let them go! Instead, I will make the people sadder. I will make them work harder." And he did just that.

Now God's people were even sadder! They worked even harder and hurt even more! There was only one thing to do: "Help us, LORD!" Moses and the people cried out to God. "Help us! DOOOOOO SOMETHING!"

The people were really, REALLY sad now. Let's cry out to God even louder with them: "Help us, LORD! Help us! DOOOOO SOMETHING!"

The LORD heard the people. He saw what the mighty, mean king did. He knew how sad His people were... and He did something AGAIN!

"What do you think the LORD did now?"

The LORD sent sad things upon the mighty, mean king, his people, and his land... but He protected His people from them all. This would show EVERYONE that the LORD was the One, True God. This would make the king free God's people.

*Story with lines separating paragraphs (**text in bold,** optional interaction cues in italics)*

The LORD sent nasty flies and gnats that swarmed and buzzed all around the king and his people...but not a one bothered God's people!

Can you buzz like a fly?

He sent lots of slippery-slidey frogs to hop all around the king and his people... and even into their houses...and even into their beds! But not a one bothered God's people!

Can you hop like a grasshopper?

He sent hungry locusts to munch up all the food of the king and his people. He made itchy, scratchy, ouchy bumps pop out all over their skin. He made other sad things happen to the king and his people (and even to their animals and their plants. But not a one bothered God's people or their animals or plants!

The mean king and his people were very sad and miserable. They didn't like all the things the LORD had sent upon them.

What do you think they looked like?

What would the mighty, mean king do now? Would he believe that the LORD is the One, True God? Now would he let God's people go free? YES, HE WOULD!

"Go away! Go home! THE LORD IS GOD!" the mighty, mean king said. "We have had enough of these sad things. We will do what your God wants us to do," he said. "God's people can go free!"

What did the mean king say? "Go away! Go home! The LORD IS GOD!"

How HAPPY Moses and Aaron were! How happy God's people were! They praised the LORD, the one, true God. He loved them and had heard their cries. He had seen what the mighty, mean king did. He knew how sad His people were... AND HE DID SOMETHING!

God's people were so happy! The LORD rescued them from the mighty, mean king. Let's cheer for God! He's not like anyone else!

How great is the LORD! He is not like anyone else!

| Big Question 4 Bible Story | use with all FIVE lessons | p.4 |

Cracking the Case: (story wrap-up for Listening Assignments)

It's time to see how we did with our Listening Assignment.

Detective Dan's Lesson #1 Listening Assignment:
1. A showdown is like a fight to see who's the best. Who won the showdown in this story? The LORD.
2. What did He prove when He won? The LORD showed that He was the one, true God.

For You and Me:
Long ago, the LORD showed He was the one, true God, and He is still the one, true God today. There's no one better to love and obey than Him. His good plans for His people and this world will always win! Let's ask Him to help us to put our trust in Him.

Detective Dan's Lesson #2 Listening Assignment:
Our Bible Verse is 1 Kings 8:23: "O LORD... there is no God like you in heaven above or on earth beneath."

1. Who didn't believe the LORD was the one, true God in our story? The mean, mighty king (Pharaoh) and his people.
2. How did the LORD show that He really was the one, true God? He rescued His people from the mean, mighty king, and did it in such great ways that even the king had to say that the LORD is God in heaven and on earth!

For You and Me:
The LORD is still the one, true God. There are none other like Him in heaven or on earth. And the amazing thing is, this great God wants us to be His people! Let's ask Him to help us to turn away from our sins and put our trust in His Son, Jesus, as our Savior. He loves to answer this prayer.

Detective Dan's Lesson #3 Listening Assignment:
I found four clues, but one of them is NOT in the story. They are: A rug; A frog; A king (Pharaoh); and Moses.

1. Which three pictures belong in the story and which one does not? The rug was not in the story.
2. How did the LORD use three things to show He was the one, true God? Moses spoke God's words to the king, but the king refused to let the people go or admit that the LORD was God. The LORD used His mighty power and sent lots of frogs and many other things the king did not like. At last, he admitted that the LORD really was the one, true God.

For You and Me:
The LORD is still the one, true God. He wants us all to love Him, know Him and obey Him. We can ask Him and He will help us. What a wonderful thing it is to be one of God's people!

Detective Dan's Lesson #4 Listening Assignment:
1. Who did the LORD prove He was in our story? The one, true God.
2. What was something God's people asked the LORD for and He answered their prayers? They asked God to rescue them.

For You and Me:
God is still the one, true God who wants us to know, love and obey Him. He still loves to rescue His people when they cry out to Him We can be His people when we turn from our sins and trust in Jesus as our Savior.

Detective Dan's Lesson #5 Listening Assignment:
1. Who did the LORD save His people from in our story? The mighty, mean king.
2. What would He send Jesus to save His people from one day? Save them from their sins.

For You and Me:
We might not need to be rescued from a mighty, mean king like God's people did long ago, but we do all need to be rescued from our sins. The LORD wants to rescue us. He sent His Son, Jesus to be our Savior. Jesus can save us from our sins and make us God's people, too, when we repent of our sins and trust in Him as our Savior.

Big Question 4 Bible Story	use with all FIVE lessons	p.5

The Gospel (story wrap-up if NOT using Listening Assignments)

Our Bible Truth is:
Can Anybody Tell Me What the LORD Is Like?
He's Not Like Anyone Else!

The LORD is the one, true God. We should all obey Him! But, like the mighty, mean king in our story, we all say "no" to God... and we deserve God's punishment! How sad!

But, oh, how kind is the LORD! If we turn away from our sins and ask Jesus to be our Savior, God will forgive us and save us!

What a wonderful beginning that will be! For then we will get to know God in our hearts. And one day, we will go to live happily with Him forever.

Let's thank God and praise God right now for sending Jesus to Let's ask Him to help us turn away from our sins and trust in Jesus as our own Savior.

Close in prayer.

Closing Unit 4 ACTS Prayer

A=Adoration C=Confession T=Thanksgiving S=Supplication

A We praise You, God. You are the one, true God in heaven above and here on earth.

C God, in our heart, we know that You are God and that we should obey You, but many times we don't want to. Please forgive us. We need a Savior!

T Thank You for not just being good and great, but being so good and so great to people like us! Thank You for caring about us so much and for wanting us to know You. And thank You so much for sending Jesus to be our Savior.

S Work deep inside our hearts. Help us to turn away from our sins and trust in Jesus as our Savior. Help us to know You and live for You. Help us to go and tell others what we've learned about You, the one, true God.

In Jesus' name we pray. Amen.

Unit 4 Discussion Sheet

use with all FIVE lessons

Use with all response activities for deeper learning

P.1

Questions to aid discussion of the key concepts and for use in games

Be familiar with these questions and answers. Look for opportunities to ask questions and talk about their answers, such as while the children work on their coloring pages, as part of their games, or during play time. Remember: your goal isn't to ask all these questions or to only talk to the children about these things. It is to be deliberate in having good conversations with them, as natural opportunities arise.

BIG QUESTION	Can Anybody Tell Me What the LORD Is Like? He's Not Like Anyone Else!
Meaning	There are many gods that people worship, but none is like the LORD. He is the one, true God. He's not like anyone else! He's always been alive--and He will never die. He's completely good and loving. He's all-powerful and all-wise. And that's just the beginning of what the LORD is like. He is so great! There will always be more of Him to know.
Discussion Questions	*choose a few* 1. Can anybody tell me what the LORD is like? *He's not like anyone else!* 2. Do people worship many different gods? *Yes, they do.* 3. Are all gods the same as the LORD? *No, there is no other god like the LORD.* 4. Who is the one, true God? *The LORD.* 5. How long has God been alive? *He's always been alive.* 6. When will God die? *Never!* 7. How good and loving is God? *He is completely good and loving!* 8. How powerful is the LORD? *He is all powerful.* 9. How wise is the LORD? *He is all wise!* 10. Will we ever know everything there is to know about God? *No, there will always be more of Him for us to know.*
THE GOSPEL	What is God's good news for you and me? *The gospel!* *The LORD is the one, true God. We should all obey Him. But, like the mighty, mean king in our story, we all say "no" to God and we deserve God's punishment! How sad! But, oh, how kind is the LORD! He sent His Son, Jesus, to save us! Jesus lived a perfect life. Then, He offered it up as the full payment for our sins when He suffered and died on the cross. Jesus didn't stay dead. On Day Three, Jesus rose from the dead, proving He had beaten sin and death for God's people. We can be God's people, too, if we turn away from our sins and trust in Jesus as our Savior. If we do, we will get to know God in our hearts, now. And one day, we will go to live with God forever. Ask God to help you trust in Jesus. He loves to answer this prayer.*

Unit 4 Discussion Sheet

Questions to aid discussion of the key concepts and for use in games

BIBLE VERSE	"O LORD... there is no God like you in heaven above or on earth beneath." 1 Kings 8:23, ESV
Meaning	The LORD is the one, true God. There is no one like Him, in heaven or earth. Let's praise Him!
Discussion Questions	*choose a few* 1. What is God's name? *The LORD.* 2. Who is the one, true God? *The LORD.* 3. Who is a god like the LORD in heaven? *There is no God like Him in heaven.* 4. Who is a god like the LORD on earth? *There is no God like Him on earth.* 5. How should we treat the LORD? *We should praise Him, love Him and obey Him! He is the one, true God.* 6. Who can help us to know the LORD, the one, true God? *He can! He loves to help us when we ask Him to!*
BIBLE STORY	**The Case of the Big Showdown**
Discussion Questions	*choose a few* 1. What is a showdown? *It is a fight to prove who is the biggest and best.* 2. Who was the showdown between in our story? *The LORD and the mighty, mean king (Pharaoh).* 3. Who won the showdown? *The LORD.* 4. What did the LORD prove by winning the showdown? *That He was the one, true God.* 5. Who needed to be rescued from the mighty, mean king? *The people of God.* 6. Who did the LORD send to rescue the people of God? *Moses.* 7. Did the mighty, mean king obey the LORD the first time He told him to let His people go? *No, he did not.* 8. What troubles did the LORD send that showed the king that the LORD really was the one, true God? *Grasshoppers, frogs, itchy sores. and other sad things.* 9. Did the mighty, mean king let God's people go? *Yes, he did in the end.* 10. Who can we cry out to when we are in trouble? *The LORD.* 11. What do we need rescuing from? *Our sins.* 12. Who can rescue us from our sins, if we ask Him to? *The LORD. We can ask Him to help us turn from our sins and trust in Jesus as our Savior. He loves to answer this prayer!*

Index of Songs

GENERAL CLASSROOM SONGS (USED EVERY LESSON, EVERY UNIT)   133
Lyrics:
The Classroom Song vs.1-4   135
Hide 'n' Seek Kids Theme Song   136
The Classroom Rules Song   136
Let's Pray Song   137
The Big Question Box Song   137
The Bible Chant Song   138
ACTS Prayer Song   138

Sheet Music :
The Classroom Song vs.1-4   139
Hide 'n' Seek Kids Theme Song   139
The Classroom Rules Song   140
Let's Pray Song   140
The Big Question Box Song   141
The Bible Chant Song   141
ACTS Prayer Song   142

UNIT 1: THE GOD WHO REVEALS HIMSELF   143
Track Numbers: 144

Unit 1 Songs Lyrics:
Big Q & A 1 Song   145
Big Question 1 Song: How Can I Know What God Is Like?   146
Unit 1 Bible Verse Song: He Who Declares His Thought   Amos 4:13, ESV   147
Extra Unit 1 Bible Verse Song: He Who Forms the Mountains Amos 4:13, ESV (different version)   148
Extra Unit 1 Bible Verse Song: For Behold   Amos 4:23, ESV (different version)   149
Extra Big Question Bible Verse Song: Behold   Amos 4:23, ESV (different version)   150
Unit 1 Hymn: Joyful, Joyful, We Adore Thee   151
Unit 1 Praise Song: Oh, Oh, Oh, How Good Is the Lord!   152

Unit 1 Songs Sheet Music
Big Q & A 1 Song   153
Big Question 1 Song: How Can I Know What God Is Like?   154
Unit 1 Bible Verse Song: He Who Declares His Thought   Amos 4:13, ESV   156
Extra Unit 1 Bible Verse Song: He Who Forms the Mountains Amos 4:13, ESV (different version)   157
Extra Unit 1 Bible Verse Song: For Behold   Amos 4:23, ESV (different version)   158
Extra Unit Bible Verse Song: Behold   Amos 4:23, ESV (different version)   159
Unit 1 Hymn: Joyful, Joyful, We Adore Thee   160
Unit 1 Praise Song: Oh, Oh, Oh, How Good Is the Lord!   160

Index of Songs, continuned

UNIT 2: GOD'S WONDERFUL WORD, THE BIBLE   161
Track Numbers: 162

Lyrics:
Big Q & A 2 Song   163
Big Question 2 Song: What's So Special About God's Word?   164
Unit 2 Bible Verse Song: Proves True Psalm 18:30, ESV   165
Extra Unit 2 Bible Verse Song: This God   Psalm 18:30,46, ESV (other version)   166
Extra Unit 2 Bible Verse Song: This God, His Way Is Perfect   Psalm 18:30,46, ESV (other version)   167
Extra Unit 2 Bible Verse Song: The Word of the Lord 1 Peter 1:24,25, ESV   168
Unit 2 Hymn: How Precious Is the Book Divine, v.1   169
Unit 2 Praise Song: The Best Book to Read Is the Bible   170

Sheet Music:
Big Q & A 2 Song   171
Big Question 2 Song: What's So Special About God's Word?   172
Unit 2 Bible Verse Song: Proves True Psalm 18:30, ESV   174
Extra Unit 2 Bible Verse Song: This God   Psalm 18:30,46, ESV (other version)   175
Extra Unit 2 Bible Verse Song: This God, His Way Is Perfect   Psalm 18:30,46, ESV (other version)   176
Extra Unit 2 Bible Verse Song: The Word of the Lord 1 Peter 1:24,25, ESV   177
Unit 2 Hymn: How Precious Is the Book Divine, v.1   178
Unit 2 Praise Song: The Best Book to Read Is the Bible   178

UNIT 3: GOD'S GOOD NEWS, THE GOSPEL   179
Track Numbers: 180

Lyrics:
Big Q & A 3 Song   181
Big Question 3 Song: What's the Gospel?   182
Unit 3 Bible Verse Song: For God So Loved the World   John 3:16 ESV   183
Extra Unit 3 Bible Verse Song: For God So Loved the World John 3:16 ESV (other version)   184
Extra Unit 3 Bible Verse Song: For God So Loved the World John 3:16 ESV (other version)   185
Unit 3 Hymn: And Can It Be, v.1 Refrain   186
Unit 3 Praise Song: I Have Decided to Follow Jesus   187

Sheet Music:
Big Q & A 3 Song   188
Big Question 3 Song: What's the Gospel?   189
Unit 3 Bible Verse Song: For God So Loved the World   John 3:16 ESV   191
Extra Unit 3 Bible Verse Song: For God So Loved the World John 3:16 ESV (other version)   192
Extra Unit 3 Bible Verse Song: For God So Loved the World John 3:16 ESV (other version)   193
Unit 3 Hymn: And Can It Be, v.1 Refrain   194
Unit 3 Praise Song: I Have Decided to Follow Jesus   194

Index of Songs, Continued

UNIT 4: THE GOD LIKE NONE OTHER 195
Track Numbers: 196

Unit 4 Songs Lyrics: 197
Big Q & A 4 Song 198
Big Question 4 Song: Can Anybody Tell Me What the LORD Is Like? 199
Unit 4 Bible Verse Song: O, O, Lord 1 Kings 8:23, ESV 200
Extra Unit 4 Bible Verse Song: In Heaven Above Kings 8:23, *ESV* 201
Extra Unit 4 Bible Verse Song: In Heaven Above or Earth Beneath Kings 8:23, *ESV (other version)* 202
Inspector Graff's Rap: The ABC's of God 204
Unit 4 Hymn: Praise Him, Praise Him, All Ye Little Children 205
Unit 4 Praise Song: God Is So Good

Unit 4 Songs Sheet Music 206
Big Q & A 4 Song 207
Big Question 4 Song: Can Anybody Tell Me What the LORD Is Like? 209
Unit 4 Bible Verse Song: O, O, Lord 1 Kings 8:23, ESV 210
Extra Unit 4 Bible Verse Song: In Heaven Above Kings 8:23, *ESV* 211
Extra Unit 4 Bible Verse Song: In Heaven Above or Earth Beneath Kings 8:23, *ESV (other version)* 212
Unit 4 Hymn: Praise Him, Praise Him, All Ye Little Children 212
Unit 4 Praise Song: God Is So Good

<u>Lyrics</u>

The Classroom Song

HSK ESV Songs, Tracks 1-4

Verse 1

Let's gather together to worship God,

Let's gather together to worship God,

Come gather now with me!

Verse 2

We've gathered together to worship God,

We've gathered together to worship God,

And now it's time to play.

Verse 3

It's time to get ready to go and tell,

It's time to get ready to go and tell,

Come gather here with me.

Verse 4

So what's our big news to go and tell,

So what's our big news to go and tell,

Can you tell me now?

Words and Music: Constance Dever ©2011

Hide 'n' Seek Kids Theme Song

HSK ESV Songs, Track 5

Come along, we're gonna Hide 'n' seek!

Hide God's Word in our heart and Him, we'll seek,

God loves to show us the truths of His Word,

That we might know Him

and live out what we've learned.

Words and Music: Constance Dever ©2015

Classroom Rules Song

HSK ESV Songs, Track 6

Shh, be quiet while someone is talking,

Raise your hand, if you have something to say,

Don't touch your friend, sitting beside you,

Obey your teachers, Be kind as you play.

These are our classroom rules,

These are our classroom rules,

They help us worship God and love one another,

These are our classroom rules.

Words and Music: Constance Dever ©2015

Lyrics

Let's Pray
HSK ESV Songs, Track 7

1-2-3!

Fold your hands,

Bow your head,

Close your eyes.

Let's pray! *(repeat)*

Words and Music: Constance Dever ©2015

Big Question Box Song
HSK ESV Songs, Track 8

The Big Question Box Song

We've got a big box,

All closed up and locked,

Filled with the truths of God's Word.

We've got a brief case,

There's no time to waste,

Come on, kids, let's open it up!

Words and Music: Constance Dever ©2015

The Bible Chant Song

HSK ESV Songs, Track 9

The Bible, the Bible,
Let's get out the Bible.
Let's hear what God has to say.
The Bible, the Bible,
God's given us the Bible.
It's His Word for us to learn and obey! Yay!

Words and Music: Constance Dever ©2015

The ACTS Prayer Song

HSK ESV Songs, Tracks 10,11

A: Adoration, God, we praise You,

C: Confession, Forgive us our sins,

T: Thanksgiving, Thank You for Jesus,

S: Supplication, Help us live like Him. (repeat)

That's the A-C-T-S prayer, my friend,

Bow your head, Close your eyes, Shhh,

Let's begin!

Words and Music: Constance Dever ©2016

The Classroom Song

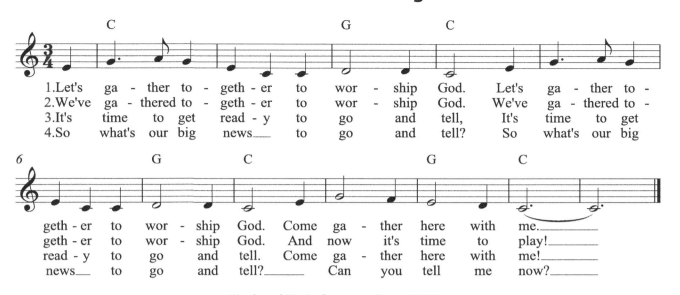

1. Let's ga - ther to - geth - er to wor - ship God. Let's ga - ther to -
2. We've ga - thered to - geth - er to wor - ship God. We've ga - thered to -
3. It's time to get read - y to go and tell, It's time to get
4. So what's our big news___ to go and tell? So what's our big

geth - er to wor - ship God. Come ga - ther here with me.___
geth - er to wor - ship God. And now it's time to play!___
read - y to go and tell. Come ga - ther here with me!___
news___ to go and tell?___ Can you tell me now?___

Words and Music: Constance Dever ©2013

Hide 'n' Seek Kids Theme Song

Come a - long, we're gon-na hide 'n' seek, Hide God's Word in our hearts, And Him, we'll seek. God

loves to show us___ the truths of His Word,___ That

we might know___ Him, and live out what we've learned.___

Words and Music: Constance Dever ©2014

The Classroom Rules Song

HSK ESV Songs, Track 6

Words and Music: Constance Dever ©2013

Let's Pray

HSK ESV Songs, Track 7

Words and Music: Constance Dever ©2013

The Big Question Box Song

HSK ESV Songs, Track 8

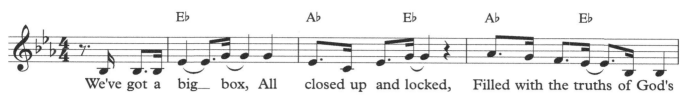

We've got a big box, All closed up and locked, Filled with the truths of God's

Word. We've got a brief case, There's

no time to waste! Come on, kids! Let's o-pen it up!

Words and Music: Constance Dever ©2016

The Bible Chant Song

HSK ESV Songs, Track 9

The Bi-ble, the Bi-ble, Let's get out the Bi-ble, Let's hear what God has to say. The

Bi-ble, the Bi-ble, God's gi-ven us the Bi-ble, It's His Word for us to learn and o-bey! Yay!

Words and Music: Constance Dever ©2013

141

The ACTS Prayer Song

A: A-do-ra tion, "God, we praise You," C: Con-fes- sion, "For - give us our sins,"

T: Thanks-giv ing, "Thank You for Je-sus, S: Sup-pli-ca-tion, "Help us live like Him."

A: A-do-ra tion, "God, we praise You," C: Con-fes- sion, "For - give us our sins,"

T: Thanks-giv ing, "Thank You for Je-sus, S: Sup-pli-ca-tion, "Help us live like Him."

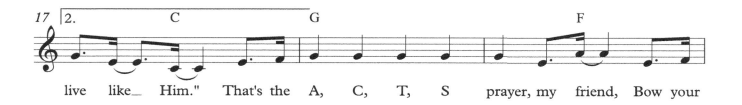

live like_ Him." That's the A, C, T, S prayer, my friend, Bow your

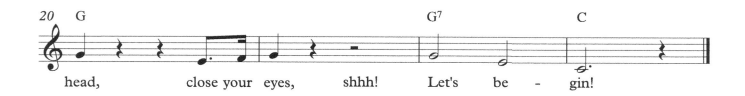

head, close your eyes, shhh! Let's be – gin!

Hide 'n' Seek Kids
Unit I: The God Who Reveals Himself
Lyrics &
Lead Sheets

Hide 'n' Seek Kids ESV Songs I Track Numbers

This is a listing of all songs mentioned in the unit curriculum. You may or may not choose to use all of the songs. They are listed in easy-reference order--NOT in the order used in the curriculum.

You may choose to simply burn a CD/load them onto an mp3 device in this order. Or, you may want to do what we do: choose the songs we want to use and create a play list of them in that order. Then, we burn a CD/upload the play list onto an mp3 device. A teacher only has to click forward to the next song, instead of hunting for the right track. The track number have been included as part of the title of each song, so teachers will still have a reference to the track number listed in the curriculum (same as those listed below), even if you change the order on your customized play list.

SONGS USED EVERY UNIT OF THE CURRICULUM
1 The Classroom Song v.1
2 The Classroom Song v.2
3 The Classroom Song v.3
4 The Classroom Song v.4
5 Hide 'n' Seek Kids Theme Song
6 The Classroom Rules Song
7 Let's Pray Song
8 The Big Question Box Song
9 The Bible Chant Song
10 ACTS Prayer Song (Short Version)
11 ACTS Prayer Song (Full Version)

> **Why the Extra Songs?**
> Hide 'n' Seek Kids is a curriculum used by children of different ages. Sometimes one of the other songs is a better fit for your kids. Or, you may simply want to teach them more songs on the same Bible Truth. Use as many or as few as you want.

UNIT 1: THE GOD WHO REVEALS HIMSELF
12 Big Q & A 1 Song
13 Big Question 1 Song: How Can I Know What God Is Like?
14,14T Big Question 1 Bible Verse Song: The LORD Declares   Amos 4:13, ESV
15 *Extra Big Question 1 Bible Verse Song: He Who Declares His Thought   Amos 4:13, ESV (different version)*
16 *Extra Big Question 1 Bible Verse Song: He Who Forms the Mountains Amos 4:13, ESV (different version)*
17 *Extra Big Question 1 Bible Verse Song: For Behold   Amos 4:23, ESV (different version)*
18 *Extra Big Question Bible Verse Song: Behold   Amos 4:23, ESV (different version)*
19 Big Question 1 Hymn: Joyful, Joyful, We Adore Thee
20 Big Question 1 Praise Song: Oh, Oh, Oh, How Good Is the Lord!

T* Tidbit   Shortened version of the Bible Verse Song

Unit I Lyrics

Big Q & A 1 Song
HSK ESV Songs 1, Track 12

How can I know what God is like,

God is like, God is like?

How can I know what God is like?

He shows me what He's like!

Words: Constance Dever Music: Adapted Nursery Rhyme ©2012

Unit I Lyrics

Big Question 1 Song:
How Can I Know What God Is Like?

HSK ESV Songs 1, Track 13

I have a very big question,
A big question 'bout God.
I have a very big question,
It's Big Question Number One,
I wanna know...

Refrain:
How can I know what God is like?
How can I know what God is like?
How can I know what God is like?
He shows me what He's like!

Verse 1:
He gave me a heart to know God,
He made everything I see.
Big tall mountains, galloping horses,
Every little bird and bee.
Everybody sing... *(Refrain)*

Verse 2:
He gave us the Bible, His Word,
To learn of His mighty deeds,
But most of all, through Jesus, His Son,
God shows Himself to me.
Everybody sing.... *(Refrain)*

Words and Music: Constance Dever ©2012

Unit I Lyrics

Unit 1 Bible Verse Song: HSK ESV Songs 1, Track 14, 14T
The LORD Declares

The LORD declares to man His thought,

The LORD declares to man His thought,

The LORD declares to man His thought,

Amos Four, thirteen.

Words: adapted from Amos 4:13 ESV   Music: Constance Dever ©2016

Unit 1 Bible Verse Song: HSK ESV Songs 1, Track 15
He Who Declares His Thought

He who declares His thought,

He who declares His thought to man.

He who declares His thought,

He who declares His thought to man.

The LORD, the LORD, is His name.

The LORD, the LORD, is His name.

The LORD, the LORD, is His name.

The LORD, the LORD, is His name.

Amos Four, thirteen.

Words: adapted from Amos 4:13 ESV   Music: Constance Dever ©2016

Tie-in: God wants us to know what He is like, so we can know Him, love Him, and praise Him. We don't have to figure out what God is like by ourselves. God show us what He's like--He declares His thoughts to us. God shows us what He's like through the spirit He put in our hearts; through His creations we see around us; through His Word, the Bible; and most of all, through His very own Son, Jesus Christ. And what's the name of the one and only true, living God? It's the LORD! Yes, the LORD is His name!

Unit 1 Extra Bible Verse Song:
He Who Forms the Mountains

HSK ESV Songs 1, Track 16

For behold,
He who forms the mountains,
Creates the wind,
and declares to man his thought,
For behold,
He who forms the mountains,
Creates the wind,
and declares to man his thought,
The LORD, the God of hosts is His name.
Amos Four, thirteen.

Words: adapted from Amos 4:13 ESV   Music: Constance Dever ©2015

Tie-in: What is the name of the one, true God? It's the LORD! Yes, the LORD is the creator of all things: the big, tall mountains, the powerful wind, the mighty angels (the hosts of heaven) and even us! God wants us to know what He is like, so we can know Him, love Him, and praise Him. We don't have to figure out what God is like by ourselves. He knows we couldn't do that! He show us what He's like and that's why he declares His thoughts to us.

Unit I Lyrics

Unit 1 Extra Bible Verse Song:
For Behold

HSK ESV Songs 1, Track 17

For behold,
He who forms the mountains,
Creates the wind,
and declares to man his thought,
For behold,
He who forms the mountains,
Creates the wind,
and declares to man his thought,
The LORD, the God of hosts,
Is His name.
The LORD, the God of hosts,
Is His name.
Amos Four, thirteen.

Words: adapted from Amos 4:13 ESV   Music: Constance Dever ©2015

Tie-in: What is the name of the one, true God? It's the LORD! Yes, the LORD is the creator of all things: the big, tall mountains, the powerful wind, the mighty angels (the hosts of heaven) and even us! God wants us to know what He is like, so we can know Him, love Him, and praise Him. We don't have to figure out what God is like by ourselves. He knows we couldn't do that! He show us what He's like and that's why he declares His thoughts to us.

Unit 1 Lyrics

Unit 1 Extra Bible Verse Song:
Behold

HSK ESV Songs 1, Track 18

Behold, for behold, Behold, for behold,

The LORD, the God of hosts is His name.

Behold, for behold, Behold, for behold,

The LORD, the God of hosts is His name.

He who forms the mountains, creates the wind,

And declares to man what is His thought.

He who forms the mountains, creates the wind,

And declares to man what is His thought.

Behold, for behold, Behold, for behold,

The LORD, the God of hosts is His name.

Behold, for behold, Behold, for behold,

The LORD, the God of hosts is His name.

Amos Four, thirteen.

Words: adapted from Amos 4:13 ESV   Music: Constance Dever ©2015

Tie-in: What is the name of the one, true God? It's the LORD! Yes, the LORD is the creator of all things: the big, tall mountains, the powerful wind, the mighty angels (the hosts of heaven) and even us! God wants us to know what He is like, so we can know Him, love Him, and praise Him. We don't have to figure out what God is like by ourselves. He knows we couldn't do that! He show us what He's like and that's why he declares His thoughts to us.

Unit 1 Lyrics

Big Question 1 Hymn:
Joyful, Joyful, We Adore Thee

HSK ESV Songs 1, Track 19

Verse 1

Joyful, joyful, we adore Thee,

God of glory, Lord of love,

Hearts unfold like flowers before Thee,

Opening to the sun above.

Verse 2

All Thy works with joy surround Thee,

Heaven an earth reflect Thy rays,

Stars and angels sing around Thee,

Center of unbroken praise.

Words: Henry van Dyke Music: Ludwig van Beethoven

Tie-in: "Children, the Lord shows us what He is like. He opens our hearts and let's us see how wonderful He is. He fills us with joy and we want to adore Him. Let's adore God right now!"

Unit 1 Lyrics

Big Question 1 Praise Song:
Oh, Oh, Oh, How Good Is the Lord!

HSK ESV Songs 1, Track 20

Verse 1

Oh! Oh! Oh! How good is the Lord,

Oh! Oh! Oh! How good is the Lord,

Oh! Oh! Oh! How good is the Lord,

I never will forget what He has done for me.

Verse 2

He shows Himself to me, How good is the Lord,

He shows Himself to me, How good is the Lord,

He shows Himself to me, How good is the Lord,

I never will forget what He has done for me.

Words and Music: Anonymous

Tie-in: "Children, How good the Lord is to show us what He's like! We would never know if He didn't show us. Let's praise Him right now!"

Big Q & A 1 Song

HSK ESV Songs 1, Track 12

How should God's peo - ple live each day? They should live like Je - sus!

How should God's peo - ple live each day? How should God's peo - ple live each day?

How should God's peo - ple live each day? They should live like Je - sus!

Words: Constance Dever Music: Adapted Nursery Rhyme ©2012

Big Question 1 Song

2

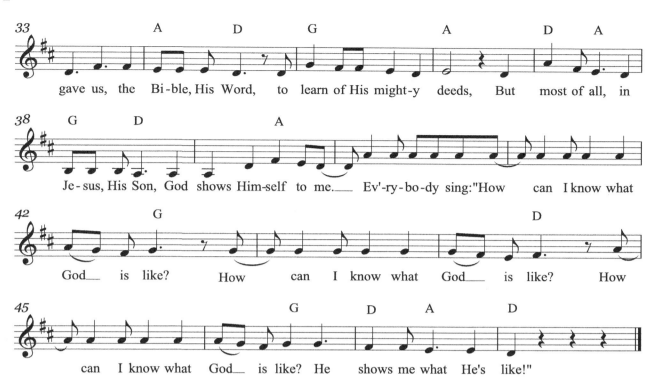

33

gave us, the Bi - ble, His Word, to learn of His might-y deeds, But most of all, in

38

Je - sus, His Son, God shows Him-self to me.___ Ev'-ry-bo-dy sing:"How can I know what

42

God___ is like? How can I know what God___ is like? How

45

can I know what God___ is like? He shows me what He's like!"

Words and Music: Constance Dever ©2012

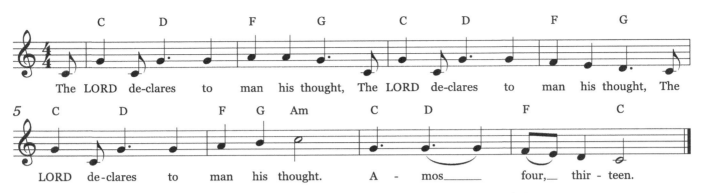

He Who Forms the Mountains
Unit 1 Extra Bible Verse

For be-hold, He___ who forms the moun-tains, cre - ates the wind, and de-

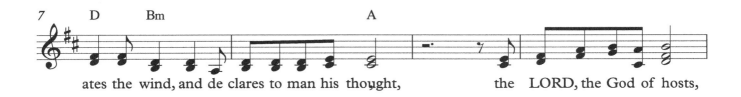

clares to man his thought, For be-hold, He___ who forms the moun-tains, cre-

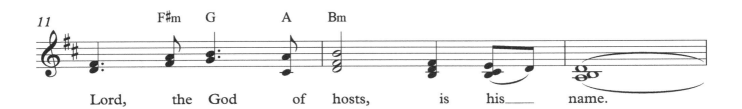

ates the wind, and de clares to man his thought, the LORD, the God of hosts,

Lord, the God of hosts, is his___ name.

A - mos Four, thir - teen.___

Words: adapted from Amos 4:13 ESV   Music: Constance Dever ©2012

For Behold

Unit 1 Extra Bible Verse

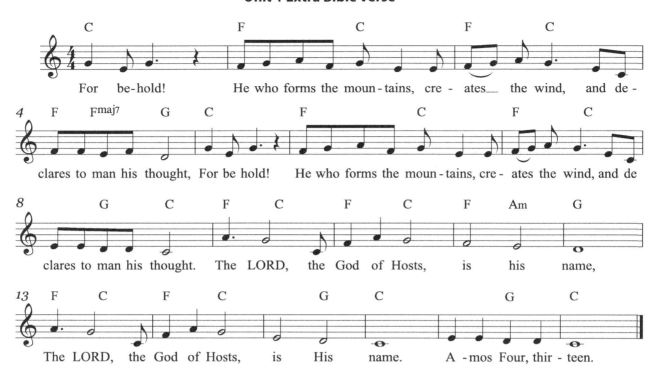

For be-hold! He who forms the moun-tains, cre - ates___ the wind, and de-

clares to man his thought, For be hold! He who forms the moun-tains, cre - ates the wind, and de

clares to man his thought. The LORD, the God of Hosts, is his name,

The LORD, the God of Hosts, is His name. A -mos Four, thir - teen.

Words: adapted from Amos 4:13 ESV   Music: Constance Dever ©2012

Behold
Unit 1 Extra Bible Verse

HSK ESV Songs 1, Track 18

Be - hold,__ For be hold,_ Be- hold,__ For be hold,_ the LORD, the

God of hosts is His name. Be -hold,__ For be hold, Be- hold,__

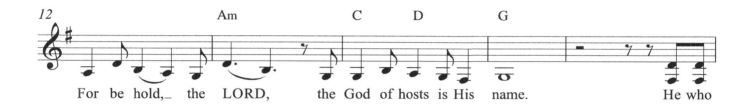

For be hold,_ the LORD, the God of hosts is His name. He who

forms the moun-tains and cre - ates the wind, de-clares to man what is His thought, He who

forms the moun-tains and cre - ates the wind, de-clares to man what is His thought.__

Be - A - mos Four, thir - teen.

Words: adapted from Amos 4:13 ESV   Music: Constance Dever ©2012

Joyful, Joyful, We Adore Thee

HSK ESV Songs 1, Track 19

Big Question 1 Hymn

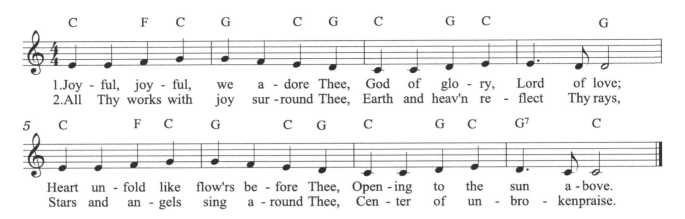

Words: Henry van Dyke   Music: Ludwig van Beethoven

Oh! Oh! Oh! How Good Is the Lord!

HSK ESV Songs 1, Track 20

Big Question 1 Praise Song

Words and Music: Anonymous

Hide 'n' Seek Kids ESV Songs 2 Track Numbers

This is a listing of all songs mentioned in the unit curriculum. You may or may not choose to use all of the songs. They are listed in easy-reference order--NOT in the order used in the curriculum.

You may choose to simply burn a CD/load them onto an mp3 device in this order. Or, you may want to do what we do: choose the songs we want to use and create a play list of them in that order. Then, we burn a CD/upload the play list onto an mp3 device. A teacher only has to click forward to the next song, instead of hunting for the right track. The track number have been included as part of the title of each song, so teachers will still have a reference to the track number listed in the curriculum (same as those listed below), even if you change the order on your customized play list.

SONGS USED EVERY UNIT OF THE CURRICULUM

1 The Classroom Song v.1
2 The Classroom Song v.2
3 The Classroom Song v.3
4 The Classroom Song v.4
5 Hide 'n' Seek Kids Theme Song
6 The Classroom Rules Song
7 Let's Pray Song
8 The Big Question Box Song
9 The Bible Chant Song
10 ACTS Prayer Song (Short Version)
11 ACTS Prayer Song (Full Version)

Why the Extra Songs?
Hide 'n' Seek Kids is a curriculum used by children of different ages. Sometimes one of the other songs is a better fit for your kids. Or, you may simply want to teach them more songs on the same Bible Truth. Use as many or as few as you want.

UNIT 2: GOD'S WONDERFUL WORD, THE BIBLE

12 Big Q & A 2 Song
13 Big Question 2 Song: What's So Special About God's Word?
14,14T Unit 2 Bible Verse Song: Proves True Psalm 18:30, ESV
15 *Extra Unit 2 Bible Verse Song: This God Psalm 18:30,46, ESV*
16 *Extra Unit 2 Bible Verse Song: This God, His Way Is Perfect   Psalm 18:30,46, ESV*
17 *Extra Unit 2 Bible Verse Song: The Word of the Lord 1 Peter 1:24,25, ESV*
18 Unit 2 Hymn: How Precious Is the Book Divine, v.1
19 Unit 2 Praise Song: The Best Book to Read Is the Bible

T* Tidbit Shortened version of the Bible Verse Song

Unit 2 Lyrics

Big Q & A 2 Song

HSK ESV Songs 2, Track 12

What's so special about the Bible?

It alone is God's Word!

It alone is God's Word!

It's always true,

It can make you wise,

It can work pow'rf'ly in your life.

It alone is God's Word!

It alone is God's Word!

Words: Constance Dever Music: Adapted Nursery Rhyme ©2012

Big Question 2 Song:
HSK ESV Songs 2, Track 13
What's So Special about the Bible?

Refrain:
What's so special about the Bible?
It alone is God's Word,
What's so special about the Bible?
It alone is God's Word,
There are millions and millions of books in the world,
But only the Bible is God's perfect Word,
There are millions and millions of books in the world,
But only the Bible is God's perfect Word.

Verse 1
God's Word was written down perfectly,
By godly men long ago,
The Holy Spirit worked through them,
Inspiring every word they wrote.

Verse 2
God's Word is powerful and living,
It changes us, deep inside,
The Holy Spirit uses it
To make God's people like Christ.

Words and Music: Constance Dever ©2012

Unit 2 Bible Verse Song:
Proves True

HSK ESV Songs 2,
Track 14,14T

This God, His ways are perfect,

The word of the LORD proves true,

This God, His ways are perfect,

The word of the LORD proves true.

This God, His ways are perfect,

The word of the LORD proves true,

This God, His ways are perfect,

The word of the LORD proves true.

Psalm Eighteen, thirty.

Words: adapted from Psalm 18:30, ESV   Music: Constance Dever ©2016

Tie-in: The LORD is like no one else. He is the one, true God. Everything He does is absolutely perfect! Everything God says is perfect, too. It is flawless. Flawless is a big word that means perfect--without even a single mistake. No, not one! God always tells us what is right and true. His Word always proves true!

Where can we read God's Word? In the Bible! It alone is God's Word. That's why we take time each day to learn from the Bible. We want to hear from God--all the wonderful things about Him; what He has done for us through Jesus, His Son; and, what good things are in store for those who love Him and live for Him. Oh, how we want to praise the LORD when we read His Word! He is the living God. He is our Savior!

Unit 2 Extra Bible Verse Song:
This God

HSK ESV Songs 2, Track 15

This God, His way is perfect,
The word of the LORD proves true,
This God, His way is perfect,
The word of the LORD proves true.

Psalm Eighteen, thirty and forty-six.

Words: adapted from Psalm 18:30, 46, ESV   Music: Constance Dever ©2016

Tie-in: The LORD is like no one else. He is the one, true God. Everything He does is absolutely perfect! Everything God says is perfect, too. It always proves true! Where can we read what He has told us? The Bible! It alone is God's Word. That's why we take time each day to learn from the Bible. We want to hear from God--all the wonderful things about Him, what He has done for us through Jesus, His Son, and what good things are in store for those who love Him and live for Him.

Unit 2 Lyrics

Unit 2 Extra Bible Verse Song:
This God, His Way Is Perfect

HSK ESV Songs 2, Track 16

This God, His way is perfect,
The word of the LORD proves true,
This God, His way is perfect,
The word of the LORD proves true.

The LORD lives, and blessed be my rock,
Exalted be the God of my salvation,
The LORD lives, and blessed be my rock,
Exalted be the God of my salvation.

This God, His way is perfect,
The word of the LORD proves true,
This God, His way is perfect,
The word of the LORD proves true.

Psalm Eighteen, thirty and forty-six.

Words: adapted from Psalm 18:30, 46, ESV   Music: Constance Dever ©2016

Tie-in: The LORD is like no one else. He is the one, true God. Everything He does is absolutely perfect! Everything God says is perfect, too. It always proves true! Where can we read what He has told us? The Bible! It alone is God's Word. That's why we take time each day to learn from the Bible. We want to hear from God--all the wonderful things about Him, what He has done for us through Jesus, His Son, and what good things are in store for those who love Him and live for Him. The LORD lives and everything He promises will come true. God's peoeple praise Him because He and His Word are so dependable. Just like a big, strong rock that can't be broken. God and His Word will always stand strong and true. Let's praise God right now!

Unit 2 Lyrics

Unit 2 Extra Bible Verse Song:
The Word of the LORD

HSK ESV Songs 2, Track 17

All flesh is like the grass,
All its glory like the flow'r,
All flesh is like the grass,
All its glory like the flow'r,

The grass withers and the flower falls,
But the word of the Lord remains,
The grass withers and the flower falls,
But the word of the Lord remains forev'r,
Yes, the word of the Lord remains forev'r.
First Peter One, twenty-four and five.

Words: adapted from 1 Peter 1:24,25 ESV   Music: Constance Dever ©2012

Tie-in: When flowers are blooming, they have such beautiful colors to look at and they smell so good. But before long, the blooms dry up and fall off.. They look ugly and they lose their good smell, too. How very different is God's Word! It is not just good for a few days. It is good forever. It is always true. It is always helpful. We can always learn from it and grow to know God better through it. Thank You, God, for giving us Your Word!

Unit 2 Lyrics

Big Question 2 Hymn:
How Precious Is the Word Divine, v.1

HSK ESV Songs 2, Track 18

Verse 1

How precious is the book divine,

By inspiration given;

Bright as a lamp its doctrines shine,

To guide our souls to heaven.

Words: William Gardiner Music: Constance Dever

Tie-in: The Bible is precious. It is no regular book. It is the only book divine, inspired by God. That means that God's Holy Spirit helped godly people write it down just right. Yes, the Bible is God's Word. In it, God tells us about Himself and how He sent Jesus to save us from our sins. He tells us how He wants us to live for Him.

Unit 2 Lyrics

Big Question 2 Praise Song:
The Best Book to Read Is the Bible

HSK ESV Songs 2, Track 19

Verse 1

The best book to read is the Bible,

The best book to read is the Bible,

It alone is God's true Word,

With the best news ever heard!

Yes! The best book to read is the Bible.

Verse 2

The best book to read is the Bible,

The best book to read is the Bible,

If you read it ev'ry day,

God will teach you His ways.

Yes! The best book to read is the Bible.

Words and Music: Anonymous

Tie-in: The Bible is the best book to read, because it alone is God's true word! In it, God tells us about Himself and the good news that He sent Jesus to save us from our sins. In it, He tells us how He wants us to live for Him. How God will bless us when we read His book, the Bible, every day!

Big Q & A 2 Song

HSK ESV Songs 2, Track 12

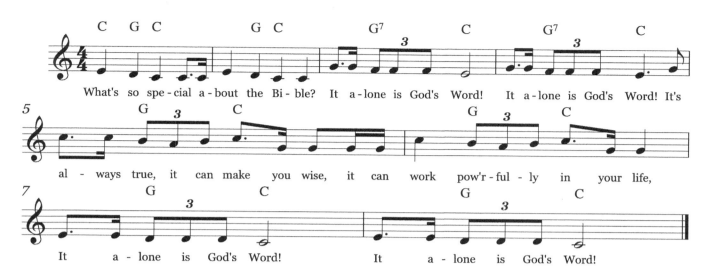

What's so spe-cial a-bout the Bi-ble? It a-lone is God's Word! It a-lone is God's Word! It's al-ways true, it can make you wise, it can work pow'r-ful-ly in your life, It a-lone is God's Word! It a-lone is God's Word!

Words: Constance Dever Music: Adapted Nursery Rhyme ©2012

Big Question 2 Song

HSK ESV Songs 2, Track 13

Words and Music: Constance Dever ©2012

Psalm 18:30 Proves True
Big Question 2 Bible Song

HSK ESV Songs 2, Track 14,14T

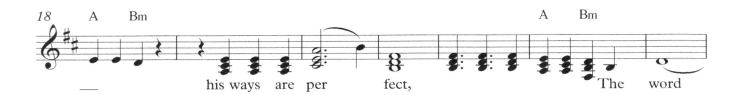

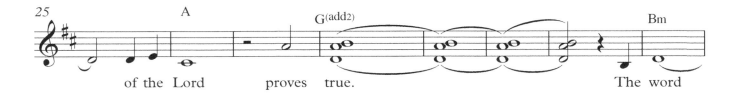

Words: adapted from Psalm 18:30, ESV   Music: Constance Dever ©2016

Psalm 18:30 This God
Extra Big Question 2 Bible Song

HSK ESV Songs 2, Track 15

This God, His ways are per-fect,   The word of the

Lord proves true.   This God, His ways are per-fect,

The word of the Lord proves true.   This God,___

___   his ways are per   fect,   The word

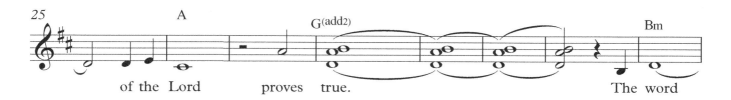

of the Lord   proves   true.   The word

of the Lord   proves   true.   Psalm Eigh-teen, thir -ty.

Words: adapted from Psalm 18:30, ESV   Music: Constance Dever ©2016

Psalm 18:30,46 God, This God, His Way Is Perfect
Extra Big Question 2 Bible Song

HSK ESV Songs 2, Track 16

This God, His way is per-fect. The word of the LORD proves true.

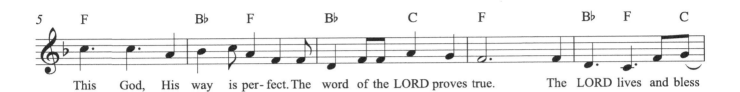

This God, His way is per-fect. The word of the LORD proves true. The LORD lives and bless

ed be my rock. Ex - alt-ed be, the God of my sal-va-tion, The LORD lives and bless

ed be my rock. Ex - alt-ed be, the God of my sal-va-tion. This God, His

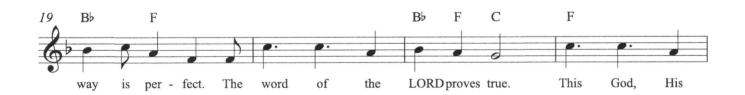

way is per-fect. The word of the LORD proves true. This God, His

way is per-fect. The word of the LORD proves true. Psalm Eigh-teen, thir-ty and for -ty six.

Words: adapted from Psalm 18:30,46 ESV   Music: Constance Dever ©2012

1 Peter 1:24,25 The Word of the Lord
Extra Big Question 2 Bible Song

HSK ESV Songs 2, Track 17

Words: adapted from 1 Peter 1:24,25 ESV   Music: Constance Dever ©2012

How Precious Is the Book Divine
Big Question 2 Hymn

HSK ESV Songs 2, Track 18

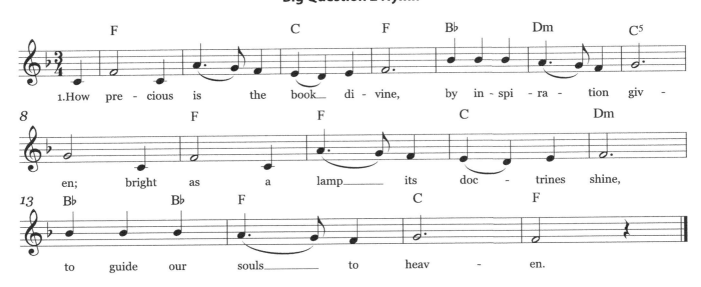

1.How pre - cious is the book di - vine, by in - spi - ra - tion giv - en; bright as a lamp its doc - trines shine, to guide our souls to heav - en.

Words: William Gardiner   Music: Constance Dever

The Best Book to Read Is the Bible
Big Question 2 Praise Song

HSK ESV Songs 2, Track 19

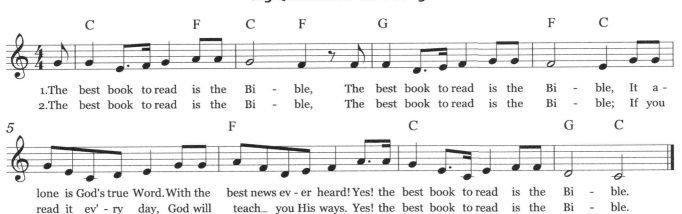

1.The best book to read is the Bi - ble, The best book to read is the Bi - ble, It a -
2.The best book to read is the Bi - ble, The best book to read is the Bi - ble; If you

lone is God's true Word. With the best news ev - er heard! Yes! the best book to read is the Bi - ble.
read it ev' - ry day, God will teach you His ways. Yes! the best book to read is the Bi - ble.

Words and Music: Anonymous

178

Hide 'n' Seek Kids ESV Songs 3 Track Numbers

This is a listing of all songs mentioned in the unit curriculum. You may or may not choose to use all of the songs. They are listed in easy-reference order--NOT in the order used in the curriculum.

You may choose to simply burn a CD/load them onto an mp3 device in this order. Or, you may want to do what we do: choose the songs we want to use and create a play list of them in that order. Then, we burn a CD/upload the play list onto an mp3 device. A teacher only has to click forward to the next song, instead of hunting for the right track. The track number have been included as part of the title of each song, so teachers will still have a reference to the track number listed in the curriculum (same as those listed below), even if you change the order on your customized play list.

SONGS USED EVERY UNIT OF THE CURRICULUM
1 The Classroom Song v.1
2 The Classroom Song v.2
3 The Classroom Song v.3
4 The Classroom Song v.4
5 Hide 'n' Seek Kids Theme Song
6 The Classroom Rules Song
7 Let's Pray Song
8 The Big Question Box Song
9 The Bible Chant Song
10 ACTS Prayer Song (Short Version)
11 ACTS Prayer Song (Full Version)

Why the Extra Songs?
Hide 'n' Seek Kids is a curriculum used by children of different ages. Sometimes one of the other songs is a better fit for your kids. Or, you may simply want to teach them more songs on the same Bible Truth. Use as many or as few as you want.

UNIT 3: GOD'S GOOD NEWS, THE GOSPEL
12 Big Q & A 3 Song
13 Big Question 3 Song: What's the Gospel?
14,14T Unit 3 Bible Verse Song: For God So Loved the World   John 3:16 ESV
15 *Extra Unit 3 Bible Verse Song: For God So Loved the World John 3:16 ESV (other version)*
16 *Extra Unit 3 Bible Verse Song: For God So Loved the World John 3:16 ESV (other version)*
17 Unit 3 Hymn: And Can It Be, v.1 Refrain
18 Unit 3 Praise Song: I Have Decided to Follow Jesus

T* Tidbit Shortened version of the Bible Verse Song

Unit 3 Lyrics

Big Q & A 3 Song

HSK ESV Songs 3, Track 12

What's the gospel?

What's the gospel?

Can you tell me what it is?

It's salvation through faith in Jesus,

That's what the gospel is. (repeat)

Words: Constance Dever Music: Adapted Nursery Rhyme ©2012

Unit 3 Lyrics

Big Question 3 Song:
HSK ESV Songs 3, Track 13
What Is the Gospel?

Refrain:
What is the gospel?
G-O-S-P-E-L?
What is the gospel?
Can anybody tell me?
What is the gospel?
Yes, I know what it is!
Salvation through faith in Christ,
That's what the gospel is.

"G" is for God, our good King and Creator,
O, we should obey Him, but instead we're disobeyers,
So S, we need a Savior to save us from our sins,
That Savior is Jesus, who "P" took the punishment.

Yes, Jesus died upon the cross, the perfect sacrifice,
Then on day three, He rose again
To prove He'd won the fight,
And now "E"everyone who repents and believes in Him,
He gives "E-L" eternal life: forever life with Him. Refrain

Unit 3 Lyrics

Unit 3 Bible Verse Song:
For God So Loved the World

HSK ESV Songs 3,
Track 14,14T

For God so loved the world,

That He gave His only Son,

That whoever believes in Him shouldn't perish,

But have eternal life.

For God so loved the world,

That He gave His only Son,

That whoever believes in Him shouldn't perish,

But have eternal life.

John Three, sixteen.

Words: adapted from John 3:16, ESV   Music: Constance Dever ©2016

Tie-in: How great is God's love for sinners like you and me, that He would send His own Son, Jesus, to suffer and die for us! Now, all who turn from their sins and trust in Jesus as their Savior will not perish. They will not receive the punishment they deserve for their sins. Jesus has already paid for their sins when He died on the cross. Because of what Jesus has done for them, these people will enjoy eternal life with God. Here on earth, they will know God in their hearts and His care in their lives. And when they die, they will go to be with Him forever! God offers us eternal life, too, when we turn away from our sins and trust in Jesus as our Savior.

Extra Unit 3 Bible Verse Song:
For God So Loved the World

HSK ESV Songs 3, Track 15

For God so loved the world,

For God so loved the world,

That He gave His only Son,

He gave His only Son,

That whoever believes in Him should not perish,

But have eternal life,

But have eternal life.

John Three, sixteen.

Words: adapted from John 3:16, ESV   Music: Constance Dever ©2012

Tie-in: How great is God's love for sinners like you and me, that He would send His own Son, Jesus, to suffer and die for us! Now, all who turn from their sins and trust in Jesus as their Savior will not perish. They will not receive the punishment they deserve for their sins. Jesus has already paid for their sins when He died on the cross. Because of what Jesus has done for them, these people will enjoy eternal life with God. Here on earth, they will know God in their hearts and His care in their lives. And when they die, they will go to be with Him forever! God offers us eternal life, too, when we turn away from our sins and trust in Jesus as our Savior.

Unit 3 Lyrics

Extra Unit 3 Bible Verse Song:
For God So Loved the World

HSK ESV Songs 3, Track 16

For God so loved the world,

That He gave His only Son, His Son,

For God so loved the world,

That He gave His only Son, His Son,

That whoever believes in Him should not perish,

But have eternal life,

That whoever believes in Him should not perish,

But have eternal life.

John Three, sixteen.

Words: adapted from John 3:16, ESV   Music: Constance Dever ©2016

Tie-in: How great is God's love for sinners like you and me, that He would send His own Son, Jesus, to suffer and die for us! Now, all who turn from their sins and trust in Jesus as their Savior will not perish. They will not receive the punishment they deserve for their sins. Jesus has already paid for their sins when He died on the cross. Because of what Jesus has done for them, these people will enjoy eternal life with God. Here on earth, they will know God in their hearts and His care in their lives. And when they die, they will go to be with Him forever! God offers us eternal life, too, when we turn away from our sins and trust in Jesus as our Savior.

<u>**Unit 3 Lyrics**</u>

Big Question 3 Hymn:
And Can It Be?

HSK ESV Songs 3, Track 17

Refrain

Amazing love, how can it be?

That thou, my God, should die for me?

Amazing love, how can it be?

That thou, my God, should die for me?

Words: Charles Wesley Music: Thomas Campbell

Tie-in: God's love is amazing! How He loves His people! They deserved the full punishment for their sins. They deserved to die and be separated from God forever. But Jesus came to die for the sins of all who would ever turn from their sins and trust in Him as their Savior. He died in their place. He took their sins. So that they could be forgiven and live as God's people forever. When we turn from our sins and trust in Jesus as our Savior, then His death pays for our sins, too. We, too, can know God now in our hearts, and one day, go to live with Him forever.

Unit 3 Lyrics

Big Question 3 Praise Song:
I Have Decided to Follow Jesus

HSK ESV Songs 3, Track 18

I have decided to follow Jesus,

I have decided to follow Jesus,

I have decided to follow Jesus,

No turning back, no turning back.

Words: Anonymous Music: Indian Folk Melody

Tie-in: God offers to forgive our sins when we turn away from sinning and trust in Jesus as our Savior. He gives us eternal life and makes us His people. God's people love God and want to please Him. Every day, they ask God to help them to follow Jesus by how they live. They want to love God and others the way Jesus did. God loves to answer this prayer. He promises to send the Holy Spirit to help them do this.

Big Q & A 3 Song

HSK ESV Songs 3, Track 12

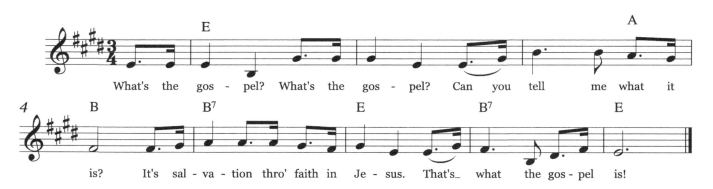

What's the gos - pel? What's the gos - pel? Can you tell me what it

is? It's sal - va - tion thro' faith in Je - sus. That's_ what the gos - pel is!

Words: Constance Dever Music: Adapted Nursery Rhyme ©2012

Big Question 3 Song

2

27

What is the Gos-pel, can an-y-bo dy tell me? What is the Gos-pel, Yes, I know what it is. Sal-

31

va - tion thru faith in Christ that's what the gos - pel is. Sal -

33 ritard

va - tion thru faith in Christ that's what the gos - pel is.

Words and Music: Constance Dever ©2012

John 3:16 For God So Loved the World
Big Question 3 Bible Verse

HSK ESV Songs 3,
Track 14,14T

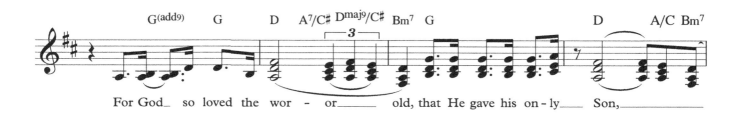

For God__ so loved the wor - or_____ old, that He gave his on-ly_____ Son,_____

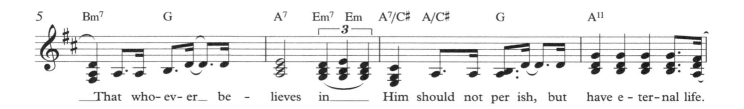

_____That who-ev-er__ be - lieves in_____ Him should not per ish, but have e - ter-nal life.

___ For God__ so loved the wor - or_____ old, that He gave his on-ly

___ Son,_____ That__ who-ev-er__ be lieves in_____ Him should not per ish, but

have e - ter - nal life.____ John Three, six - teen.

Words: adapted from John 3:16, ESV   Music: Constance Dever ©2012

John 3:16 For God So Loved the World

Extra Big Question 3 Bible Verse

HSK ESV Songs 3, Track 15

Words: adapted from John 3:16, ESV   Music: Constance Dever ©2012

John 3:16 For God So Loved the World

Extra Big Question 3 Bible Verse

HSK ESV Songs 3, Track 16

Words: adapted from John 3:16, ESV   Music: Constance Dever ©2012

And Can It Be?
Big Question 3 Hymn

HSK ESV Songs 3, Track 17

1

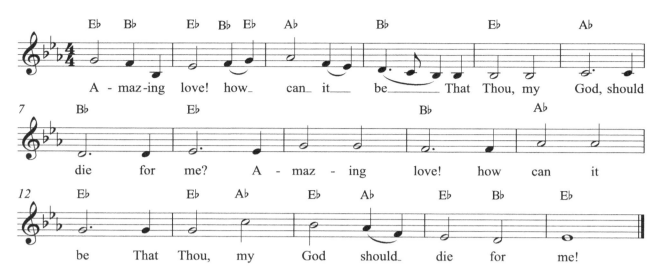

Words: Charles Wesley   Music: Thomas Campbell

I Have Decided to Follow Jesus
Big Question 3 Praise Song

HSK ESV Songs 3, Track 18

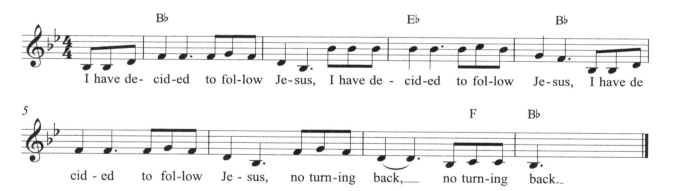

Words: Anonymous   Music: Indian Folk Melody

Hide 'n' Seek Kids ESV Songs 4 Track Numbers

This is a listing of all songs mentioned in the unit curriculum. You may or may not choose to use all of the songs. They are listed in easy-reference order--NOT in the order used in the curriculum. You may choose to simply burn a CD/load them onto an mp3 device in this order. Or, you may want to do what we do: choose the songs we want to use and create a play list of them in that order. Then, we burn a CD/upload the play list onto an mp3 device. A teacher only has to click forward to the next song, instead of hunting for the right track. The track number have been included as part of the title of each song, so teachers will still have a reference to the track number listed in the curriculum (same as those listed below), even if you change the order on your customized play list.

SONGS USED EVERY UNIT OF THE CURRICULUM

1 The Classroom Song v.1
2 The Classroom Song v.2
3 The Classroom Song v.3
4 The Classroom Song v.4
5 Hide 'n' Seek Kids Theme Song
6 The Classroom Rules Song
7 Let's Pray Song
8 The Big Question Box Song
9 The Bible Chant Song
10 ACTS Prayer Song (Short Version)
11 ACTS Prayer Song (Full Version)

> **Why the Extra Songs?**
> Hide 'n' Seek Kids is a curriculum used by children of different ages. Sometimes one of the other songs is a better fit for your kids. Or, you may simply want to teach them more songs on the same Bible Truth. Use as many or as few as you want.

UNIT 4: THE GOD LIKE NONE OTHER

12 Big Q & A 4 Song
13 Big Question 4 Song: Can Anybody Tell Me What the LORD Is Like?
14 Inspector Graff's Rap: The ABC's of God
15,15T Unit 4 Bible Verse Song: O, O, LORD 1 Kings 8:23, ESV
16 *Extra Unit 4 Bible Verse Song: In Heaven Above* Kings 8:23, *ESV (short version)*
17 *Extra Unit 4 Bible Verse Song: In Heaven Above* Kings 8:23, *ESV (full version)*
18 *Extra Unit 4 Bible Verse Song: In Heaven Above or Earth Beneath* Kings 8:23, *ESV (other version)*
19 Unit 4 Hymn: Praise Him, Praise Him, All Ye Little Children
20 Unit 4 Praise Song: God Is So Good

T* Tidbit   Shortened version of the Bible Verse Song

Unit 4 Lyrics

Big Q & A 4 Song

HSK ESV Songs 4, Track 12

Can anybody tell me,
Tell me, tell me,
Can anybody tell me,
What the LORD is like?
He's not like anyone else,
Anyone else, anyone else,
He's not like anyone else,
That's what the LORD is like.

Words: Constance Dever Music: Adapted Nursery Rhyme ©2012

Big Question 4 Song:
HSK ESV Songs 4, Track 13
Can Anybody Tell Me What the LORD Is Like?

Refrain:
Tell me, can anybody tell me,
Tell me, what the LORD is like?
Tell me, can anybody tell me,
Tell me, what the LORD is like?
He's not like anyone else,
He's not like anyone else,
He's not like anyone else,
He's not like anyone else,

He's Omniscient! *(He knows all things)*
Omnipresent! *(He's everywhere you can be)*
Omni-benevolent! *(He's always good!)*
and Omnipotent! *(He can do all things!) Refrain*

He's Immutable! *(He never changes!)*
He's Infallible! *(He makes no mistakes!)*
He's Infinite! *(There's always more of Him to know!)*
And purely Righteous!
(He has no sin! Not even a teeny, tiny speck!) Refrain

Words and Music: Constance Dever ©2012

Unit 4 Bible Verse Song:

HSK ESV Songs 4,
Tracks 15, 15T

O, O LORD

O, O, LORD,

There is no, no God like You,

O, O, LORD,

There is no God like You.

O, O, LORD,

There is no, no God like You,

First Kings Eight, twenty-three.

Words: adapted from 1 Kings 8:23, ESV   Music: Constance Dever ©2015

Tie-in: The LORD is the one, true God. There is no one like Him, in heaven or earth. Let's praise Him!

Unit 4 Lyrics

Unit 4 Extra Bible Verse Song:
In Heaven Above

HSK ESV Songs 4, Tracks 16,17

O LORD, there is no God like you.
In heaven above or on earth beneath,
O LORD, there is no God like you.
In heaven above or on earth beneath. (repeat)

In heaven above,
Or earth beneath,
There is no God like you.
In heaven above,
Or earth beneath,
There is no God like you. (repeat)

First Kings Eight, twenty-three.

Words: adapted from 1 Kings 8:23, ESV   Music: Constance Dever ©2015

Tie-in: The LORD is the one, true God. There is no one like Him, in heaven or earth. Let's praise Him!

Unit 4 Extra Bible Verse Song:
In Heaven Above or Earth Beneath

HSK ESV Songs 4, Track 18

In heaven above or earth beneath,
There is no God like you.
In heaven above or earth beneath,
There is no God like you.
O LORD, there is no God like you.
O LORD, there is no God like you.
In heaven above or earth beneath,
There is no God like you.
In heaven above or earth beneath,
There is no God like you.
O LORD, there is no God like you.
O LORD, there is no God like you.
O LORD, there is no God like you.
O LORD, there is no God like you.
First Kings Chapter Eight, twenty-three.

Words: adapted from 1 Kings 8:23, ESV   Music: Constance Dever ©2015

Tie-in: The LORD is the one, true God. There is no one like Him, in heaven or earth. Let's praise Him!

Inspector Graff's Rap
HSK ESV Songs 4, Track 14

So you say that the Lord's not like anyone else,
That He's in a category all by Himself,
Well, that's cool, y'all, 'cuz I agree,
Come praise the Lord with me! Come 'on!

Refrain:
Come, little children,
Gonna say my ABC's of God,
Yes, come draw near, little children,
Gonna say 'em for all to hear. (Repeat)

The Lord is ABLE, He is BLESSED,
He is full of COMPASSION, is COMPLETE DELIGHTFULNESS,
He sits ENTHRONED above the cherubim,
There's no one, I mean no one who's EXALTED like Him!
The Lord is FORGIVING, FULL of GLORY He shines,
He's His people's HELPER, INTERCEDES all the time,
He's also our JUDGE and our KING supreme,
He's the LORD, the LIVING ONE, robed in MAJESTY.

So we've just described some of who the Lord is,
Using words from A to M.
And it's clear there's no one like Him.
Now let's go from N to Z,
Come, praise the Lord with me. (Refrain)

Unit 4 Lyrics

Inspector Graff's Rap, continued

The Lord NEEDS NOTHING, NOT even sleep;
He's the ONE, true God and PROVIDER of true PEACE;
He QUIETS His people with His love;
He REDEEMED them from hell
By the power of His blood—Jesus;
The Lord is SOVEREIGN, He is TRUTHFUL and UPRIGHT,
Over death He's VICTORIOUS and He's WONDERF'LY WISE;
He's our eXCELLENT God, He's real name is YAHWEH,
He is full of ZEAL, and His good plans win always!

Now I've said my ABC's,
Come and praise the Lord with me!
Now I've said my ABC's,
Won't you come and praise the Lord with me,
Come on! (Refrain)

Now we know our ABC's,
And you'll have to agree,
He's not like anyone else,
He's in a category all by Himself,
He's in a category all by Himself.

A,B,C,D,E,F,G,
H,I,J,K,L,M,N,O,P,
Q,R,S,T,U,V,W,X,Y and Zzz.

Words and Music: Constance Dever, Julian White ©2012

Unit 4 Lyrics

Big Question 4 Hymn:
Praise Him, Praise Him, All Ye Little Children

HSK ESV Songs 4, Track 19

Praise Him, praise Him,
All ye little children,
God is love (powerful, holy),
God is love (powerful, holy),
Praise Him, praise Him,
All ye little children,
God is love (powerful, holy),
Praise Him, praise Him,
All ye little children,
God is love (powerful, holy).

Words: Carey Bonner, Constance Dever Music Anonymous

Tie-in: ""Children God is so good, so powerful and so holy! Let's praise Him!

Unit 4 Lyrics

Big Question 4 Praise Song:
God Is So Good

HSK ESV Songs 4, Track 20

God is so good (powerful, holy),

God is so good (powerful, holy),

God is so good (powerful, holy),

He's so good (powerful, holy) to me.

Words and Music: Anonymous

Tie-in: "Children God is so good, so powerful and so holy! Let's praise Him!

Big Q & A 4 Song

Can an-y-bo-dy tell me, tell me, tell me, Can an-y-bo-dy tell me, what the Lord is like? He's not like an-y-one else, an-y-one else, an-y-one else, He's not like an y-one else, That's what the Lord is like!

Words: Constance Dever Music: Adapted Nursery Rhyme ©2012

Big Question 4 Song

HSK ESV Songs 4, Track 13

He's not like a-ny-one else, He's not like a-ny-one else!___ He's Im-

mu-ta-ble!_ (He ne-ver chan-ges!) In-fal-li-ble! (He makes no mis-takes!) He's

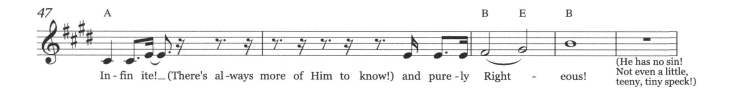

In-fin-ite!_ (There's al-ways more of Him to know!) and pure-ly Right - eous!

(He has no sin!
Not even a little,
teeny, tiny speck!)

Tell me, can a-ny-bo-dy tell me, Tell me, What the LORD is like?

Tell me, can a-ny-bo-dy tell me, Tell__ me, what the LORD is like? He's not like

a - ny-one else,_ He's not like a-ny-one else!___ He's not like

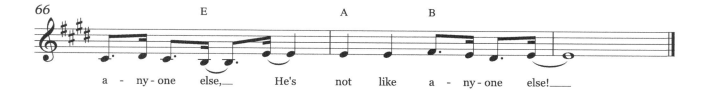

a - ny-one else,___ He's not like a-ny-one else!___

Words and Music: Constance Dever ©2012

O, O LORD

HSK ESV Songs 4, Tracks 15, 15T

Unit 4 Bible Verse

O, O, LORD, there is no, no god like You! O, O, LORD, there is no god like You!

O, O, LORD, there is no, no god like You! First Kings____ eight, twen-ty three.

Words: adapted from 1 Kings 8:23, ESV   Music: Constance Dever ©2012

1 Kings 8:23 In Heaven Above

Big Question 4 Bible Verse

Words: adapted from 1 Kings 8:23, ESV   Music: Constance Dever ©2012

1 Kings 8:23 In Heaven Above or Earth Beneath
Big Question 4 Bible Verse

HSK ESV Songs 4, Track 18

In heav-en a bove or earth be neath, there is no god like You. In

heav-en a bove or earth be neath, there is no god like You. O Lord, there is,

no god like You. O Lord, there is, no god like You. In

O Lord, there is, no god like You. O Lord, there is,

no god like You. FirstKings Chap-ter Eight, twen-ty three.

Words: adapted from 1 Kings 8:23, ESV   Music: Constance Dever ©2012

211

Praise Him, Praise Him, All Ye Little Children
HSK ESV Songs 4, Track 19
Big Question 4 Hymn

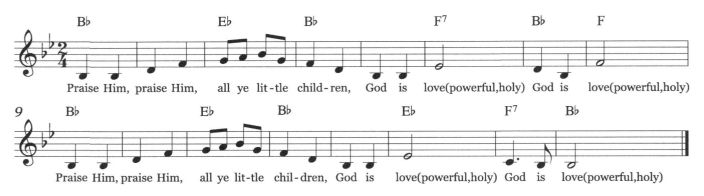

Words: Carey Bonner, Constance Dever   Music: Anonymous

God Is So Good
HSK ESV Songs 4, Track 20
Big Question 4 Praise Song

Words and Music: Anonymous

Hide 'n' Seek Kids

Appendix B:
Games

Index of Games

List of Supplies Needed to Make All Games 185

Bible Verse Games 185
Lily Pad Jump 186
Animal Cube 187
Simon Says How 188
Bean Bag Catch 189
Slap, Clap and Stack 190
Freeze 'n' Say 191
Fill 'er Up 192
Loud and Soft, Big and Little 193
Roll 'n' Toss 194
Duck, Duck, Goose 195
Detective Mission Madness Practice 196
Block Clapping 197
Meet, Greet and Keep It Up

Music, Movement & Memory Activities 198
Thumping Drums 199
Say, Spring Up and Shout 200
Freeze Frame 201
Egg Shakers 202
Jingle Bell Hands 203
Big Voice, Little Voice 204
Sing, Dance and Fall Down 205
Bottle Shakers 206
March 'n' Say 207
Clap, Tap and Say 208
Block Clappers 209
Musical Squares 210
Lullabies, Bells and Lions

Bible Story Review Games 211
Who's in the Basket? 212
Run to the Grocery Store 213
Treasure Hunt 214
Take Me through the Tunnel 215
Missing in Action 216
Hide 'n' Seek Kids Clue Hunt 218
Who's Inside? 219
Look Who's Coning Down the Tracks 220
Going Fishing 221
Pony Express 222
Clothespin Line Up and Drop 223
Fix Up the Mix Up

Master Supplies List for All Hide 'n' Seek Kids Games

Hide 'n' Seek Kids uses many games. The good news is, they are simply made and they are re-used throughout the whole curriculum. Make sure you save the games you make and it will save you a lot of time later.

This is the full list of the games and the supplies needed in the Hide 'n' Seek Kids Curriculum. I **would highly suggest you do this!** Get the prep work over with at the beginning and coast your way through years of enjoyment! Store them in ziploc bags or baskets and pull them out when needed. So simple!

Bible Verse Games

Lily Pad Jump
- Cube-shaped cardboard box,
- paper,
- glue,
- marker

Animal Cube
- Cube-shaped cardboard box,
- paper,
- glue,
- marker

Simon Says How
- Cube-shaped Cardboard box
- Paper, glue, and a marker

Bean Bag Catch
- 1 bean bag per every 2 children (or every child)
- NOTE: Can also fill socks with beans and tie open end to make beanbags.

Slap, Clap and Stack
- 10 or 12 Blocks or other stackable objects

Freeze 'n' Say
- Music and CD/Tape player

Fill 'er Up
- 1 bean bag per child
- NOTE: Can also fill socks with beans and tie open end to make beanbags.
- Cardboard box or laundry basket
- Carpet squares, 1 per child

Bible Verse Games

Loud and Soft, Big and Little
- none

Roll 'n' Toss
- Cube-shaped Cardboard box
- Paper, glue, and a marker
- 1 bouncy ball per 2 children

Duck, Duck, Goose
- none

Detective Mission Madness Practice
- Detective Gear, such as a trench coat, sunglasses, and a hat

Master Supplies List for all Hide 'n' Seek Kids Games, continued

Music, Movement & Memory

Thumping Drums
- 1 Oatmeal container/coffee can with lid per drum
- Tape
- Popcorn, rice, beans, etc.
- Wooden spoons, dowels, unsharpened pencils, if desired, for mallets

Say, Spring Up and Shout
- Bean bags, one per child

Freeze Frame
- Some kind of fun hat or clothing for the leader to wear

Egg Shakers
- Empty Easter eggs
- Rice, beans, buttons, pennies, popcorn, beads, small nails or bolts, etc.
- Glue and glue gun OR strong packing tape

Jingle Bell Hands
- 1 6" piece of sturdy string
- 4 or 5 jingle bells, available in most craft shops

Big Voice, Little Voice
- none

Music, Movement & Memory
- 1 oatmeal container/coffee can with lid per drum
- Tape
- Popcorn, rice, beans, etc.
- Wooden spoons, dowels, unsharpened pencils, if desired, for mallets

Bottle Shakers
- 1 empty 16 oz. soda bottle per shaker
- Rice, beans, buttons, pennies, popcorn, beads, small nails or bolts, etc.
- Glue and glue gun OR strong packing tape

Clap, Tap and Say
- none

Music, Movement & Memory

March 'n' Say
- Optional: A fun hat for the leader of the march, or for everyone in the march

Block Clappers
- 2 wooden blocks per child, preferably about 3"x 2", as found in many children's block sets

Master Supplies List for all Hide 'n' Seek Kids Games, continued

Story Review Games

Who's Inside?
- 10 different containers with lids

Look Who's Coming Down the Tracks
- Two shoe boxes
- 6' or so of rope
- Optional: Engineer's hat

Going Fishing
- One long wooden dowel, yardstick, etc. per fishing pole
- Yarn
- Paper clip per fishing pole
- Rope
- Two chairs
- Blanket
- Box/bucket/container
- Bucket

Pony Express
- Small manila envelopes, one per flannel graph figure
- Kid's small backpack or a tote bag with a strap
- Basket
- Cowboy hat
- Stick horse or a broom

Clothespin Line Up and Drop
- Rope
- Clothespins, the hinged type
- Shoe box
- Tape

Missing in Action
- None

Hide 'n' Seek Kids Detective Clue Hunt
- Variety of interesting items that have one or more places to Hide a storyboard picture
- Detective Hat
- 4 False Clues (included on the next page)
- CD Player and Hide 'n' Seek Kids Theme Song

Take Me Through the Tunnel
- Chairs or Table
- Sheet or blanket
- Box

Story Review Games

Who's in the Basket?
- Blanket
- Basket

Run to the Grocery Store
- Grocery bag or kid's grocery cart
- Empty food cartons

Treasure Hunt
- 10 small lidded plastic containers or boxes (like from a jewelry store) or wooden, hinged boxes from a craft store
- Various decorating supplies, such as fake craft jewels, glitter, glitter glue, foil paper, gold spray paint
- glue

Bible Verse Game

intake or Response Activity to learn Bible verse

Lily Pad Jump

Materials

Bible Verse sign from the curriculum
Hide 'n' Seek Kids Discussion Questions (optional)
Cube-shaped cardboard box, paper, glue, marker

Preparation

Make a die out of the cardboard box as follows:
1. Cut the paper into the size of one side of the cube.
2. Use it as a pattern to make six pieces (one for each side of the cube).
3. Glue each piece of paper onto each side of the cube.
4. Write the numbers 1-6 on the each side of the cube like a die.

Learning the Verse

Choose the whole verse or an appropriate length portion of the verse to learn. Read the verse slowly and explain it to them. A simple explanation is included on the back of the Bible Truth sign. Practice saying the verse with the children a few times.

Playing the Game

1. Tell children that they will be froggies, leaping from lily pad to lily pad. Everyone will say the verse together, then you (or a very good, well-behaved listening "froggie") will roll the die and see how many leaps all the froggies will make before them stop.

2. Have them practice leaping. Warn them to watch out for their other froggie friends so that no one gets hurt. Practice stopping.

3. Have everyone get in froggie position. Roll die and tell them how many leaps they will leap. Say the verse together. At your signal, everyone leaps as you (or you and they) count out the number of leaps together: "1, 2, 3, stop!" etc. Repeat. If desired, you can also ask them a question about the verse after every turn or every few turns. See the Hide n" Seek Kids Discussion Sheet for possible questions.

Bible Verse Game

intake or Response Activity to learn Bible verse

Animal Cube

Materials
Bible Verse sign from the curriculum
Hide 'n' Seek Kids Discussion Questions (optional)
Cube-shaped cardboard box
Paper, glue, and a marker

Preparation
1. Cut the paper into the size of one side of the cube. Use it as a pattern to make six pieces (one for each side of the cube) Draw a simple animal picture on each piece of paper. Possibilities would be: rabbit, monkey, elephant, bird, fish, and a horse. Glue each picture onto each side of the cube.

Learning the Verse
Choose the whole verse or an appropriate length portion of the verse to learn. Read the verse slowly and explain it to them. A simple explanation is included on the back of the Bible Truth sign. Practice saying the verse with the children a few times.

Playing the Game
1. Tell the children they will be playing a game in which they must move like six different animals. Have them practice the movements for each of the animals on your cube. (Rabbit: leaping; monkey: scratching under arms and saying "ooh-ooh, ahh-ahh"; Elephant: swinging arms like a trunk and making trumpet sound; Bird: flapping arms like wings; Fish: palms together, weaving them in a serpentine action, saying "blub-blub"; horse: galloping/prancing and neighing).

2. Show the children the cube with the animal pictures on it, just like the ones they've practiced. Tell them that you will roll the dice and everyone (at your signal) will begin making the movement for that animal. Tell them that they must stop in place and be very quiet when they hear a certain noise (such as a whistle, a bell ring, you clap, etc.). Tell them that you will be watching them. And that children who are very good at listening and stopping when you say so will get a chance to toss the cube for everyone. Practice tossing the cube, making the movements and stopping with the children.

3. Now it's time to play the whole game. Choose a child to roll the cube and say which animal is picked and what action they will do for the animal. Have everyone say the verse, then at your cue, let the children act out the animal until you tell them to stop (a bell or whistle can be used to give the start and stop signals).

4. Choose another child and repeat. If desired, you can also ask them a question about the verse after every turn or every few turns. See the Hide 'n' Seek Kids Discussion Sheet for possible questions.

Other Option: If children get really good at this, you can challenge them by saying the verse while they make the movement.

Bible Verse Game

intake or Response Activity to learn Bible verse

Simon Says How

Materials

Bible Verse sign from the curriculum
Hide 'n' Seek Kids Discussion Questions (optional)
Cube-shaped Cardboard box
Paper, glue, and a marker
Die Number and Action Chart (see below)

Preparation

Make a die out of the cardboard box as follows:

1. Cut the paper into the size of one side of the cube. Use it as a pattern to make six pieces (one for each side of the cube)
2. Glue each piece of paper onto each side of the cube.
3. Write the numbers 1-6 on the each side of the cube like a die.
4. Make a sign as follows:

    1 = Head   2 = Feet
    3 = Hands   4 = Hands and Feet
    5 = Laying Down   6 = Eyes Closed

Learning the Verse

Choose the whole verse or an appropriate length portion of the verse to learn. Read the verse slowly and explain it to them. A simple explanation is included on the back of the Bible Truth sign. Practice saying the verse with the children a few times.

Playing the Game

1. Have the children spread out facing the leader.

2. Tell the children that they are going to play "Simon Says How", a game in which everyone will take turns making up different actions that they will do while saying the verse.

3. Explain that "Simon" will roll the die and make up actions that use the parts of the body that correspond to the number on the chart. Everyone else will then recite the verse while standing still. Then challenge them to recite it again while doing the actions "Simon" made up at the same time.

4. Simon will then choose another person to be Simon in his place. Repeat. If desired, you can also ask them a question about the verse after every turn or every few turns. See the Hide 'n' Seek Kids Discussion Sheet for possible
    questions.

Bible Verse Game

intake or Response Activity to learn Bible verse

Bean Bag Catch

Materials

Bible Verse sign from the curriculum

Hide 'n' Seek Discussion Sheet (optional)

1 bean bag per every 2 children (or every child)

NOTE: Can also fill socks with beans and tie open end to make beanbags.

Preparation

None.

Learning the Verse

Choose the whole verse or an appropriate length portion of the verse to learn. Read the verse slowly and explain it to them. A simple explanation is included on the back of the Bible Truth sign. Practice saying the verse with the children a few times.

Playing the Game

1. Have the children stand in two long lines, with their partners facing each other at arm's length apart.

2. Give out a bean bag to each person in one of the long lines. (Partners will not have one.) Have everyone say the verse together, then throw the bean bag to their partners, trying to catch the bean bag. (NOTE: no one is "out" if they don't catch it.)

3. Have both lines of children take a step back.

4. Say the verse all together again, then throw the bean bags again.

5. Repeat as frequently as desired. If desired, you can also ask them a question about the verse after every turn or every few turns. See the Hide 'n' Seek Discussion Sheet for possible questions.

Bible Verse Game

intake or Response Activity to learn Bible verse

Slap, Clap and Stack

Materials

Bible Verse sign from the curriculum
Hide 'n' Seek Discussion Sheet (optional)
10 or 12 Blocks or other stackable objects

Preparation

None.

Learning the Verse

Choose the whole verse or an appropriate length portion of the verse to learn. Read the verse slowly and explain to them. A simple explanation is included on the back of the Bible Truth sign. Practice saying the verse with the children a few times.

Playing the Game

1. Tell the children that they are going to learn the verse while working together to make the largest stack of blocks/
   objects they can. After each time they say the verse, a child gets to pick out an object to put on the tower. Teacher will help them balance it in place.

2. Have everyone sit down in a circle around the stacking area. Say the verse together. If desired, you can add a motion
   the children do each time they say the verse, such as clap, stomp feet, etc. This will add movement to this game. Choose a child to pick out an object. Help the child put it in place.

3. Continue adding objects/blocks until all objects are used up or the tower falls down.

4. Repeat as desired. If desired, you can also ask them a question about the verse after every turn or every few turns. See the Hide 'n' Seek Discussion Sheet for possible questions.

Bible Verse Game

intake or Response Activity to learn Bible verse

Freeze 'n' Say

Materials
Bible Verse sign from the curriculum
Hide 'n' Seek Kids Discussion Questions (optional)
Music and CD/Tape player

Preparation
None.

Learning the Verse
Choose the whole verse or an appropriate length portion of the verse to learn. Read the verse slowly and explain it to them. A simple explanation is included on the back of the Bible Truth sign. Practice saying the verse with the children a few times.

Playing the Game
1. Play some of the music for the children. Tell them that they will move around the room as you tell them (marching, leaping, clapping, etc.) while they hear the music. They will stop and freeze in whatever position they are in when the music stops. Practice this with them.

2. When they have the concept down, add saying the verse when the music stops and they are in their frozen position.

3. After they say the verse, then tell them how you want them to move when the music starts again. You can take their suggestions for movement ideas, too.

4. Start the music up again and continue. Repeat as frequently as desired. If desired, you can also ask them a question about the verse after every turn or every few turns. See the Hide 'n' Seek Kids Discussion Sheet for possible questions.

Bible Verse Game

intake or Response Activity to learn Bible verse

Fill 'er Up

Materials
Bible Verse sign from the curriculum
Hide 'n' Seek Kids Discussion Questions (optional)
1 bean bag per child
NOTE: Can also fill socks with beans and tie open end to make beanbags.
Cardboard box or laundry basket
Carpet squares, 1 per child

Preparation
1. Put box/basket in a central location.
2. Place carpet squares equidistant about 2' from center box/basket. These will be for the children to sit on.

Learning the Verse
Choose the whole verse or an appropriate length portion of the verse to learn. Read the verse slowly and explain it to them. A simple explanation is included on the back of the Bible Truth sign. Practice saying the verse with the children a few times.

Playing the Game
1. Have the children stand on a carpet square.

2. Tell them that they will be saying the verse, then—on your signal—they will trying to throw as many of their bean bags as they can into the box/basket target in the middle.

3. As they get good at throwing their bean bags in, have the children move back their carpet squares.

4. Repeat verse before toss. If desired, you can also ask them a question about the verse after every few tosses. See the Hide 'n' Seek Kids Discussion Sheet for possible questions.

Bible Verse Game

intake or Response Activity to learn Bible verse

Loud and Soft, Big and Little

Materials

Bible Verse sign from the curriculum
Hide 'n' Seek Kids Discussion Questions (optional)

Preparation

None.

Learning the Verse

Choose the whole verse or an appropriate length portion of the verse to learn. Read the verse slowly and explain it to them. A simple explanation is included on the back of the Bible Truth sign. Practice saying the verse with the children a few times.

Playing the Game

1. Tell the children: "Let's practice our Bible verse with a game."

2. "First let's say our verse together," (say it a couple times).

3. "Now let's see how quietly we can whisper it! Can you say it quietly like I am?" Have everyone follow your voice as it gets quiet, then loud, then medium, etc. Quiet them, then repeat. If desired, you can also ask them a question about the verse after they repeat the verse a few times. See the Hide 'n' Seek Kids Discussion Sheet for possible questions.

NOTE: You may find it easier for the children to follow getting louder and softer by lowering your hands when you are getting quieter and then raising your hands when you are getting louder.

Bible Verse Game

intake or Response Activity to learn Bible verse

Roll 'n' Toss

Materials

Bible Verse sign from the curriculum
Hide 'n' Seek Kids Discussion Questions (optional)
Cube-shaped Cardboard box
Paper, glue, and a marker
1 bouncy ball per 2 children

Preparation

1. Cut the paper into the size of one side of the cube. Use it as a pattern to make six pieces (one for each side of the cube)

2. Glue each piece of paper onto each side of the cube.

3. Write different actions on each side of the cube: Roll, Bounce, Overhand Toss, Close Eyes and Roll, Backwards Roll (through legs), Underhand Toss.

Learning the Verse

Choose the whole verse or an appropriate length portion of the verse to learn. Read the verse slowly and explain it to them. A simple explanation is included on the back of the Bible Truth sign. Practice saying the verse with the children a few times.

Playing the Game

1. Have the children spread out facing the leader.

Playing the Game

1. Tell the children they will be throwing a ball to a partner in the different ways you have written on the cube (show them the cube).

2. Have the children stand in two long lines, with their partners facing each other about 9-12' apart (whatever seems to be a good tossing/rolling distance for your children).

3. Give out the ball to each person in one of the long lines. (Partners will not have one.)

4. Practice each of the different ball actions, then begin the game.

5. Have everyone say the verse together. Toss the cube and tell everyone what the motion will be. At your signal, have one partner roll, toss, etc. the ball to the other. After all the partners have received the balls and every-one is back in line. Have everyone say the verse together, then toss the cube again. If desired, you can also ask them a question about the verse after every few rolls. See the Hide 'n' Seek Kids Discussion Sheet for possible questions.

Bible Verse Game

intake or Response Activity to learn Bible verse

Duck, Duck, Goose

Materials

Bible Verse sign from the curriculum

Hide 'n' Seek Kids Discussion Questions (optional)

Preparation

None.

Learning the Verse

Choose the whole verse or an appropriate length portion of the verse to learn. Read the verse slowly and explain it to them. A simple explanation is included on the back of the Bible Truth sign. Practice saying the verse with the children a few times.

Playing the Game

1. Have the children sit in a circle, cross-legged on the floor.

2. Choose a child to be "It". "It" will walk around behind the seated children, tapping each one on the head, the whole group recites the verse, saying one word for each head tap.

3. The child whose head is the last one to be tapped must get up and chase "It", hoping to tag "It" before "It" can get around the circle and sit down in the open spot in the circle.

4. If the child does tag "It" then he may take his place in the circle. If not, then the new child is "It." If desired, you can also ask them a question about the verse before repeating. See the Hide 'n' Seek Kids Discussion Sheet for possible questions.

5. Repeat as frequently as desired.

Bible Verse Game

intake or Response Activity to learn Bible verse

Detective Mission Madness Practice

Materials
Bible Verse sign from the curriculum
Hide 'n' Seek Kids Discussion Questions (optional)
Hide 'n' Seek Kids Theme Song and/or Bible verse song
Detective Gear, such as a trench coat, sunglasses, and a hat

Preparation
None.

Learning the Verse
Choose the whole verse or an appropriate length portion of the verse to learn. Read the verse slowly and explain it to them. A simple explanation is included on the back of the Bible Truth sign. Practice saying the verse with the children a few times.

Playing the Game
1. Tell the children that a detective is someone who gets paid to find answers to questions. Hide 'n' Seek Kids are like detectives, looking for answers to big questions about God. Sometimes detectives have to do all sorts of things to get answers to their questions and solve the case they are working on. In this game, they will practice some sneaky detective moves.

2. Put on the detective costume, telling the children that you will start out the game as the Chief Detective.

3. As you play the Hide 'n' Seek Kids theme song, you will lead the children in practicing one of their moves, such as swimming across a deep river. . (Other possible actions would be crawling, hand over eye looking around left and right; walking backwards, shuffling, stooping, and crawling..)

4. When the song finishes, the children will sit down and everyone will say the verse together. If desired, you can also ask them a question about the verse. See the Hide 'n' Seek Kids Discussion Sheet for possible questions.

5. Choose a child to take your place as Chief Detective. Repeat activity, choosing another detective move. Play continues as time and attention span allow.

Bible Verse Game

intake or Response Activity to learn Bible verse

Block Clapping

Materials

Bible Verse sign from the curriculum

Hide 'n' Seek Kids Discussion Questions (optional)

2 wooden blocks per child, preferably about 3"x 2", as found in many children's block sets

Preparation

None.

Learning the Verse

Choose the whole verse or an appropriate length portion of the verse to learn. Read the verse slowly and explain it to them. A simple explanation is included on the back of the Bible Truth sign. Practice saying the verse with the children a few times.

Playing the Game

1. Show the children the clapping blocks and tell them: "We are going to use our Bible verse to play a game. But first, we need to practice saying the verse." (Practice saying it a couple of times).

2. Hand out the clapping blocks and let the children clap them a while (without saying the verse), then quiet them.

3. Then tell them, "OK, let's try saying our verse and block clapping at the same time!" Lead the children in reciting the verse and clapping with each word. Or, you can have the children clap the blocks together a certain number of times, then say the verse after the last clap. If desired, you can also ask them a question about the verse before repeating. See the Hide 'n' Seek Kids Discussion Questions for possible questions.

4. Repeat as frequently as desired.

Bible Verse Game

intake or Response Activity to learn Bible verse

Meet, Greet and Keep It Up

Materials

Bible Verse sign from the curriculum
Hide 'n' Seek Kids Discussion Questions (optional)
16 oz. cups, 1 per child (with some extras)
2 pieces of rope as long as a line of children
Masking tape

Preparation

1. Line up the 2 pieces of rope about 6' apart.
2. Put down a piece of masking tape the same length as the ropes, running parallel to the ropes midway between the 2 ropes.

Learning the Verse

Choose the whole verse or an appropriate length portion of the verse to learn. Read the verse slowly and explain it to them. A simple explanation is included on the back of the Bible Truth sign. Practice saying the verse with the children a few times.

Playing the Game

1. Break the children into partners. Have them stand in two long lines, with their partners facing each other about 6' apart.

2. Tell the children they will be meeting and greeting their partners with a handshake at the masking tape in the middle, then turning around and going back to their place along the rope. Have them practice this.

3. Now tell them, that they will also be balancing a cup on their head while they do this.

4. Give out a cup to everyone. Have them practice balancing the cup on their heads.

5. Now play the game. Have everyone say the verse together. Then have them put the cups on their heads. At your signal, have them walk to the middle, greet their partner with a handshake, turn around and go back— trying to keep the cup balanced on their head the whole time. (There is no penalty for cups falling off.)

6. Have everyone settle back in place in the line, with the cups off their heads. Say the verse together again, put the cups back on their heads, then walk to greet partner again, etc.

7. You can move the ropes back gradually so the children can try to do it from further and further apart.

8. If desired, you can also ask them a question about the verse after every few turns. See the Hide 'n' Seek Kids Discussion Questions for possible questions.

Music, Movement & Memory Activity

Intake or Response Activity to learn the Big Question, Bible verse and Unit music

Thumping Drums

Materials
CD of unit music
Hide 'n' Seek Kids Discussion Questions (optional)
1 Oatmeal container/coffee can with lid per drum
Tape
Popcorn, rice, beans, etc.
Wooden spoons, dowels, unsharpened pencils, if desired, for mallets

How to Make
1. Tape the lid of empty oatmeal or coffee cans in place. (If want to make a snare drum, add popcorn, rice, etc. in the empty container before taping shut.)

2. Children can either tap drum with hands or you can give them 2 wooden spoons, wooden dowels or unsharpened pencils with wooden spools glue gunned to an end as mallets.

What to Do
1. Show the children the thumping drums. Tell them. "I'm going to say God's Word and make a joyful noise to Him with these thumping drums. Come and join me!

2. "First, let's sing our Bible verse song/Big Question song/Praise Song/Hymn together (say the verse a couple of times, if using it.)"

3. "Now let's make that joyful noise to the LORD!" Hand out the drums (and mallets) and let the children beat them awhile. Quiet them, then repeat.

4. If desired, you can ask the children a question related to the verse/the songs they are singing, using the Hide 'n' Seek Kids Discussion Sheet after each time (or every few times) you sing the song/say the verse.

NOTE: Younger children may need to sing the Bible verse/Big Question song/etc, then thump. But, as the children get older, they may be able to sing the song(s) AND thump at the same time.

Music, Movement & Memory Activity

Intake or Response Activity to learn the Big Question, Bible verse and Unit music

Say, Spring Up and Shout

Materials
CD of unit music
Hide 'n' Seek Kids Discussion Questions (optional)
Optional: Bean bags, one per child

What to Do

1. Tell the children: "We're going to sing our Bible verse/Big Question/other song and make a joyful noise to God, crouching down like this (Crouch down). Then at the end, we're going to spring up and shout, "Amen, I agree!"

2. "So first, let's sing our Bible verse/Big Question Song together as we crouch down." (Crouch down, say the verse a couple of times.)

3. "Now let's jump up and say, "AMEN! I agree!" After everyone springs up and says "Amen," quiet them, then repeat.

4. If desired, when the children get the crouching and jumping down, you might give them a bean bag to toss in the air as they spring up. Practicing tossing up in the air rather than AT others.

5. If desired, you can ask the children a question related to the verse/the songs they are singing, using the Hide n' Seek Kids Discussion Sheet after each time (or every few times) you sing the song/say the verse.

Music, Movement & Memory Activity

Intake or Response Activity to learn the Big Question, Bible verse and Unit music

Freeze Frame

Materials

CD of unit music

Hide 'n' Seek Kids Discussion Sheet Questions (optional)

Some kind of fun hat or clothing for the leader to wear

What to Do

1. Tell the children. "I'm going to sing God's Word and make a joyful noise to Him...but I'm going to freeze in place in between songs. Come and join me!

2. Choose one child to be the leader. Help them put on the leader hat/clothing.

3. Have the kids march around behind the leader, singing the song of your choice.

4. Have the children freeze in place when you stop the song at a random point.

5. When everyone is frozen, have the children tell you what the next word/phrase to the song.

6. If desired, you can ask the children a question related to the words or another question from the Hide 'n' Seek Kids Discussion Sheet after each time (or every few times) you freeze the song.

7. Choose another leader and play the song again, stopping on a different word from the song to highlight.

Music, Movement & Memory Activity

Intake or Response Activity to learn the Big Question, Bible verse and Unit music

Egg Shakers

Materials
CD of unit music
Hide 'n' Seek Kids Discussion Sheet (optional)
Empty Easter eggs
Rice, beans, buttons, pennies, popcorn, beads, small nails or bolts, etc.
Glue and glue gun OR strong packing tape

How to Make
1. Fill empty Easter eggs with different small objects such as rice, beans, pennies, buttons, popcorn, beads, small nails or bolts, etc., then seal lid shut with glue gun or with packing tape. Different objects make different sounds. Different amounts of the same object make different sounds, too. The children will enjoy the variety.

What to Do
1. Show the children the egg shakers and tell them. "I'm going to sing our Bible verse/Big Question/other song and make a joyful noise to God with these egg shakers. Come and join me!

2. "First, let's sing the Bible verse/ Big Question song together on our own (sing the song a couple of times.) Now let's make that joyful noise to the LORD!"

3. Hand out the egg shakers and let the children shake them a while (without singing), then quiet them.

4. Then tell them, "OK, let's try singing and shaking our eggs at the same time!" Lead the children in song and shaking.

5. If desired, you can ask the children a question related to the verse/the songs they are singing, using the Hide 'n' Seek Discussion Sheet after each time (or every few times) you sing the song/say the verse.

NOTE: Younger children may need to sing the Bible verse/Big Question song/etc, then shake. But, as the children get older, they may be able to sing the song(s) AND shake at the same time.

Music, Movement & Memory Activity

Intake or Response Activity to learn the Big Question, Bible verse and Unit music

Jingle Bell Hands

Materials
CD of unit music
Hide 'n' Seek Kids Discussion Questions (optional)
1 6" piece of sturdy string
4 or 5 jingle bells, available in most craft shops

How to Make
1. Cut a piece of string about 6" long.

2. Thread 4 or 5 jingle bells onto string, securely tying each in place with a knot before adding the next one. Tie the ends together. Children can either wear these like a bracelet or can hold them in their hands.

What to Do
1. Show the children the bottle shakers and tell them, "I'm going to sing our Bible verse/Big Question song and make a joyful noise to God with these bottle shakers. Come and join me! First, let's sing the Bible verse/ Big Question/etc. song together on our own (sing the song a couple of times.) Now let's make that joyful noise to the LORD!"

2. Hand out the jingle hand bells and let the children jingle them a while (without singing), then quiet them.

3. Then tell them, "OK, let's try singing and jingling at the same time!" Lead the children in singing and jingling.

4. If desired, you can ask the children a question related to the verse/the songs they are singing, using the Hide 'n' Seek Discussion Sheet after each time (or every few times) you sing the song/say the verse.

NOTE: Younger children may need to sing the Bible verse/Big Question song/etc, then jingle. But, as the children get older, they may be able to sing the song(s) AND jingle at the same time.

Music, Movement & Memory Activity

Intake or Response Activity to learn the Big Question, Bible verse and Unit music

Big Voice, Little Voice

Materials
    CD of unit music
    Hide 'n' Seek Kids Discussion Questions (optional)

What to Do
1. Tell the children: "I'm going to sing our Bible verse/Big Question song and make a joyful noise to Him quietly and loudly! Come and join me!"

2. "First let's sing our Bible verse/Big Question Song together," (sing the song a time or two)

3. "Now let's see how quietly we can whisper it! Can you sing it quietly like I am?" Have everyone follow your voice as it gets quiet, then loud, then medium, etc. Quiet them, then repeat.

4. If desired, you can ask the children a question related to the verse/the songs they are singing, using the Hide 'n' Seek Kids Discussion Sheet after each time (or every few times) you sing the song/say the verse.

NOTE: You may find it easier for the children to follow getting louder and softer by lowering your hands when you are getting quieter and then raising your hands when you are getting louder.

Music, Movement & Memory Activity

Intake or Response Activity to learn the Big Question, Bible verse and Unit music

Sing, Dance and Fall Down

Materials
CD of unit music
Hide 'n' Seek Kids Discussion Questions (optional)
1 oatmeal container/coffee can with lid per drum
Tape
Popcorn, rice, beans, etc.
Wooden spoons, dowels, unsharpened pencils, if desired, for mallets

How to Make
1. Tape the lid of empty oatmeal or coffee cans in place. (If want to make a snare drum, add popcorn, rice, etc. in the empty container before taping shut.)

2. Children can either tap drum with hands or you can give them 2 wooden spoons, wooden dowels or unsharpened pencils with wooden spools glue gunned to an end as mallets.

What to Do
1. Tell the children: "I'm going to sing our Bible verse/Big Question/etc. song and make a joyful noise to Him with my body by dancing to some music…then falling down when it stops. Come and join me!"

2. "First let's sing our Bible verse/Big Question Song together." (sing the song a time or two).

3. "Now let's dance as we sing our song. Then fall down when we finish. Let's dance." Have everyone dance and sing the song. When you finish, say, "Everyone fall down!" Quiet the children, then repeat.

4. If desired, you can ask the children a question related to the verse/the songs they are singing, using the Hide 'n' Seek Kids Discussion Sheet after each time (or every few times) you sing the song/say the verse.

Music, Movement & Memory Activity

Intake or Response Activity to learn the Big Question, Bible verse and Unit music

Bottle Shakers

Materials
CD of unit music
Hide 'n' Seek Kids Discussion Questions (optional)
1 empty 16 oz. soda bottle per shaker
Rice, beans, buttons, pennies, popcorn, beads, small nails or bolts, etc.
Glue and glue gun OR strong packing tape

How to Make
1. Fill empty 16 oz.. soda bottles with different small objects such as rice, beans, pennies, buttons, popcorn, beads, small nails or bolts, etc.

2. Seal lid shut with glue gun or with packing tape. Different objects make different sounds. Different amounts of the same object make different sounds, too. The children will enjoy the variety.

What to Do
1. Show the children the bottle shakers and tell them. "I'm going to sing our Bible verse/Big Question song and make a joyful noise to God with these bottle shakers. Come and join me! First, let's sing the Bible verse/ Big Question/etc. song together on our own (sing the song a couple of times.) Now let's make that joyful noise to the LORD!"

2. Hand out the bottle shakers and let the children shake them a while (without singing), then quiet them.

3. Then tell them, "OK, let's try singing and shaking at the same time!" Lead the children in song and shaking.

4. If desired, you can ask the children a question related to the verse/the songs they are singing, using the Hide 'n' Seek Kids Discussion Sheet after each time (or every few times) you sing the song/say the verse.

NOTE: Younger children may need to sing the Bible verse/Big Question song/etc, then shake. But, as the children get older, they may be able to sing the song(s) AND shake at the same time.

Music, Movement & Memory Activity

Intake or Response Activity to learn the Big Question, Bible verse and Unit music

March 'n' Say

Materials
> CD of unit music
> Hide 'n' Seek Kids Discussion Questions (optional)
> Optional: A fun hat for the leader of the march, or for everyone in the march

What to Do

1. Tell them, "I'm going to say God's Word and make a joyful noise to Him by marching. Come and join me!"

2. "First let's sing our Bible verse/Big Question Song together." (sing a time or two)

3. "Now let's march around as we sing!"

4. If desired, let the leader of the march (you the first time, then pick different children), wear a fun hat as he/she leads. Or, have hats for everyone to wear.

5. If desired, you can ask the children a question related to the verse/the songs they are singing, using the Hide 'n' Seek Kids Discussion Sheet after each time (or every few times) you sing the song/say the verse.

NOTE: Younger children may need to sing the Bible verse/Big Question song/etc, then thump. But, as the children get older, they may be able to sing the song(s) AND thump at the same time.

Music, Movement & Memory Activity

Intake or Response Activity to learn the Big Question, Bible verse and Unit music

Clap, Tap and Say

Materials
  CD of unit music
  Hide 'n' Seek Kids Discussion Questions (optional)

What to Do

1. Tell the children: "I'm going to sing our Bible verse/Big Question/etc. song and make a joyful noise to Him with my body by clapping and tapping. Come and join me!"

2. First let's sing our Bible verse song/Big Question song/Praise Song/Hymn together (say the verse a couple of times, if using it.)

3. "Now let's clap and tap! Can you do what I'm doing?" Have everyone follow your motions as you clap your hands, tap your head, hit your knees together, rub your belly, etc. for a while. Quiet them, then repeat. If desired, have different children think up different motions.

4. If desired, you can ask the children a question related to the verse/the songs they are singing, using the Hide 'n' Seek Kids Discussion Sheet after each time (or every few times) you sing the song/say the verse.

NOTE: Younger children may need to sing the Bible verse/Big Question song/etc, then clap, tap, etc. But, as the children get older, they may be able to sing the song(s) AND do the motions at the same time.

Music, Movement & Memory Activity

Intake or Response Activity to learn the Big Question, Bible verse and Unit music

Block Clappers

Materials
CD of unit music
Hide 'n' Seek Kids Discussion Questions (optional)
2 wooden blocks per child, preferably about 3"x 2", as found in many children's block sets

What to Do
1. Show the children the clapping blocks . Tell them, "I'm going to say God's Word and make a joyful noise to Him with these clapping blocks. Come and join me!

2. First let's sing our Bible verse song/Big Question song/Praise Song/Hymn together (say the verse a couple of times, if using it.)

3. Now let's make that joyful noise to the LORD!" Hand out the clapping blocks and let the children clap them a while (without singing), then quiet them.

4. Then tell them, "OK, let's try singing and block clapping at the same time!" Lead the children in song and clapping.

5. If desired, you can ask the children a question related to the verse/the songs they are singing, using the Hide 'n' Seek Kids Discussion Sheet after each time (or every few times) you sing the song/say the verse.

NOTE: Younger children may need to sing the Bible verse/Big Question song/etc, then clap. But, as the children get older, they may be able to sing the song(s) AND clap at the same time.

Music, Movement & Memory Activity

Intake or Response Activity to learn the Big Question, Bible verse and Unit music

Musical Squares

Materials

    CD of unit music

    Carpet Squares, enough for all of the children (or chairs)

    Hide 'n' Seek Kids Discussion Questions (optional)

What to Do

1. Set out the squares/chairs in a circle. Ask the children to sit down on their square/chair.

2. Tell the children they will march around behind the squares/chairs as you play the Big Question Song/Bible verse song/Hymn/Praise Song/etc. When the music stops, they are to sit down on the nearest square/chair island.

3. Play the music, sing the song as the children make swimming motion with their arms to it. Stop the music and have the children sit down on the nearest square/chair.

3. If desired, you can ask the children a question related to the verse/the songs (or the lesson concepts) they are singing, using the Hide 'n' Seek Kids Discussion Questions, after each time (or every few times) they sit down.

Music, Movement & Memory Activity

Intake or Response Activity to learn the Big Question, Bible verse and Unit music

Lullabies, Bells and Lions

Materials
CD of unit music
Bell
Hide 'n' Seek Kids Discussion Questions (optional)

What to Do

1. Tell the children: "We're going to pretend to go to sleep as children, but wake up like an animal. Everyone sit down and let's sing our lullaby before we go to bed. When you hear the morning bell ring, you can pretend to be the animal I say until you hear the bedtime bell ring and you have to sit back down.

2. Ring the bell and say, "It's time for bed, it's time for bed! Sit down where you are, you sleepy heads!" Have all the children sit down in place. Then say, "Before we go to sleep, we have to sing our bedtime lullaby. Let's sing our Bible verse song/Big Question song/Praise Song/Hymn." Have the children sing the song with you, then tell them, "Shhh. Lay down! It's time for bed!"

3. Have all the children lay down and be very still and quiet like they are sleeping for a few minutes. Then say, "Sleeping, sleeping, look at all the sleeping children. But when the morning bell rang, they all woke up, and were lions (or whatever animal you choose) all day!"

3. All the children will get up and pretend to be the animal. After a few moments, ring the bell and say, "It's time for bed, it's time for bed! Sit down where you are, you sleepy heads!"

4. If desired, you can ask the children a question related to the verse/the songs they are singing, using the Hide 'n' Seek Kids Discussion Questions after each time (or every few times) you sing the lullaby song.

Bible Story Review Game

Response Activity to review the story and key concepts

Who's in the Basket?

Materials
   Bible Truth storyboard pictures
   Hide 'n' Seek Kids Discussion Questions
   Blanket
   Basket

Preparation
None.

Playing the Game

1. Hide one of the pictures in the basket and cover it up with the blanket.

2. Ask the children: "Who's in the basket? Would you like to look?" Have chose a child to take off the blanket and pull out the picture to show the rest of the children. Say: "Look! It's ------" The children or you or you and the children can answer with who it is. For more fun, have a little song like "Pop! Goes the Weasel" you hum each time before the child pulls the blanket off Or, just count "1, 2, 3, GO!" and pull the blanket off quickly. If desired, you may also want to ask the children a question about the picture/the story as the picture is identified, using the Hide 'n' Seek Kids Discussion Sheet for suggestions.

3. Repeat as frequently as desired.

Bible Story Review Game

Response Activity to review the story and key concepts

Run to the Grocery Store

Materials
Bible Truth storyboard pictures
Hide 'n' Seek Kids Discussion Questions
Grocery bag or kid's grocery cart
Empty food cartons

Preparation
1. Put a clue inside each food container.

2. Set out the containers on a table or shelf at one end of the room.

3. Set up the story board at the other end, with the shopping cart or bag.

Playing the Game
1. Have the children assemble near the storyboard.

2. Have them take turns pushing the grocery cart/carrying the grocery bag to the other end of the room and choosing a food item. If desired, tell the children which food item you want them to pick out each time.

3. When the child returns with the food, have them open the container and pull out the picture. If desired, you may also want to ask the children a question about the picture/the story as the picture is identified, using the Hide 'n' Seek Kids Discussion Sheet for suggestions.

4. Ask the class what the picture is, then add it to the story board, gradually reproducing the story.

Bible Story Review Game

Response Activity to review the story and key concepts

Treasure Hunt

Materials

Bible Truth storyboard pictures

Hide 'n' Seek Kids Discussion Questions

10 small lidded plastic containers or boxes (like from a jewelry store) or wooden, hinged boxes from a craft store

Various decorating supplies, such as fake craft jewels, glitter, glitter glue, foil paper, gold spray paint

glue

Preparation

Before playing the game, you will need to make your treasure boxes:

1. Collect 10 small lidded plastic containers or lidded boxes (like from a jewelry story), just large enough to put the Bible story pictures in. Alternatively, you can also purchase 10 hinged wooden boxes from a craft store. These make marvelous treasure boxes.

2. Decorate each container/box with the jewels, glitter, paper, gold paint, etc to give them a "treasure-y" look.

Right before Class:

1. Put a Bible story picture in each container and Hide them around the room.

2. You may want to review the story and the pictures before class.

Playing the Game

1. Tell the children that you are going on a treasure hunt and need their help finding all the treasure hidden around the room.

2. Have the children take turns finding the treasure boxes and bringing them to you.

3. Remove each picture as the box is found and ask the children review questions about the character from the Bible story. If desired, you can simply put each picture on the floor, table, or storyboard as it is found, then ask questions about the Bible story when you have collected them all. (See the Hide 'n' Seek Kids Discussion Sheet for possible questions.)

4. Remember to store your boxes after the game, keeping them for the next time you play.

5. Game continues as time allows or until you have retrieved and reviewed all the pictures and the story.

Bible Story Review Game

Response Activity to review the story and key concepts

Take Me Through the Tunnel

Materials
   Bible Truth storyboard pictures and Storyboard
   Hide 'n' Seek Kids Discussion Questions
   Chairs or Table
   Sheet or blanket
   Box

Preparation
1. Construct a tunnel using the sheet draped over a table/chairs.
2. Put the flannelgraph figures in a box in the "tunnel."

Playing the Game
1. Have the children take turns crawling through the tunnel, retrieving one of the pictures.

2. When the child comes out of the tunnel, he shows the figure to the other children from them to name.

3. Have the children name the character; and, if desired, answer a question (see Hide 'n' Seek Kids Discussion Sheet) about what they did in the story.

4. Have the child stick the picture on the storyboard, gradually recreating the scene as the game progresses.

Bible Story Review Game

Response Activity to review the story and key concepts

Missing in Action

Materials
Bible Truth storyboard pictures and Storyboard
Hide 'n' Seek Kids Discussion Questions

Preparation
1. Put all the story pictures up on the storyboard, recreating the scene from the story. .

Playing the Game
1. Review the story briefly, pointing to the figures on the story board background as you go. Have the children help you, if desired.

2. Tell the children that someone from the story is about to go "Missing in Action" and they have to guess who it is. Have the children cover their eyes and take one figure off the board.

3. Have the children open their eyes and figure out who is missing.

4. Put the picture back on the board. Take another picture off the board, having a child choose who will go missing in action this time.

5. If desired, you can ask the children a question related to story each time/every few times a picture is put up, using the Hide 'n' Seek Kids Discussion Sheet.

Bible Story Review Game

Response Activity to review the story and key concepts

Hide 'n' Seek Kids Clue Hunt

Materials
Bible Truth storyboard pictures
Hide 'n' Seek Kids Discussion Questions
Variety of interesting items that have one or more places to Hide a storyboard picture
Detective Hat
4+ False Clue Pictures--pictures that aren't in the story (included on the next page)
CD Player and Hide 'n' Seek Kids Theme Song

Preparation
1. Collect a variety of interesting items, that some way to Hide a picture, such as an old box with a lid, wallet, purse, clothing with pockets, a book, etc. If your items have MORE than one place to Hide things, that is even better.

2. Cut out/Print out the false clue pictures included with the game.

3. Hide each story picture inside one of the items.

4. Set out the items for the children to see, telling them that each of them have an important clue in them. Most of them are from the story, but a few are not. Tell them that it is the job of the Deep Down Detectives to find the hidden clues and decide if they belong in the story or not.

Playing the Game
1. Have the children line up. Play the Hide 'n' Seek Kids Theme Song and lead the children in marching around the room and then back to their places to sit down as it ends. (This is merely an energy-release tactic). Have the children take turns choosing an item, finding the clue you have hidden within it. Have the child/the class decide if the clue belongs in the story or not. If it belongs in the story, have them tell how, or, you could ask the children a question about the picture, using the Hide 'n' Seek Kids Discussion Sheet for suggestions.

2. Continue until all the clues have been found.

3. If desired, you can have the child who will choose the next clue to lead the class in marching to the theme song before they choose their clue.

Bible Story Review Game

Response Activity to review the story and key concepts

Hide 'n' Seek Kids Detective Clue Hunt, continued

False Clues (use as many as you want)

Bible Story Review Game

Response Activity to review the story and key concepts

Who's Inside?

Materials
Bible Truth storyboard pictures (and/or other objects that remind you of things from the story)
Hide 'n' Seek Kids Discussion Questions
10 different containers with lids

Preparation
1. Put in various pictures/objects in each container and shut.

2. Line up all the containers or put them in a big bag, such as a trash bag.

Playing the Game
1. Have 10 different sized/colored lidded containers with shaded sides, all big enough to fit the laminated pictures or other objects from the story or concept. Have the children take turns choosing a container (from the bag) and opening it. Each time ask: "Who's inside?" Child/children/you/you and children can answer together. If desired, you may also want to ask the children a question about the picture/the story as each picture/object is identified using the Hide 'n' Seek Kids Discussion Sheet for suggestions.

2. Repeat.

Bible Story Review Game

Response Activity to review the story and key concepts

Look Who's Coming Down the Tracks

Materials
Bible Truth storyboard pictures
Hide 'n' Seek Kids Discussion Questions
Two shoe boxes
6' or so of rope
Optional: Engineer's hat

Preparation
1. Make a "train" with two cars made with the two shoe boxes strung together with rope.

2. Poke a hole through the front short side of the shoe box that will be the back "car."

3. Poke a hole through the front and back short sides of the shoe box that will be the front "car."

4. Thread the rope through these holes, tying knots near the inside and outside of each to keep the car securely in place.

Playing the Game
1. Put a picture in each "car" of the train (out of the sight of the children). Say, "Look who's coming down the track!"

2. Hand the end of the rope to a child and have them pull it around to where the other participating children are saying "Choo! Choo! Choo! Choo!" (you can have all the children say this, just the child pulling, you and the child, etc.)

3. After the child pulls it to where the children are say, "Train, stop!"

4. Pull out the pictures, show them to the children and ask, "Who's on our train?"

5. If desired, you can ask the children a question related to the picture/story, from the Hide 'n' Seek Kids Discussion Sheet.

Tip: For more fun, have a train engineer's hat for the child pulling the train to wear.

Bible Story Review Game

Response Activity to review the story and key concepts

Going Fishing

Materials
Bible Truth storyboard pictures
Hide 'n' Seek Kids Discussion Questions
One long wooden dowel, yardstick, etc. per fishing pole
Yarn
Paper clip per fishing pole
Rope
Two chairs
Blanket
Box/bucket/container
Bucket

Preparation

1. Make fishing poles out of long wooden dowels, yardsticks, etc with a piece of yarn for fishing line and a paper clip for a hook.

2. Attach a picture to the end of each pole.

3. Tie a rope between two chairs and drape a piece of cloth or a blanket over the rope. Lay the poles against the blanket so that the tips and the fishing line drape over the other side and drop down into a bucket/box on the other side.

4. Place other bucket on the side the children and the ends of the fishing rods are. This will be the "holding tank" for the fish when they are caught.

Playing the Game

1. Ask the children, "Would you like to go fishing in my pond today?"

2. "Let's see what you'll catch." The child chooses one of the poles, pulls it up and see what's on the end.

3. Say "Looks like you've caught a big one! Pull it out!"

4. As the child pulls up the fishing rod and reveals what is on the end, ask the children, "Who did you catch?" If desired, you may also want to ask the children a question about the picture/the story as each "fish" is caught, using the Hide 'n' Seek Kids Discussion Sheet for suggestions.

5. Have the child put the "fish" in the holding tank.

6. If desired, when all the fish are caught, take them out of the holding tank and review the "catch of the day."

Bible Story Review Game

Response Activity to review the story and key concepts

Pony Express

Materials

> Bible Truth storyboard pictures
> Hide 'n' Seek Kids Discussion Questions
> Small manila envelopes, one per flannel graph figure
> Kid's small backpack or a tote bag with a strap
> Basket
> Cowboy hat
> Stick horse or a broom

Preparation

1. Tell the children that long ago cowboys used to pick up the mail, put it in their bags and ride it fast from town to town on their horses. This was called the Pony Express. Today, they will practice riding for the Pony Express and bring the mail back to the class.

Playing the Game

1. Show the children how to ride the stick horse down to the other end, pick up a piece of mail from the basket, put it in their bag, then ride it back to the class. Take the envelope out of the bag and open it, showing them the picture inside. Ask the children who/what the picture is and then put it on the storyboard. If desired, you may also want to ask the children a question about the picture/the story as the picture is identified, using the Hide 'n' Seek Kids Discussion Sheet for suggestions.

2. Have the children take turns riding the Pony Express, each time adding the new figure to the storyboard until the story is recreated on it.

Bible Story Review Game

Response Activity to review the story and key concepts

Clothespin Line Up and Drop

Materials
Bible Truth storyboard pictures
Hide 'n' Seek Kids Discussion Questions
Rope
Clothespins, the hinged type
Shoe box
Tape

Preparation
1. Attach a spring-type clothespin to some of the laminated storyboard pictures and put them in a shoe box with
   the lid taped on one side like a hinge and with a hole in the top.

2. Hang up a short rope (in an out-of-traffic-flow location) between two chairs.

Playing the Game
1. Open the shoe box and say, "It's time to say hello to our story friends!"

2. Pull the pictures out one at a time, saying "Hello, so-and-so, each time you pick up a picture and clip them to the rope.

3. When all are pinned up say, "It's time to say goodbye to so-and-so." Can you find so-and-so?" Then have the child point out the right figure on the clothesline, take it off the rope, reattaching the clothespin and handing it to the child. If desired, you may also want to ask the children a question about the picture/the story as the picture is identified, using the Hide 'n' Seek Kids Discussion Sheet for suggestions.

4. Have a container/bucket/shoe box and say, "Say, goodbye!" letting the child drop the clothespin in the bucket and put the picture through the slot in the shoe box.

Bible Story Review Game

Response Activity to review the story and key concepts

Fix Up the Mix Up

Materials

Bible Truth storyboard pictures

Hide 'n' Seek Kids Discussion Questions

Preparation

None.

Playing the Game

1. Take all the Storyboard pictures and mix them up in a pile in front of the children.

2. Tell them that the story pictures are all mixed up and you need help fixing them up again.

3. Let the children take turns picking a picture out of the pile and re-constructing the story on the storyboard. If desired, you may also want to ask the children a question about the picture/the story as each picture/object is identified using the Hide 'n' Seek Kids Discussion Sheet for suggestions.

Hide 'n' Seek Kids

Appendix C: Crafts and Take Home Sheets

Index of Crafts and Take Home Sheets

Unit 1

Lesson 1 Coloring Sheet/Take Home Sheet   227
Lesson 2 Coloring Sheet/Take Home Sheet   229
Lesson 3 Coloring Sheet/Take Home Sheet   231
Lesson 4 Coloring Sheet/Take Home Sheet   233
Lesson 5 Coloring Sheet/Take Home Sheet   235
Big Question 1 Bible Story and Key Concepts to Take Home   237
Extra Craft 1: Big Question and Answer Craft   243
Extra Craft 2: Bible Verse Craft   247
Extra Craft 3: Bible Story Jigsaw Puzzle Picture   251

Unit 2

Lesson 1 Coloring Sheet/Take Home Sheet   253
Lesson 2 Coloring Sheet/Take Home Sheet   255
Lesson 3 Coloring Sheet/Take Home Sheet   257
Lesson 4 Coloring Sheet/Take Home Sheet   259
Lesson 5 Coloring Sheet/Take Home Sheet   261
Big Question 2 Bible Story and Key Concepts to Take Home   263
Extra Craft 1: Big Question and Answer Craft   269
Extra Craft 2: Bible Verse Craft   273
Extra Craft 3: Bible Story Jigsaw Puzzle Picture   277

Unit 3

Lesson 1 Coloring Sheet/Take Home Sheet   279
Lesson 2 Coloring Sheet/Take Home Sheet   281
Lesson 3 Coloring Sheet/Take Home Sheet   283
Lesson 4 Coloring Sheet/Take Home Sheet   285
Lesson 5 Coloring Sheet/Take Home Sheet   287
Big Question 3 Bible Story and Key Concepts to Take Home   289
Extra Craft 1: Big Question and Answer Craft   295
Extra Craft 2: Bible Verse Craft   299
Extra Craft 3: Bible Story Jigsaw Puzzle Picture   303

Unit 4

Lesson 1 Coloring Sheet/Take Home Sheet   305
Lesson 2 Coloring Sheet/Take Home Sheet   307
Lesson 3 Coloring Sheet/Take Home Sheet   309
Lesson 4 Coloring Sheet/Take Home Sheet   311
Lesson 5 Coloring Sheet/Take Home Sheet   313
Big Question 4 Bible Story and Key Concepts to Take Home   315
Extra Craft 1: Big Question and Answer Craft   321
Extra Craft 2: Bible Verse Craft   325
Extra Craft 3: Bible Story Jigsaw Puzzle Picture   329

Hide 'n' Seek Kids

Unit I Take Home Resources The God Who Reveals Himself

BIG QUESTION 1

How can I know what God is like?

ANSWER:
He shows me what He's like!

Hide 'n' Seek Kids Sneaky Seekers
hiding God's Word in our hearts, seeking to know God Himself

Big Question I, Lesson I Take Home Sheet

Big Question 1: How Can I Know What God Is Like?
   Answer: He Shows Me What He's Like!

Meaning:

God made us. He wants us to know what He is like, so we can know Him, love Him, and praise Him. God shows us what He is like: through the spirit He put in our hearts; through all of His creations we see around us; through His Word, the Bible; and most of all, through His very own Son, Jesus Christ.

How do I know this is true? The Bible tells me so:

"He who declares to man what is His thought...The LORD, the God of hosts, is His name." Amos 4:13, ESV

Some Questions for You

1. Can You Fix the Big Question and Answer?
How can I know what God is like? He snows me what He's like!
Answer: How can I know what God is like? He SHOWS me what He's like!

2. Who can show us what God is like? *God can!*

3. What is the best first step we can ask God to do to show us what He's like? *We can ask God to show us what He's like. We can ask Him to work in our heart, that we would turn away from our sins and trust in Jesus as our Savior. He delights to do these things!*

Let's Pray!

A   We praise You, God. You show us what You are like!

C   God, in our heart, we know that You are God and that we should obey You, but many times we don't want to. Please forgive us. Please change our hearts so they want to know and obey You.

T   Thank You for helping us to learn more about You. Thank You for wanting us to know You. Thank You for giving us a heart to know You; and, for making this world that shows us what You are like. Thank You for what we learn about You in Your Word, the Bible. And most of all, thank You for showing us what You are like in Your Son, Jesus.

S   Work deep inside our hearts. Help us to turn away from our sins and trust in Jesus as our Savior. Help us to know You. Put in our hearts the special kind of happy only You can give. Help us to go and tell others what we've learned.

   In Jesus' name we pray. Amen.

Let's Sing Our Big Question and Answer!

Big Q & A 1 Song *from Hide 'n' Seek Kids ESV Songs 1, track 12*

How can I know what God is like?
God is like? God is like?
How can I know what God is like?
He shows me what He's like!

Song Question: How can I know what God is like?
   Answer: *He shows me what He's like!*

Go to the Hide 'n' Seek Kids Parent Resources for Unit 1 to get the Bible story and many more resources and songs for this unit at praisefactory.org

The LORD!

"He who declares to man His thought. The LORD, the God of hosts, is His name." Amos 4:13, ESV

Hide 'n' Seek Kids Sneaky Seekers
hiding God's Word in our hearts, seeking to know God Himself

Big Question I, Lesson 2 Take Home Sheet

Big Question 1: How Can I Know What God Is Like?
   Answer: He Shows Me What He's Like!

How do I know this is true? The Bible tells me so:

"He who declares to man what is His thought...The LORD, the God of hosts, is His name." Amos 4:13, ESV

Meaning:

God wants us to know what He is like, so we can know Him, love Him, and praise Him. We don't have to figure out what God is like by ourselves. God show us what He's like--He declares His thoughts to us.

God shows us what He's like through the spirit He put in our hearts; through His creations we see around us; through His Word, the Bible; and most of all, through His very own Son, Jesus Christ.

And what's the name of the one and only true, living God? It's the LORD! Yes, the LORD is His name!

Some Questions for You

1. What's the missing word to the Bible verse?
"He who declares to man His thought. The _____ , the God of hosts, is His name."
Answer: LORD.

2. What does God declare to us? *His thoughts! He shows us what He's like!*

Let's Pray!

A   We praise You, God. You show us what You are like!

C   God, in our heart, we know that You are God and that we should obey You, but many times we don't want to. Please forgive us. Please change our hearts so they want to know and obey You.

T   Thank You for helping us to learn more about You. Thank You for wanting us to know You. Thank You for giving us a heart to know You; and. for making this world that shows us what You are like. Thank You for what we learn about You in Your Word, the Bible. And most of all, thank You for showing us what You are like in Your Son, Jesus.

S   Work deep inside our hearts. Help us to turn away from our sins and trust in Jesus as our Savior. Help us to know You. Put in our hearts the special kind of happy only You can give. Help us to go and tell others what we've learned.

   In Jesus' name we pray. Amen.

Let's Sing Our Bible Verse!

Big Question 1 Bible Verse Song *from Hide 'n' Seek Kids ESV Songs 1, track 14,14T*

The LORD declares to man his thought,
The LORD declares to man his thought,
The LORD declares to man his thought,
Amos Four, thirteen.

Song Question: What does the LORD declare to man? *His thought. That means He shows us what He's like!*

Go to the Hide 'n' Seek Kids Parent Resources for Unit 1 to get the Bible story and many more resources for this unit at www.praisefactory.org

Which three pictures belong in the story ? Put an "X" in the box next to each of these.
What did God use three of these things to show Simeon?

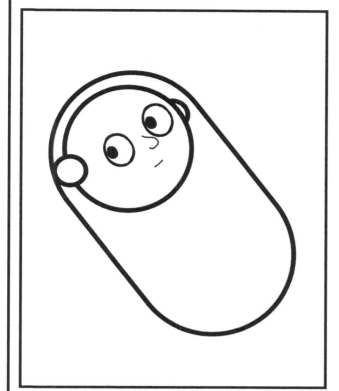

☐ **Baby Jesus**

☐ **Chair**

☐ **Bible**

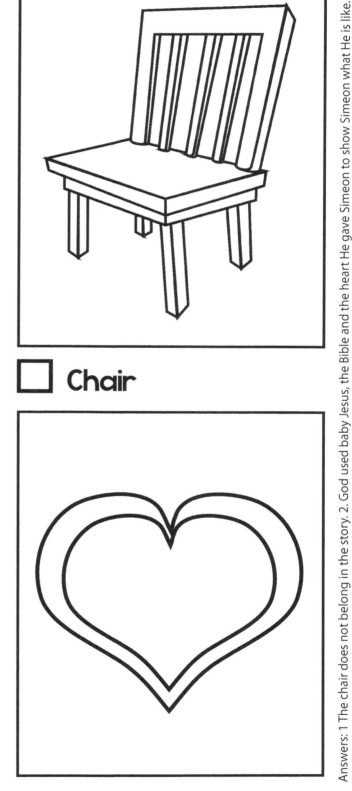

☐ **Heart**

Answers: 1 The chair does not belong in the story. 2. God used baby Jesus, the Bible and the heart He gave Simeon to show Simeon what He is like.

Hide 'n' Seek Kids Sneaky Seekers
hiding God's Word in our hearts, seeking to know God Himself

Big Question I, Lesson 3 Take Home Sheet

Big Question 1: How Can I Know What God Is Like?
Answer: He Shows Me What He's Like!

Meaning:

God made us. He wants us to know what He is like, so we can know Him, love Him, and praise Him. God shows us what He is like: through the spirit He put in our hearts; through all of His creations we see around us; through His Word, the Bible; and most of all, through His very own Son, Jesus Christ.

How do I know this is true? The Bible tells me so:

"He who declares to man what is His thought...The LORD, the God of hosts, is His name." Amos 4:13, ESV

Some Questions for You

1. **Who wanted to know more and more about God in our story?** *Simeon.*
2. **Who showed Simeon what God was like?** *God.*
3. **What are some things God used to show Simeon what He was like?** *The heart God gave Simeon to know and love Him; everything Simeon saw around him that God made; the Bible, God's Word; and Jesus, God's Son.*
3. **Who can show me what God is like?** *God can.*
4. **What can I do to help God show me what He's like?** *I can ask Him to show me what He is like. I can ask Him to work in my heart. I can ask Him to show me what He's like as I look at what He's made. I can listen to the Bible and learn about Jesus. I can turn away from my sins and trust in Jesus as my Savior.*

Let's Pray!

A   We praise You, God. You show us what You are like!

C   God, in our heart, we know that You are God and that we should obey You, but many times we don't want to. Please forgive us. Please change our hearts so they want to know and obey You.

T   Thank You for helping us to learn more about You. Thank You for wanting us to know You. Thank You for giving us a heart to know You; and. for making this world that shows us what You are like. Thank You for what we learn about You in Your Word, the Bible. And most of all, thank You for showing us what You are like in Your Son, Jesus.

S   Work deep inside our hearts. Help us to turn away from our sins and trust in Jesus as our Savior. Help us to know You. Put in our hearts the special kind of happy only You can give. Help us to go and tell others what we've learned.

In Jesus' name we pray. Amen.

Let's Sing about Our Big Question and Answer!

Big Question 1 (Action Rhyme) Song *from Hide 'n' Seek Kids ESV Songs 1, track 13*

I have a very big question,
a big question 'bout God,
I have a very big question,
It's Big Question Number One, *hold up 1 finger*
I wanna know...

Refrain:
How can I know what God is like?
How can I know what God is like?
How can I know what God is like?
He shows me what He's like!

Verse 1:
My heart can know and love God,   *place hand over heart*
He made everything I see.   *cup hand over eye & look around*
Big tall mountain, galloping horses,   *gallop in place*
Every little bird and bee. *Refrain*

Verse 2:
He gave us the Bible, His Word,   *make open book with flat hands*
To learn of His might deeds,   *hold up flexed arm*
But most of all, through Jesus, His Son,
God shows Himself to me.   *Refrain*   *point to self*

Song Question: What are four ways God shows us what He's like? *The heart He gave us to know and love Him; everything we see around us that He made; the Bible, the perfect Word of God; and most of all, through Jesus, God's Son.*

Go to the Hide 'n' Seek Kids Parent Resources for Unit 1 to get the Bible story and many more resources for this unit at www.praisefactory.org

HSK BQ1 L3 Coloring Sheet/Take Home pg.2

Thank You, God!

Simeon wanted to know more and more about what God is like. He thanked God for sending Jesus to show us what God is like and to be the Savior to save us from our sins. Let's thank God, too!

HSK BQ 1 L4 Coloring Sheet/Take Home pg.1

Hide 'n' Seek Kids Sneaky Seekers
hiding God's Word in our hearts, seeking to know God Himself

Big Question I, Lesson 4 Take Home Sheet

Big Question 1: How Can I Know What God Is Like?
   Answer: He Shows Me What He's Like!

Meaning:

God made us. He wants us to know what He is like, so we can know Him, love Him, and praise Him. God shows us what He is like: through the spirit He put in our hearts; through all of His creations we see around us; through His Word, the Bible; and most of all, through His very own Son, Jesus Christ.

How do I know this is true? The Bible tells me so:

"He who declares to man what is His thought...The LORD, the God of hosts, is His name." Amos 4:13, ESV

Some Questions for You

1. What's something we can thank God for? *For sending Jesus to save sinners like you and me. For wanting us to know what He is like.*

2. What is something I can ask God to do inside of me, if I want to know what He's like? *I can ask God to show me what He is like. I can ask Him to work in my heart. I can ask Him to show me what He's like as I look at what He's made. I can listen to the Bible and learn about Jesus. I can turn away from my sins and trust in Jesus as my Savior.*

Let's Pray!

A   We praise You, God. You show us what You are like!

C   God, in our heart, we know that You are God and that we should obey You, but many times we don't want to. Please forgive us. Please change our hearts so they want to know and obey You.

T   Thank You for helping us to learn more about You. Thank You for wanting us to know You. Thank You for giving us a heart to know You; and. for making this world that shows us what You are like. Thank You for what we learn about You in Your Word, the Bible. And most of all, thank You for showing us what You are like in Your Son, Jesus.

S   Work deep inside our hearts. Help us to turn away from our sins and trust in Jesus as our Savior. Help us to know You. Put in our hearts the special kind of happy only You can give. Help us to go and tell others what we've learned.

   In Jesus' name we pray. Amen.

Let's Praise God Right Now!

Big Question 1 Hymn: Joyful, Joyful, We Adore Thee *from Hide 'n' Seek Kids ESV Songs 1, track 19*

Verse 1
Joyful, joyful, we adore Thee,
God of heaven, Lord of love,
Hearts unfold like flowers before Thee,
Opening to the sun above.

Verse 2
All Thy works in joy surround Thee,
Heaven and earth reflect Thy rays,
Stars and angels sing before Thee,
Center of unbroken praise.

Words: Henry van Dyke   Music: Ludwig van Beethoven

Song Question: What's something we can praise God for? *For being the God of heaven and the Lord of love. He gives us a heart that can know Him and adore Him.*

Go to the Hide 'n' Seek Kids Parent Resources for Unit 1 to get the Bible story and many more resources for this unit at www.praisefactory.org

Simeon was so happy to see baby Jesus! He praised God for sending Him to be our Savior. Now all who turn away from their sins and trust in Jesus as their Savior are forgiven their sins. They will know God in their heart now, and one day, they will go to live with Him forever in heaven. That will be happiest of all!

Hide 'n' Seek Kids Sneaky Seekers
hiding God's Word in our hearts, seeking to know God Himself

Big Question I, Lesson 5 Take Home Sheet

Big Question 1: How Can I Know What God Is Like?
  Answer: He Shows Me What He's Like!

Meaning:

God made us. He wants us to know what He is like, so we can know Him, love Him, and praise Him. God shows us what He is like: through the spirit He put in our hearts; through all of His creations we see around us; through His Word, the Bible; and most of all, through His very own Son, Jesus Christ.

How do I know this is true? The Bible tells me so:

"He who declares to man what is His thought...The LORD, the God of hosts, is His name." Amos 4:13, ESV

Some Questions for You

1. Simeon was so happy so see Jesus. Why? What did he know Jesus had come to do? *Jesus came to show us what God is like. And most of all, He came to be the Savior of all who turn away from their sins and trust in Jesus as their Savior.*

2. Can Jesus be our Savior? How? *Yes! Jesus came to save all who turn away from their sins and trust in Him as their Savior. If we do this, Jesus will save us, too. We can know the happiness of knowing God in our heart even today. And one day, He will take us to live with Him forever in heaven. That will be happiest of all!*

Let's Pray!

A We praise You, God. You show us what You are like!

C God, in our heart, we know that You are God and that we should obey You, but many times we don't want to. Please forgive us. Please change our hearts so they want to know and obey You.

T Thank You for helping us to learn more about You. Thank You for wanting us to know You. Thank You for giving us a heart to know You; and. for making this world that shows us what You are like. Thank You for what we learn about You in Your Word, the Bible. And most of all, thank You for showing us what You are like in Your Son, Jesus.

S Work deep inside our hearts. Help us to turn away from our sins and trust in Jesus as our Savior. Help us to know You. Put in our hearts the special kind of happy only You can give. Help us to go and tell others what we've learned.

  In Jesus' name we pray. Amen.

Let's Praise God Right Now!

Big Question 1 Praise Song: Oh, Oh, Oh, How Good is the Lord *from Hide 'n' Seek Kids ESV Songs 1, track 20*

Oh, oh, oh, how good is the Lord!
Oh, oh, oh, how good is the Lord!
Oh, oh, oh, how good is the Lord!
I never will forget what He has done for me.

He shows Himself to me, how good is the Lord!
He shows Himself to me, how good is the Lord!
He shows Himself to me, how good is the Lord!
I never will forget what He has done for me.

Song Question: We praise God for being so good and for showing us what He's like. God has done so many good things for us, but what is the very best thing He has done for us? *He sent Jesus to be the Savior for all who would turn away from their sins and trust in Him as their Savior.*

Go to the Hide 'n' Seek Kids Parent Resources for Unit 1 to get the Bible story and many more resources for this unit at www.praisefactory.org

HSK BQ1 L5 Coloring Sheet/Take Home pg.2

Hide 'n' Seek Kids Sneaky Seekers
hiding God's Word in our hearts, seeking to know God Himself

BIG QUESTION I BIBLE STORY & KEY CONCEPTS

Dear Parents,

Big Question #I is: How Can I Know What God Is Like? Your child is learning that "God Shows Us What He's Like!"

Here's a copy of the Bible story they are learning along with the "Listening Assignment" for each lesson. These assignments provide a different teaching emphasis for each lesson, helping the children dig deeper into each Bible truth. They match up with your child's take home for each lesson. We hope that these resources help your family to further "Hide God's Word in your heart and SEEK to know God, Himself!" Happy hiding and seeking!

•many more resources for this Big Question came be found online at www.praisefactory.org•

Listening Assignments for Big Question I Bible Story:
"The Case of the Old Man Who Looked for God"
Luke 2:25-32

(Note: These questions are most appropriate for older preschoolers)

Detective Dan's Lesson #1 Listening Assignment:
As you listen to the story, see if you can figure out:
1. Who was the old man who looked for God?
2. How did he find out what God was like?

Detective Dan's Lesson #2 Listening Assignment:
Our Bible verse is Amos 4:13: "He who declares to man what is His thought...The LORD, the God of hosts, is His name."

As you listen to the story, see if you can figure out:
1. Who did the LORD declare His thoughts to?
2. What book did the Lord use to declare His thoughts?

Detective Dan's Lesson #3 Listening Assignment:
I found four clues, but one of them is NOT in the story.
They are: baby Jesus, a chair, God's Word (on a scroll, like in Bible times) and a heart.
(these pictures are found on your child's Lesson 3 take home sheet)

I need to know:
1. Which three pictures belong in the story and which one does not?
2. What did God use three of these things to show Simeon?

Detective Dan's Lesson #4 Listening Assignment:
As you listen to the story, see if you can figure out:
1. Who did Simeon want to know more and more?
2. What was something Simeon thanked God for?

Detective Dan's Lesson #5 Listening Assignment:
As you listen to the story, see if you can figure out:
1. Why was Simeon so happy to see baby Jesus?
2. What did God send Jesus to do?

Read the questions, then say,
"Ok, Hide 'n' Seekers! Put on your best listening ears and see if you can find the answers these questions. When I finish reading the story, we will see if we can answer all the questions."

Big Question I Bible Story	use with all FIVE lessons	p.2

"The Case of the Old Man Who Looked for God" Luke 2:25-32

Story with lines separating paragraphs (text in bold, optional interaction cues in italics)

Simeon was a very, very old man.

Have you seen a very old man? They often have gray hair and sometimes even have a long, grey beard. Simeon looked like that!

Simeon knew and loved God in his heart.

Can you point to where your heart is?

But oh, how Simeon wanted to know more about God and what He is like!

Simeon knew God created the whole world. He could learn more about God, as he looked at all that God had made. There was so much to see!

The big, tall mountains,

Can you stretch up your arms really high like a tall mountain?

the galloping horses,

When horses gallop they run really, really fast and make lots of noise with their feet. Can you stomp your feet like you were a galloping horse?

the flying birds,

Let's flap our arms like birds!

the buzzing bees.

What sound does a buzzing bee make?

Simeon could see how wonderful God was in all the things He had made. But oh, how Simeon wanted to know more about God and what He is like!

Simeon read the Bible, God's Word, too.

Where's our Bible? Have children point to your Bible.

He learned that God is good and great, loving and wise.

But oh, how Simeon wanted to know more about God and what He is like!

Big Question I Bible Story use with all FIVE lessons **p.3**

Story with lines separating paragraphs (text in bold, optional interaction cues in italics)

Then one day, something very good happened to Simeon. God gave Simeon a wonderful promise: "I am sending My Son, Jesus, here to earth. He will show people what I am like, and will make the way for them to know and love Me. He will bring My forgiveness to everyone who trusts in Him as their Savior! They will know Me in their heart. Then one day, they will come to live happily with Me forever!" God promised. "And Simeon, you will get to see My Son, Jesus, at my Temple-Church before you die!" God told Simeon.

Simeon gathered with other people to worship God at a special place called the Temple. Where do we gather together to worship God? Why, it's right here! We're in it now! It's a church!

How excited Simeon was! Oh, how wonderful it would be to see God's very own Son!

Simeon went to God's Temple-Church.

Walk! Walk! Walk! Here goes Simeon to God's Temple-Church. Can you make a walking noise with your feet?

And who did Simeon see when he got there? Mary and Joseph. And who were they carrying? Baby Jesus, God's Son!

Pretend to hold a baby in your arms.

Simeon was very happy to see baby Jesus, God's Son, just as God had promised!

Yes, there was Jesus, just a little baby! But Jesus wouldn't stay a baby. He would grow up, up, up. He would tell everyone about God. He would show them what God is like. And, He would die on the cross to save God's people. They would be forgiven by God for disobeying Him! Yay!

Let's cheer really loud! Yay!

Then on Day One, Two, Three, Jesus would rise up from the dead, showing He had really done it! Yes, God's people were forgiven! Jesus had beaten sin and death for them! Yay!

Let's cheer really loud again! Yay!

One day, old Simeon died. Was that a sad day for Simeon? No, it was not!

Shake your head "no."

That was the day when God brought Simeon to live with Him in heaven. That's what made that day, Simeon's happiest day ever.

Now Simeon would really get to know how wonderful God is... more and more, forever and ever!

Simeon is so happy in heaven where he lives happily with God forever. Let's cheer really loud! Yay!

Big Question I Bible Story   use with all FIVE lessons   p.4

Cracking the Case: (story wrap-up for Listening Assignments)

It's time to see how we did with our Listening Assignment.

Detective Dan's Lesson #1 Listening Assignment:
1. Who was the old man who looked for God?
Simeon.
2. How did he find out what God was like?
He knew God in his heart; he saw what God was like as he looked around him at the things God had made; he learned about Him in the Bible, God's Word; and most of all, he knew what God was like through His Son, Jesus.

For You and Me:
Like Simeon, we can know what God is like. God has given us a heart to know and love Him. We can look around us and see what He's like in the things He has made. We can learn about Him in the Bible; and, we can know what He's like most of all when we learn about Jesus. We can ask God to show us what He's like and help us to know and love Him. He delights to do this!

Detective Dan's Lesson #2 Listening Assignment:
Our Bible Verse is: Amos 4:13:
"He who declares to man what is His thought...The LORD, the God of hosts, is His name."

1. Who did the LORD declare His thoughts to?
Simeon.
2. What book did the LORD use to declare His thoughts? The Bible, God's Word.

For You and Me:
The LORD can show us what He's like, through the special hearts He gave us, as we look around at all the amazing things He has made. He can declare His thoughts to us as we read the Bible, His Word and learn about His Son, Jesus Ask God to show Himself to you! He delights to do this!

Detective Dan's Lesson #3 Listening Assignment:
I found four clues, but one of them is NOT in the story. They are: baby Jesus, a chair, God's Word (on a scroll, like in Bible times) and a heart.

I need to know:
1. Which three pictures belong in the story and which one does not? The chair does not belong.
2. What did God use three of these things to show Simeon? God used baby Jesus, the Bible and the heart He gave Simeon to show Simeon what He is like.

For You and Me:
The LORD wants to show us what He's like, too. He can use the heart He's given us, the Bible, and Jesus to show us what He's like, too.

Detective Dan's Lesson #4 Listening Assignment:
1. Who did Simeon want to know more and more about? God.
2. What was something Simeon thanked God for?
Simeon thanked God for keeping His promise to let him see Jesus before he died. He was so happy to know that the time had come for God to save His people through Jesus.

For You and Me:
Like Simeon, we can thank God for sending Jesus to save sinners, like you and me.

Detective Dan's Lesson #5 Listening Assignment:
1. Why was Simeon so happy to see baby Jesus?
He knew that the time had come for God to save God's people from their sins through Jesus.
2. What did God send Jesus to do? God sent Jesus to show us what He's like. And, to take the punishment for the sins of God's people so they could know God and be His people forever.

For You and Me:
God can show us what He's like through His Son, Jesus. Jesus can save us from our sins and make us God's people, too, when we repent of our sins and trust in Him as our Savior.

Big Question I Bible Story   use with all FIVE lessons   p.5

The Gospel (story wrap-up if NOT using Listening Assignments)

Our Bible Truth is:
How Can I Know What God Is Like?
He Shows Me What He's Like!

God showed Simeon what He is like, and He can show us, too! We can ask Him to work in our heart and help us to turn away from disobeying Him and trust in Jesus as our Savior. When we do, God will forgive our sins and save us! He will live in our heart, helping us to know Him right now. He will satisfy our heart, giving us a special kind of happiness that comes only from knowing Him. And one day, we will go to live with Him in heaven forever. That will be best of all!

Close in prayer.

Closing Unit 1 ACTS Prayer

A=Adoration C=Confession T=Thanksgiving S=Supplication

A We praise You, God. You show us what You are like!

C LORD, in our heart we know that You are God. We know we should obey You, but many times we don't want to. Please forgive us. We need a Savior!

T Thank You for wanting us to know You. Thank You for giving us a heart to know You; and, for making this world that shows us what You are like. Thank You for what we learn about You in Your Word, the Bible. And most of all, thank You for showing us what You are like in Your Son, Jesus.

S Work deep inside our hearts. Help us to turn away from our sins and trust in Jesus as our Savior. Help us to know You. Put in our hearts the special kind of happy that comes only from knowing You. Help us to go and tell others what we've learned.

   In Jesus' name we pray. Amen.

HSK Sneaky Seekers: Big Question I Key Concepts   p.6

UNIT 1: The God Who Reveals Himself

Unit Big Question (and Answer): "How Can I Know What God Is Like? He Shows Me What He's Like!"

Meaning:

God made us. He wants us to know what He is like, so we can know Him, love Him, and praise Him.

God shows us what He is like by the heart He gave us to know and love Him; through all of His creations we see around us; through His Word, the Bible; and most of all, through His very own Son, Jesus Christ.

Unit 1 Bible Verse: Amos 4:13 ESV

"He who declares to man what is His thought...The LORD, the God of hosts, is His name."

Meaning:

God wants us to know what He is like, so we can know Him, love Him, and praise Him. We don't have to figure out what God is like by ourselves. God show us what He's like--He declares His thoughts to us.

God shows us what He's like through the spirit He put in our hearts; through His creations we see around us; through His Word, the Bible; and most of all, through His very own Son, Jesus Christ.

And what's the name of the one and only true, living God? It's the LORD! Yes, the LORD is His name!

Unit 1 ACTS Prayer

A   We praise You, God. You show us what You are like!

C   LORD, in our heart we know that You are God. We know we should obey You, but many times we don't want to. Please forgive us. We need a Savior!

T   Thank You for wanting us to know You. Thank You for giving us a heart to know You; and, for making this world that shows us what You are like. Thank You for what we learn about You in Your Word, the Bible. And most of all, thank You for showing us what You are like in Your Son, Jesus.

S   Work deep inside our hearts. Help us to turn away from our sins and trust in Jesus as our Savior. Help us to know You. Put in our hearts the special kind of happy that comes only from knowing You. Help us to go and tell others what we've learned. In Jesus' name we pray. Amen.

Unit 1 Story

The Case of the Old Man Who Looked for God
Luke 2:25-32

Songs Used in Unit 1   *listen to or download songs for free at https://praisefactory.org: Hide n Seek Kids Music page*

Big Q & A 1 Song
Big Question 1 Song
Big Question 1 Bible Verse Song: "The LORD Declares" Amos 4:13, ESV
Extra Bible Verse Song: "He Who Declares His Thought" Amos 4:13, ESV
Extra Bible Verse Song: "He Who Forms the Mountains" Amos 4:13, ESV
Extra Bible Verse Song: "For Behold" Amos 4:13, ESV
Extra Bible Verse Song: "Behold" Amos 4:13, ESV
Big Question 1 Hymn: Joyful, Joyful, We Adore Thee
Big Question 1 Praise Song: Oh! Oh! Oh! How Good is the Lord

Unit I Big Question and Answer Extra Craft

Coloring, Gluing and Sticking Activity

Craft Description
Children will color and decorate the number associated with the Big Question they are learning.

Supplies
White paper (cardstock is best)
Crayons, colored pencils, markers
Glue sticks
Small decorating items, such as glitter glue, colored paper dots (made with a hole punch), small fabric scraps, pom poms, sequins, small tissue or foil pieces, etc.

Preparation
1. Print out copies of the Big Question and Answer and the Number onto separate sheets of paper.
2. Cut out the circle around the number.
3. Set out coloring and decorating supplies.
4. Make an example of each card to show the children.

Directions
1. Show the children your example, telling them they are decorating and practicing the Big Question and Answer to go and tell their families and friends.
2. Have children first color their Big Question and Answer sheets,
3. Then have them use the additional decorating suppiles to fill in the space around their number.
4. Glue the number in place.
5. Write child's name on card.
6. Allow cards to dry.

If you don't want to use the extra decorating supplies, just have the children coloring in their numbers and glue them in place on their Big Question and Answer sheet.

Practice Telling
Have the children practice holding up the Big Question and saying it. You can have fun with this by having the children mimic when you raise it up, how you say it, etc. a sort of Simon Says element.

Unit 1 Bible Verse Craft: Amos 4:13 Extra Craft

Accordion Picture

Bible Verse: "He who declares to man what is His thought...The LORD, the God of hosts, is His name."
Amos 4:13, ESV

Craft Description
Children will make an accordion folded sign that folds out and reveals a person and the Bible verse.

Supplies
White paper or cardstock
Man print out
Crayons
Tape

Preparation
1. Print out onto the paper the two parts of the picture, one set per child.
2. Tape the halves of paper along the short side, so that the "person" is properly connected in the middle.
3. Set out crayons.
4. Make an example of the craft for the children to see.

Directions
1. Show the children your example, telling them that they are making this so that can go and tell their parents and friends this week the Bible verse they are learning.
2. Have the children color in the "man" on their paper.
3. Write child's name on card.
4. Fold the paper backwards and forwards in approximately 1" segments, as if making a homemade paper fan. Folds should run across the short side of page.

Practice Telling
Have the children practice telling the Bible verse by squatting down and whispering, "He who declares to..." Then, on the word "man, have the children jump up and unfold their picture to reveal the "man." They can shout out loud the word "man" and the rest of the verse: "what is His thought. The LORD, the God of hosts, is His name." You also can play the Big Question 1 Bible Verse songs and practice as you sing.

"He who declares to....

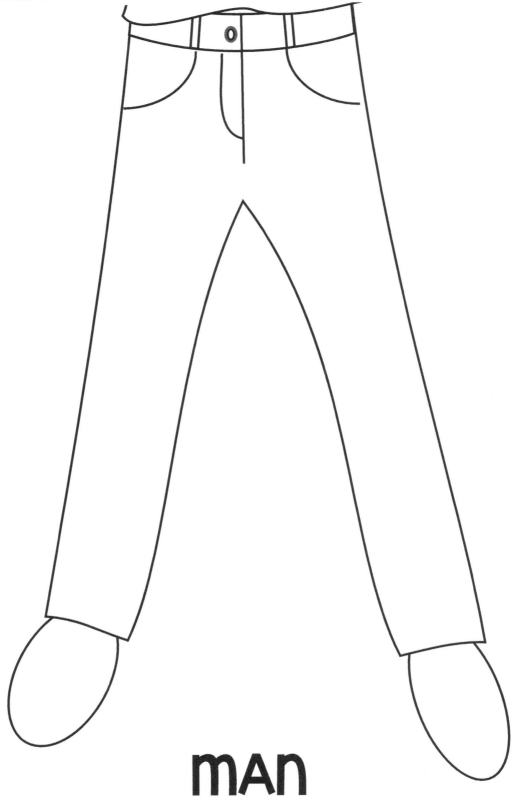

mAn
His thought.
The LORD, the God of hosts, is His name."
Amos 4:13, ESV

The Case of the Old Man Who Looked for God: Luke 2:25-32 Jigsaw Puzzle Page

Make copies of picture and cut out into an appropriate number of pieces for your children. Or, can print out color versions of this puzzle by downloading from praisefactory.org

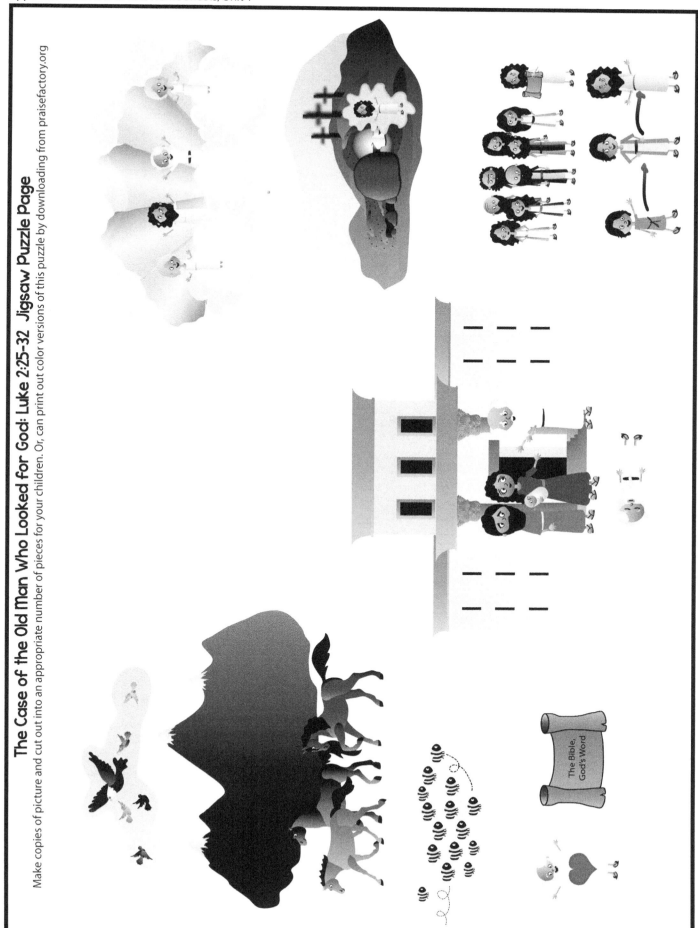

BIG QUESTION 2

What's so special about the Bible?

God's Word

The Bible

ANSWER:

It alone is God's Word!

Hide 'n' Seek Kids Sneaky Seekers
hiding God's Word in our hearts, seeking to know God Himself

Big Question 2, Lesson I Take Home Sheet

Big Question 2: What's So Special about the Bible?
   Answer: It Alone Is God's Word!

Meaning:

There are millions of books in the world, but none is like the Bible. It alone is God's perfect Word! God made sure it was written down just right. It tells us everything we need to know God and how to live for Him. It is powerful to do everything God wants it to do. Everything else in this world may come and go, but God's Word will last forever. It will always prove true.

How do I know this is true? The Bible tells me so:

"This God--His ways are perfect. The word of the LORD proves true. The Lord lives, and blessed be my rock, and exalted be the God of my salvation." Psalm 18:30,46

Some Questions for You

1. Can You Fix the Big Question and Answer?
What's So Special about the Bible? It is some of God's Word!
Answer: No! What's So Special about the Bible? It ALONE is God's Word!

2. Who does the Bible tell us about God? *Everything we need to know about Him.*

3. What is God's good news for you and me that God gives us in His Word, the Bible? *The gospel!*
The Bible tells us so many good and important things. But, the very, very, very best thing it tells us is how we can be saved from our sins. What does the Bible say? It tells us that even though we are sinners who deserved God's punishment for our sins, God sent His Son to save us. He promises to forgive the sins of all who turn away from disobeying Him and trust in Jesus as their Savior. God will help us to do this, if we ask Him. He loves to answer this prayer!

Let's Pray!

A   We praise You, God. You are perfect, and everything You tell us in Your Word, the Bible, always proves true.

C   God, we know You are perfect and everything You say is true, but too many times we still don't trust You or obey Your Word. Please forgive us! We need Jesus to be our Savior!

T   Thank You for giving us Your words, written down perfectly in the Bible. Thank You that we can always know what is right and true when we read Your Word, the Bible. And thank You for all the wonderful things You tell us in the Bible, especially the stories about Jesus.

S   Work deep inside our hearts. Help us to turn away from our sins and trust in Jesus as our Savior. Help us to want to read Your Word. Help us to know You better as we learn. Help us to go and tell others how they can learn about You in Your wonderful Word, the Bible. In Jesus' name we pray. Amen.

Let's Sing Our Big Question and Answer!

Big Q & A 2 Song *from Hide 'n' Seek Kids ESV Songs 2, track 12*

What's so special about the Bible?
It alone is God's Word!
It alone is God's Word!
It's always true,
It can make you wise,
It can work pow'rf'ly in your life.
It alone is God's Word!
It alone is God's Word!

Song Question: What's so special about the Bible?
   Answer: *It alone is God's Word!*

Go to the Hide 'n' Seek Kids Parent Resources for Unit 2 to get the Bible story and many more resources and songs for this unit at praisefactory.org
HSK BQ2 L1 Coloring Sheet/Take Home pg.2

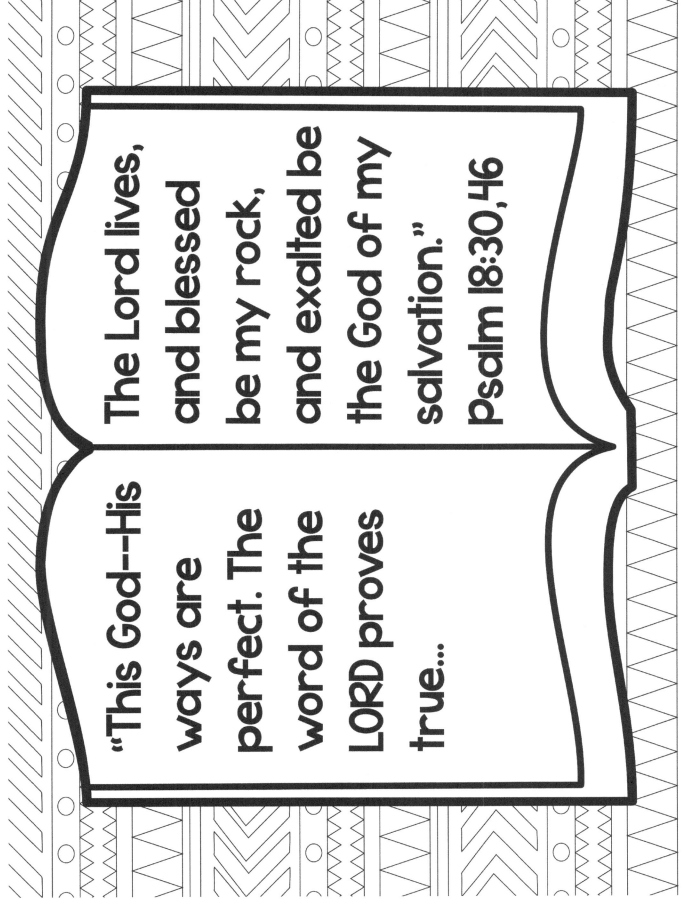

"This God--His ways are perfect. The word of the LORD proves true...

The Lord lives, and blessed be my rock, and exalted be the God of my salvation." Psalm 18:30,46

Hide 'n' Seek Kids Sneaky Seekers
hiding God's Word in our hearts, seeking to know God Himself

Big Question 2, Lesson 2 Take Home Sheet

Big Question 2: What's So Special about the Bible?
        Answer: It Alone Is God's Word!

How do I know this is true? The Bible tells me so:

"This God--His ways are perfect. The word of the LORD proves true. The Lord lives, and blessed be my rock,
  and exalted be the God of my salvation." Psalm 18:30,46

Meaning:

The LORD is like no one else. He is the one, true God. Everything He does is absolutely perfect! Everything God says is
perfect, too. It is flawless. Flawless is a big word that means perfect--without even a single mistake. No, not one! God
always tells us what is right and true. His Word always proves true!

Where can we read God's Word? In the Bible! It alone is God's Word. That's why we take time each day to learn from the
Bible. We want to hear from God--all the wonderful things about Him; what He has done for us through Jesus, His Son;
and, what good things are in store for those who love Him and live for Him. Oh, how we want to praise the LORD when
we read His Word! He is the living God. He is our Savior!

Some Questions for You

1. What's the missing word to the Bible verse?
"This God--His ways are perfect. The _____ of the LORD proves true. The Lord lives, and blessed be my rock,
      and exalted be the God of my salvation."
Answer: word.

2. What always proves true? *The Bible! It alone is God's Word!*

Let's Pray!

A   We praise You, God. You are perfect, and everything You tell us in Your Word, the Bible, always proves true.

C   God, we know You are perfect and everything You say is true, but too many times we still don't trust You or obey Your
     Word. Please forgive us! We need Jesus to be our Savior!

T   Thank You for giving us Your words, written down perfectly in the Bible. Thank You that we can always know what is
     right and true when we read Your Word, the Bible. And thank You for all the wonderful things You tell us in the Bible,
     especially the stories about Jesus.

S   Work deep inside our hearts. Help us to turn away from our sins and trust in Jesus as our Savior. Help us to want to
     read Your Word. Help us to know You better as we learn. Help us to go and tell others how they can learn about You in
     Your wonderful Word, the Bible. In Jesus' name we pray. Amen.

Let's Sing Our Bible Verse!

Big Question 2 Bible Verse Song *from Hide 'n' Seek Kids ESV Songs 2, track 14,14T*

This God, His ways are perfect,
The word of the LORD proves true,
This God, His ways are perfect,
The word of the LORD proves true. *Repeat*

Psalm Eighteen, thirty.

Song Questions: Who is perfect? *The LORD!* What is His Word like? *It proves true. That means it's perfect, too!*

Go to the Hide 'n' Seek Kids Parent Resources for Unit 2 to get the Bible story and many more resources for this unit at www.praisefactory.org

Which of these things did Grandma Lois and Mother Eunice NOT give to Timothy? Put an "X" in the box next to each of these. Which did Grandma Lois and Mother Eunice think was most important of all?

☐ **Zebra**

☐ **God's Word, the Bible**

☐ **Food**

☐ **Clothes**

Answers: 1.The zebra. 2. God's Word, the Bible, was most important of all.

Hide 'n' Seek Kids Sneaky Seekers
hiding God's Word in our hearts, seeking to know God Himself

Big Question 2, Lesson 3 Take Home Sheet

Big Question 2: What's So Special about the Bible?
Answer: It Alone Is God's Word!

Meaning:

There are millions of books in the world, but none is like the Bible. It alone is God's perfect Word! God made sure it was written down just right. It tells us everything we need to know God and how to live for Him. It is powerful to do everything God wants it to do. Everything else in this world may come and go, but God's Word will last forever. It will always prove true.

How do I know this is true? The Bible tells me so:

"This God--His ways are perfect. The word of the LORD proves true. The Lord lives, and blessed be my rock, and exalted be the God of my salvation." Psalm 18:30,46

Some Questions for You

1. How long will God's Word last? *Forever!*

2. What will always prove true? *The Bible! It is God's perfect Word.*

3. Who can help me to understand God's Word, the Bible? *God can.*

4. What does the Bible tell me to do if I want to know God? *It tells me to ask God to forgive my sins and to ask Jesus to be my Savior. God will help us do this, if we ask Him. He loves to answer this prayer!*

Let's Pray!

A We praise You, God. You are perfect, and everything You tell us in Your Word, the Bible, always proves true.

C God, we know You are perfect and everything You say is true, but too many times we still don't trust You or obey Your Word. Please forgive us! We need Jesus to be our Savior!

T Thank You for giving us Your words, written down perfectly in the Bible. Thank You that we can always know what is right and true when we read Your Word, the Bible. And thank You for all the wonderful things You tell us in the Bible, especially the stories about Jesus.

S Work deep inside our hearts. Help us to turn away from our sins and trust in Jesus as our Savior. Help us to want to read Your Word. Help us to know You better as we learn. Help us to go and tell others how they can learn about You in Your wonderful Word, the Bible. In Jesus' name we pray. Amen.

Let's Sing about Our Big Question and Answer!

Big Question 2 (Action Rhyme) Song *from Hide 'n' Seek Kids ESV Songs 2, track 13*

Refrain:
What's so special about the Bible?
It alone is God's Word,   *(point up to God)*
What's so special about the Bible?
It alone is God's Word.   *(point up to God)*

There are millions and millions of books
   in the world,
But only the Bible is God's perfect Word,
There are millions and millions of books
   in the world,
But only the Bible is God's perfect Word.

Verse 1:
God's Word was written down perfectly,   *(use index of one hand to*
By godly men long ago,   *pretend to write on open*
The Holy Spirit worked through them,   *palm of the other hand*
Inspiring every word they wrote. *Refrain*

Verse 2:
God's Word is powerful and living,
It changes us, deep inside,   *(touch heart)*
The Holy Spirit uses it
To make God's people like Christ. *Refrain*

Song Question: Who helped godly people write down God's Word perfectly? *The Holy Spirit. He worked in their hearts and inspired every word they wrote.*

Go to the Hide 'n' Seek Kids Parent Resources for Unit 2 to get the Bible story and many more resources for this unit at www.praisefactory.org

HSK BQ 2 L3 Coloring Sheet/Take Home pg.2

God, We Thank You!

Grandma Lois and Mother Eunice wanted Timothy to know and love God most of all. They taught Timothy about God from His Word, the Bible. They thanked God for working in Timothy's heart and helping him trust in Jesus as his Savior. God can work in our hearts, too. Let's ask Him to help us now!

HSK BQ 2 L4 Coloring Sheet/Take Home pg.1

Hide 'n' Seek Kids Sneaky Seekers
hiding God's Word in our hearts, seeking to know God Himself

Big Question 2, Lesson 4 Take Home Sheet

Big Question 2: What's So Special about the Bible?
   Answer: It Alone Is God's Word!

Meaning:

There are millions of books in the world, but none is like the Bible. It alone is God's perfect Word! God made sure it was written down just right. It tells us everything we need to know God and how to live for Him. It is powerful to do everything God wants it to do. Everything else in this world may come and go, but God's Word will last forever. It will always prove true.

How do I know this is true? The Bible tells me so:

"This God--His ways are perfect. The word of the LORD proves true. The Lord lives, and blessed be my rock, and exalted be the God of my salvation." Psalm 18:30,46

Some Questions for You

1. What's something I can thank God for giving me? *The Bible, His perfect Word.*

2. What is something I can ask God to help me with as I learn His Word, the Bible? *I can ask God to show me what He is like. I can ask Him to work in my heart and help me understand His Word. I can Him to use it to help me to turn away from my sins and trust in Jesus as my Savior.*

Let's Pray!

A We praise You, God. You are perfect, and everything You tell us in Your Word, the Bible, always proves true.

C God, we know You are perfect and everything You say is true, but too many times we still don't trust You or obey Your Word. Please forgive us! We need Jesus to be our Savior!

T Thank You for giving us Your words, written down perfectly in the Bible. Thank You that we can always know what is right and true when we read Your Word, the Bible. And thank You for all the wonderful things You tell us in the Bible, especially the stories about Jesus.

S Work deep inside our hearts. Help us to turn away from our sins and trust in Jesus as our Savior. Help us to want to read Your Word. Help us to know You better as we learn. Help us to go and tell others how they can learn about You in Your wonderful Word, the Bible.

In Jesus' name we pray. Amen.

Let's Praise God Right Now!

Big Question 2 Hymn: How Precious Is the Book Divine *from Hide 'n' Seek Kids ESV Songs 2, track 18*

Verse 1
How precious is the book divine,
By inspiration given;
Bright as a lamp its doctrines shine,
To guide our souls to heaven.

Words: William Gardiner   Music: Constance Dever

Song Question: What's something we can praise God for? *For being the God who gives us the Bible and makes it perfect. We can trust it to tell us what God is like. It tells us how we can be saved through Jesus and how God wants us to live.*

Go to the Hide 'n' Seek Kids Parent Resources for Unit 2 to get the Bible story and many more resources for this unit at www.praisefactory.org

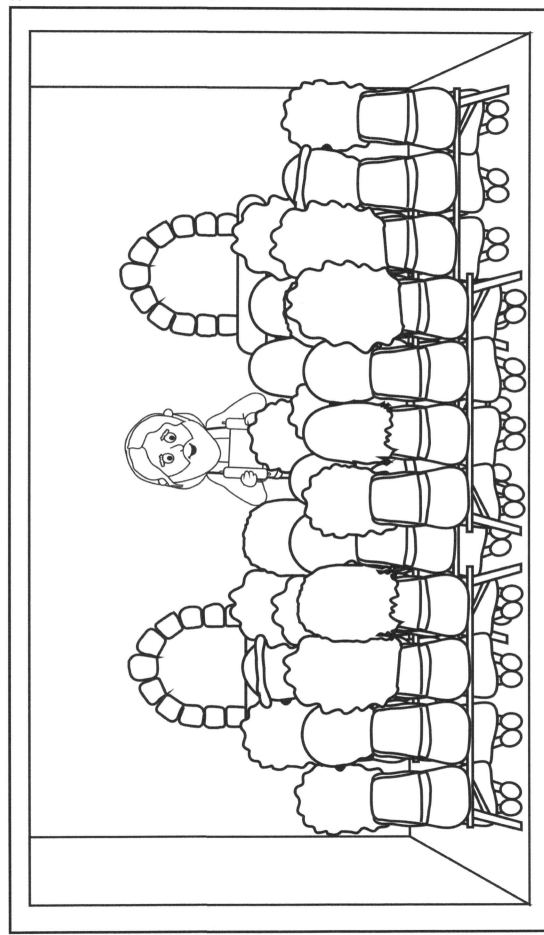

Timothy learned God's Word when he was a little boy. God worked in his heart as he listened. He turned away from his sins and trusted in Jesus as his Savior. God kept working in his heart, changing him in more and more wonderful ways.

And what did Timothy do when he grew up? He became a pastor. He wanted to care for God's people and teach them God's Word. He wanted them to come to know Jesus as their Savior, just as he did!

HSK BQ 2 L5 Coloring Sheet/Take Home pg.1

Hide 'n' Seek Kids Sneaky Seekers
hiding God's Word in our hearts, seeking to know God Himself

Big Question 2, Lesson 5 Take Home Sheet

Big Question 2: What's So Special about the Bible?
   Answer: It Alone Is God's Word!

Meaning:

There are millions of books in the world, but none is like the Bible. It alone is God's perfect Word! God made sure it was written down just right. It tells us everything we need to know God and how to live for Him. It is powerful to do everything God wants it to do. Everything else in this world may come and go, but God's Word will last forever. It will always prove true.

How do I know this is true? The Bible tells me so:

"This God--His ways are perfect. The word of the LORD proves true. The Lord lives, and blessed be my rock, and exalted be the God of my salvation." Psalm 18:30,46

Some Questions for You

1. What happened in Timothy's heart as he listened to God's Word, the Bible? *God worked in his heart. He turned away from his sins and trust in Jesus as his Savior. Then God kept working in his heart, changing him in wonderful ways, more and more.*

2. Can Jesus be our Savior? How? *Yes! Jesus came to save all who turn away from their sins and trust in Him as their Savior. If we do this, Jesus will save us, too. We can know the happiness of knowing God in our heart even today. And one day, He will take us to live with Him forever in heaven. That will be happiest of all!*

Let's Pray!

A We praise You, God. You are perfect, and everything You tell us in Your Word, the Bible, always proves true.

C God, we know You are perfect and everything You say is true, but too many times we still don't trust You or obey Your Word. Please forgive us! We need Jesus to be our Savior!

T Thank You for giving us Your words, written down perfectly in the Bible. Thank You that we can always know what is right and true when we read Your Word, the Bible. And thank You for all the wonderful things You tell us in the Bible, especially the stories about Jesus.

S Work deep inside our hearts. Help us to turn away from our sins and trust in Jesus as our Savior. Help us to want to read Your Word. Help us to know You better as we learn. Help us to go and tell others how they can learn about You in Your wonderful Word, the Bible.

In Jesus' name we pray. Amen.

Let's Praise God Right Now!

Big Question 2 Praise Song: The Best Book to Read Is the Bible *from Hide 'n' Seek Kids ESV Songs 2, track 19*

Verse 1
The best book to read is the Bible,
The best book to read is the Bible,
It alone is God's true Word,
With the best news ever heard!
Yes! The best book to read is the Bible.

Verse 2
The best book to read is the Bible,
The best book to read is the Bible,
If you read it ev'ry day,
God will teach you His ways.
Yes! The best book to read is the Bible.

Song Question: We praise God for being the giver of His true word to us. What is that best news that He gives us in the Bible? *He sent Jesus to be the Savior for all who would turn away from their sins and trust in Him as their Savior.*

Go to the Hide 'n' Seek Kids Parent Resources for Unit 2 to get the Bible story and many more resources for this unit at www.praisefactory.org
HSK BQ2 L5 Coloring Sheet/Take Home pg.2

Hide 'n' Seek Kids Sneaky Seekers
hiding God's Word in our hearts, seeking to know God Himself

BIG QUESTION 2 BIBLE STORY & KEY CONCEPTS

Dear Parents,

Big Question #2 is: What's So Special about the Bible? It Alone Is God's Word!"

Here's a copy of the Bible story they are learning along with the "Listening Assignment" for each lesson. These assignments provide a different teaching emphasis for each lesson, helping the children dig deeper into each Bible truth. They match up with your child's take home for each lesson. We hope that these resources help your family to further "Hide God's Word in your heart and SEEK to know God, Himself!" Happy hiding and seeking!

•many more resources for this Big Question came be found online at www.praisefactory..org•

Listening Assignments for Big Question 2 Bible Story:
"The Case of the Women's Best Gift"
I Timothy

(Note: These questions are most appropriate for older preschoolers)

Detective Dan's Lesson #1 Listening Assignment:

I need to find out:
1. Who are the women in our story?
2. What was their best gift and who did they give it to?

Detective Dan's Lesson #2 Listening Assignment:

Our Bible verse is Psalm 18:30,46: "This God--His ways are perfect. The word of the LORD proves true. The Lord lives, and blessed be my rock, and exalted be the God of my salvation."

As you listen to the story, see if you can figure out:
1. Who in our story knew that God and His Word were perfect?
2. Who did they teach God's Word to?

Detective Dan's Lesson #3 Listening Assignment:

I found four clues, but one of them is NOT in the story.
They are: Food, a zebra, God's Word (on a scroll, like in Bible times) and some clothes.
Hold up each of the four pictures for the children to see as you identify them. Better yet, put them up on your flannelgraph board, off to one side.

I need to know:
1. Which of these things did Grandma Lois and Mother Eunice NOT give to Timothy?
2. Which of these things did they think was most important of all?

Detective Dan's Lesson #4 Listening Assignment:

As you listen to the story, see if you can figure out:
1. Who did Grandma Lois and Mother Eunice want Timothy to know and love most of all?
2. What book did they thank God for giving to them?

Detective Dan's Lesson #5 Listening Assignment:

As you listen to the story, see if you can figure out:
1. What happened in Timothy's heart as he listened to God's Word, the Bible?
2. What good news from the Bible did Timothy preach about when he grew up?

Read the questions, THEN SAY,

"Ok, Hide 'n' Seeker! Put on your best listening ears and see if you can find the answers to Detective Dan's questions. When I finish telling the story, we'll see what we come up with."

| Big Question 2 Bible Story | use with all FIVE lessons | p.2 |

"The Case of the Women's Best Gift" I Timothy

Story with lines separating paragraphs (text in bold, optional interaction cues in italics)

Grandma Lois and Mother Eunice loved the Bible. They loved what the Bible told them about God and His Son, Jesus. They loved how it worked in their heart and helped them know God and live for Him! If Grandma Lois and Mother Eunice knew one thing, it was that there was NO BOOK like the Bible! It alone was God's Word! It was always true. They could count on it.

Do you see a Bible in this room? Point to it.

Now, Mother Eunice had a little boy named Timothy. She and Grandma Lois loved Timothy very, very much. And because they loved him, they hugged him…and they fed him good food…and they gave him clothes to wear…and a good place to sleep at night. They taught good manners and how to do his chores and all sorts of things that would help him grow up to be a fine, young man one day.

Do you have a mother or a grandmother? What kinds of things do they do for you because they love you?

But most of all, because Grandma Lois and Mother Eunice loved Timothy so much, they wanted him to know and love God. And oh, how they wanted Timothy to turn away from his sins and trust in Jesus as his Savior!

So, Grandma Lois and Mother Eunice taught Timothy every day from the only book in the whole, wide world where the truths about God are written down just right. Can you guess what that book is?

Can you guess what that book is called? (I bet you can!) Let's say its name all together—The Bible!

The Bible, yes, the Bible was that one, special book. It alone is God's Word and Grandma Lois and Mother Eunice knew it.

The Bible is a very BIG book filled with so many good stories and so many important truths about God. There was so, so much to teach Timothy!

Hold up your Bible and show the children how big it is. Open it up and show them all the words on the pages.

But of everything in the whole Bible, Grandma Lois and Mother Eunice most wanted Timothy to know one thing.

Can you guess what it is?

They wanted him to know the gospel—the good news of Jesus. They wanted him to know how he could become one of God's people.

"Long ago, God created the whole world, Timothy," they told him. "He gave us His good laws to live by, but we all choose to disobey them, Timothy. "We need a Savior to save us from our sins and God sent that Savior to us! It's Jesus!" Grandma Lois and Mother Eunice taught Timothy. "We hope one day you will ask Jesus to forgive your sins and trust in Him as your Savior like we have, Timothy," they told him. "There's nothing better than knowing God and living for Him."

Big Question 2 Bible Story
use with all FIVE lessons

Story with lines separating paragraphs (text in bold, optional interaction cues in italics)

At first, Timothy just listened and learned as Grandma Lois and Mother Eunice taught him from the Bible. But after a while, something wonderful happened: God's Word began to work powerfully in Timothy's heart and mind, helping him to believe.

"God, I believe what is written in Your Word, the Bible. I believe in Your Son, Jesus, and trust in Him as my Savior. Please forgive me for disobeying You. I want to live my life for you. Please save me!" Timothy prayed.

God was happy to answer Timothy's prayers. And Timothy was happy to be one of God's people!

Did you know that we can become God's people, too, when we pray like Timothy did, for God to forgive our sins and help us to trust in Jesus as our Savior? It's true!

But that was only the beginning. Now Timothy wanted to learn from the Bible more than ever! He wanted to know more about God and love Him more, too. too. He wanted God's Word to go on working inside his heart, changing him more and more, too.

And that's just what happened! As Timothy kept learning from the Bible, God's Word, it kept on working inside him. And Timothy, the little boy, grew up and up and up to be Timothy, the man with a heart full of love for God, His Word, and His people.

A grown-up man needs a grown up man's job. And what job do you think God gave Timothy to do?

What job do you think Timothy did?

God called Timothy to be a pastor—a man who teaches God's Word to God's people and loves them as they gather together as a church.

Now others gathered around Timothy as he preached to them the same truths from the God's Word that Grandma Lois and Mother Eunice had taught him long ago as a little boy!

How happy Grandma Lois and Mother Eunice must have been! What a great work God had done in Timothy through His Word, the Bible! And now God was even using Timothy to do a great work in the hearts of others, too!

Let's clap and say, "Yay!" for all the good things God did in Timothy through His Word, the Bible!

Big Question 2 Bible Story   use with all FIVE lessons   p.4

Cracking the Case: (story wrap-up for Listening Assignments)

It's time to see how we did with our Listening Assignment.

Detective Dan's Lesson #1 Listening Assignment:
1. Who are the women in our story? Grandma Lois and Mother Eunice.
2. What was their best gift and who did they give it to? Their best gift was teaching God's Word and the good news of Jesus. They taught it to Timothy, Mother Eunice's son.

For You and Me:
Timothy learned God's truths in the Bible and so are you...right now! God used His Word, the Bible, to work in Timothy's heart and help him trust in Jesus as His Savior. God can use His Word to work inside of us, too.

Detective Dan's Lesson #2 Listening Assignment:
Our Bible verse is Psalm 18:30,46:
"This God--His ways are perfect. The word of the LORD proves true. The Lord lives, and blessed be my rock, and exalted be the God of my salvation."

1. Who in our story knew that God and His Word were perfect? Grandma Lois and Mother Eunice.
2. Who did they teach God's Word to? Timothy.

For You and Me:
God is the living God! He and His Word, the Bible, are still perfect! God's Word will always prove true. We can trust in God and His Word, just like Grandma Lois, Mother Eunice and Timothy did!

Detective Dan's Lesson #3 Listening Assignment:
I found four clues, but one of them is NOT in the story. They are: Food, a zebra, God's Word (on a scroll, like in Bible times) and some clothes.

1. Which of these things did Grandma Lois and Mother Eunice NOT give to Timothy? The zebra.
2. Which of these things did they think was most important of all? God's Word, the Bible.

For You and Me:
Like Timothy, we have people who love us and who give us many good things. But of everything we can ever have, learning God's Word, the Bible is the most important of all. Ask them to help you learn God's Word.

Detective Dan's Lesson #4 Listening Assignment:
1. Who did Grandma Lois and Mother Eunice want Timothy to know and love most of all? God.
2. What book did they thank God for giving to them?
The Bible, God's Word.

For You and Me:
God is the person best person we can know and love, too. God can use His Word to do wonderful things in our hearts, too. Grandma Lois, Mother Eunice and Timothy knew this. Let's thank God for His Word, the Bible. Let's ask Him to use it to do wonderful things in our hearts, too.

Detective Dan's Lesson #5 Listening Assignment:
1. What happened in Timothy's heart as he listened to God's Word, the Bible? God worked in his heart. He turned away from his sins and trust in Jesus as his Savior. Then God kept working in his heart, changing him in wonderful ways, more and more.
2. What good news from the Bible did Timothy preach about when he grew up? God will forgive us our sins and make us His people when we repent and trust in Jesus as our Savior.

For You and Me:
God can use His perfect Word, the Bible, to help us know Him and to change us in wonderful ways. Jesus can save us from our sins and make us God's people, too, when we repent of our sins and trust in Him as our Savior.

Big Question 2 Bible Story   use with all FIVE lessons   **p.5**

The Gospel (story wrap-up if NOT using Listening Assignments)

Our Bible Truth is:
What's So Special about the Bible?
It Alone Is God's Word!

God used His Word, the Bible, to work inside Timothy in wonderful ways. He can work in our hearts, too. We can ask Him to work in our heart and help us to turn away from disobeying Him and trust in Jesus as our Savior. When we do, God will forgive our sins and save us! He will live in our heart, helping us to know Him right now. He will satisfy our heart, giving us a special kind of happiness that comes only from knowing Him. And one day, we will go to live with Him in heaven forever. That will be best of all!

Close in prayer.

Closing Unit 2 ACTS Prayer

A=Adoration C=Confession T=Thanksgiving S=Supplication

A   We praise You, God. You are perfect, and everything You tell us always proves true.

C   God, we know You are perfect and everything You say is true, but too many times we still don't trust You or obey Your Word. Please forgive us! We need Jesus to be our Savior!

T   Thank You for giving us Your words, written down perfectly in the Bible. Thank You that we can always know what is right and true when we read Your Word, the Bible. And thank You for all the wonderful things You tell us in the Bible, especially the stories about Jesus.

S   Work deep inside our hearts. Help us to turn away from our sins and trust in Jesus as our Savior. Help us to want to read Your Word. Help us to know You better as we learn. Help us to go and tell others how they can learn about You in Your wonderful Word, the Bible.

In Jesus' name we pray. Amen.

UNIT 2: God's Wonderful Word, the Bible

Unit Big Question (and Answer): "What's So Special about the Bible? It Alone Is God's Word!"

Meaning:

There are millions of books in the world, but none is like the Bible. It alone is God's perfect Word! God made sure it was written down just right. It tells us everything we need to know God and how to live for Him. It is powerful to do everything God wants it to do. Everything else in this world may come and go, but God's Word will last forever. It will always prove true.

Unit 2 Bible Verse: Psalm 18:30, 46 ESV

"This God--His ways are perfect. The word of the LORD proves true. The Lord lives, and blessed be my rock, and exalted be the God of my salvation."

Meaning:

The LORD is like no one else. He is the one, true God. Everything He does is absolutely perfect! Everything God says is perfect, too. It is flawless. Flawless is a big word that means perfect--without even a single mistake. No, not one! God always tells us what is right and true. His Word always proves true!

Where can we read God's Word? In the Bible! It alone is God's Word. That's why we take time each day to learn from the Bible. We want to hear from God--all the wonderful things about Him; what He has done for us through Jesus, His Son; and, what good things are in store for those who love Him and live for Him. Oh, how we want to praise the LORD when we read His Word! He is the living God. He is our Savior!

Unit 2 ACTS Prayer

A We praise You, God. You are perfect, and everything You tell us in Your Word, the Bible, always proves true.

C God, we know You are perfect and everything You say is true, but too many times we still don't trust You or obey Your Word. Please forgive us! We need Jesus to be our Savior!

T Thank You for giving us Your words, written down perfectly in the Bible. Thank You that we can always know what is right and true when we read Your Word, the Bible. And thank You for all the wonderful things You tell us in the Bible, especially the stories about Jesus.

S Work deep inside our hearts. Help us to turn away from our sins and trust in Jesus as our Savior. Help us to want to read Your Word. Help us to know You better as we learn. Help us to go and tell others how they can learn about You in Your wonderful Word, the Bible. In Jesus' name we pray. Amen.

Unit 2 Story

The Case of the Women's Best Gift
1 Timothy

Songs Used in Unit 2   *listen to or download songs for free at https://praisefactory.org: Hide n Seek Kids Music page*

Big Q & A 2 Song
Big Question 2 Song: What's So Special About God's Word?
Unit 2 Bible Verse Song: Proves True Psalm 18:30, 46 ESV
Extra Unit 2 Bible Verse Song: This God, His Way Is Perfect   Psalm 18:30,46, ESV (other version)
Extra Unit 2 Bible Verse Song: The Word of the Lord 1 Peter 1:24,25, ESV
Unit 2 Hymn: How Precious Is the Book Divine, v.1
Unit 2 Praise Song: The Best Book to Read Is the Bible

Unit 2 Big Question and Answer Extra Craft

Coloring, Gluing and Sticking Activity

Craft Description
Children will color and decorate the number associated with the Big Question they are learning.

Supplies
White paper (cardstock is best)
Crayons, colored pencils, markers
Glue sticks
Small decorating items, such as glitter glue, colored paper dots (made with a hole punch), small fabric scraps, pom poms, sequins, small tissue or foil pieces, etc.

Preparation
1. Print out copies of the Big Question and Answer and the Number onto separate sheets of paper.
2. Cut out the circle around the number.
3. Set out coloring and decorating supplies.
4. Make an example of each card to show the children.

Directions
1. Show the children your example, telling them they are decorating and practicing the Big Question and Answer to go and tell their families and friends.
2. Have children first color their Big Question and Answer sheets,
3. Then have them use the additional decorating suppiles to fill in the space around their number.
4. Glue the number in place.
5. Write child's name on card.
6. Allow cards to dry.

If you don't want to use the extra decorating supplies, just have the children coloring in their numbers and glue them in place on their Big Question and Answer sheet.

Practice Telling
Have the children practice holding up the Big Question and saying it. You can have fun with this by having the children mimic when you raise it up, how you say it, etc. a sort of Simon Says element.

What's So Special about the Bible?

It Alone Is God's Word!

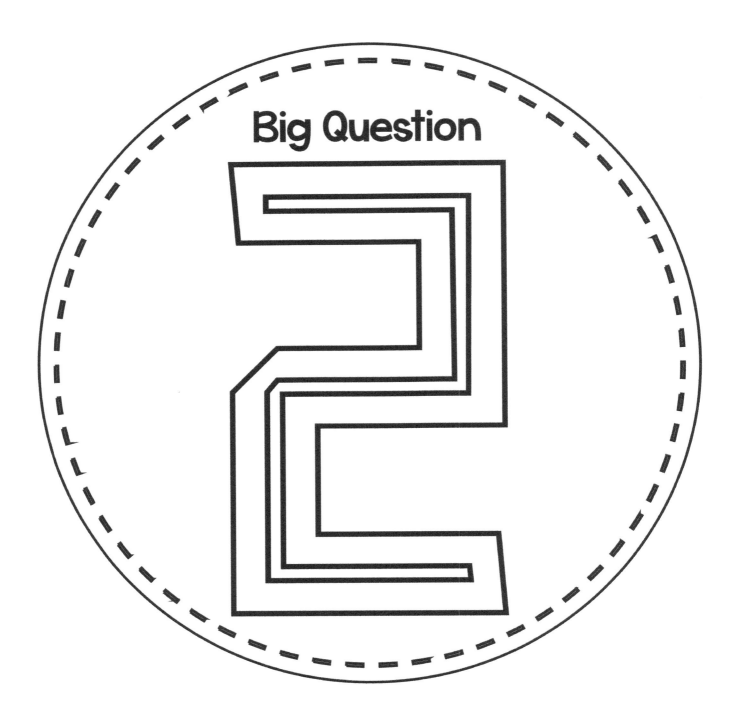

Big Question

Unit 2 Bible Verse Extra Craft: Psalm 18:30

Bible Verse Book

Bible Verse: "This God--His ways are perfect. The word of the LORD proves true." Psalm 18:30

Craft Description
Children will decorate a little "Bible" book that opens up to reveal the end of the Bible verse.

Supplies
White paper or cardstock
Bible inside and outside page
Crayons
If desired, use glitter and glue/glitter glue pens

Preparation
1. Print out onto the two sides of the Bible onto the back and front of one piece of paper.
2. Set out crayons. glitter and glue (or glitter glue pens).
3. Make an example of the craft for the children to see.

Directions
1. Show the children your example, telling them that they are making this so that can go and tell their parents and friends this week the Bible verse they are learning.
2. Have the children color in the words and pattern on the front cover of the Bible.
3. Have the children color in the word "True" and "Psalm 18:30" on the inside of the Bible. Or, they can use glitter to fill in all of the letters of the word. If working with youngest children, you might want to put the glue in the letter sections for them, then let them sprinkle the glitter on.
4. Allow card to dry before folding down middle.
5. Write child's name on card.

Practice Telling
Have the children practice telling the Bible verse by holding up their Bibles, front cover showing. Say the words to the verse together: Psalm 18:30 "This God--His ways are perfect. The word of the LORD proves..."

Then, on the word "true", have the children open up their Bibles to reveal the "true" as they say it and the Bible reference. You also can play the Big Question 2 Bible Verse songs and practice as you sing. This makes a fun listening and learning activity.

Holy Bible

"The word of the LORD proves ..."

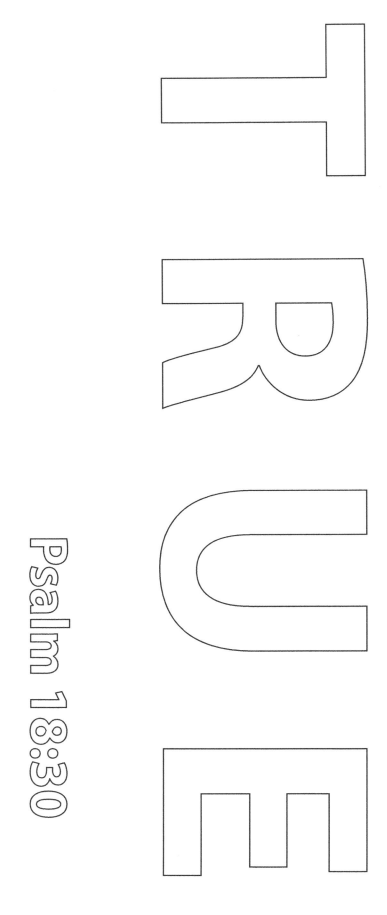

The Case of the Women's Best Gift   I Timothy Jigsaw Puzzle Page

Make copies of picture and cut out into an appropriate number of pieces for your children. Or, can print out color versions of this puzzle by downloading from praisefactorycurriculum.org

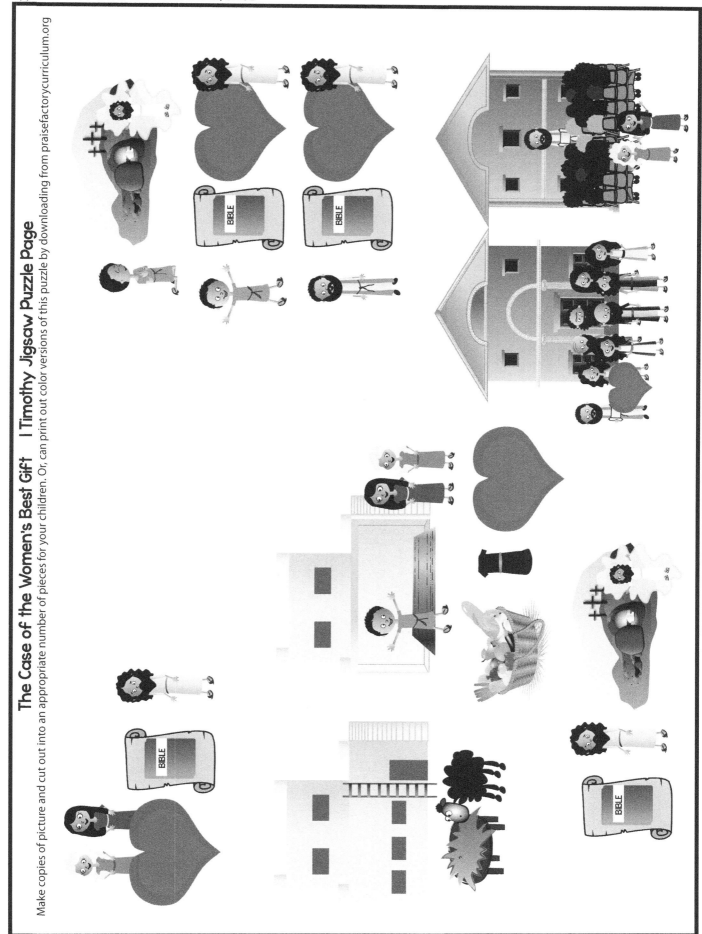

Hide 'n' Seek Kids

Unit 3 Take Home Resources
The Good News of God, the Gospel

What Is the Gospel?

ANSWER:

It's Salvation through Faith in Jesus!

Hide 'n' Seek Kids Sneaky Seekers
hiding God's Word in our hearts, seeking to know God Himself

Big Question 3, Lesson I Take Home Sheet

Big Question 3: What Is the Gospel?
>   **Answer:** It's Salvation through Faith in Jesus Christ!

Meaning:

Gospel means "good news." In the Bible, the gospel is the good news that God sent His Son, Jesus, to save sinners like you and me from the punishment we deserve for our sins. Jesus did this when He suffered and died on the cross, giving His perfect life as the full payment for our sins. This salvation is for all who turn away from their sins and trust in Jesus as their Savior. It is a gift God offers to us, too. Now that is good news, indeed!

How do I know this is true? The Bible tells me so:

"For God so loved the world, that he gave his only Son, that whoever believes in him should not perish but have eternal life." John 3:16, ESV

Some Questions for You

1. Can You Fix the Big Question and Answer?
What is the gospel? It's salvation through sneezes!
Answer: No! That's silly! What is the gospel? It's salvation through Jesus, God's Son!

2. Who can we ask to help us find salvation through Jesus? *God! He loves to help us when we ask Him.*

3. What does God tell us to do, if we want to be saved through Jesus? *We can ask God to help us to turn away from our sins and trust in Jesus as our Savior. It is His free gift to us!*

Let's Pray!

A   We praise You, God. You love us so much! You, Yourself, have chosen to send a Savior to save us!

C   God, in our heart, we know that You are God and that we should obey You, but many times we don't. We are all sinners who deserve Your punishment for disobeying You. Oh, how we need a Savior!

T   Thank You for sending Your dear Son, Jesus to be that Savior. Thank You for making the way for our sins to be forgiven.

S   Work deep inside our hearts. Help us to turn away from our sins and trust in Jesus as our Savior. Help us to know You and live for You. Help us to go and tell others the good news of the gospel, too. In Jesus' name we pray. In Jesus' name we pray. Amen.

Let's Sing Our Big Question and Answer!

Big Q & A 3 Song   *from Hide 'n' Seek Kids ESV Songs 3, track 12*

What's the gospel?
What's the gospel?
Can you tell me what it is?
It's salvation through faith in Jesus,
That's what the gospel is. (repeat)

Song Question: What's the Gospel?
>   **Answer:** *It's salvation through faith in Jesus.*

Go to the Hide 'n' Seek Kids Parent Resources for Unit 3 to get the Bible story and many more resources and songs for this unit at praisefactory.org

"For God so loved the world, that he gave his only Son, that whoever believes in him should not perish but have eternal life." John 3:16, ESV

Hide 'n' Seek Kids Sneaky Seekers
hiding God's Word in our hearts, seeking to know God Himself

Big Question 3, Lesson 2 Take Home Sheet

Big Question 3: What Is the Gospel?
    Answer: It's Salvation through Faith in Jesus Christ!

How do I know this is true? The Bible tells me so:

"For God so loved the world, that he gave his only Son, that whoever believes in him should not perish but have eternal life." John 3:16, ESV

Meaning:

How great is God's love for sinners like you and me, that He would send His own Son, Jesus, to suffer and die for us! Now, all who turn from their sins and trust in Jesus as their Savior will not perish. They will not receive the punishment they deserve for their sins. Jesus has already paid for their sins when He died on the cross. Because of what Jesus has done for them, these people will enjoy eternal life with God. Here on earth, they will know God in their hearts and His care in their lives. And when they die, they will go to be with Him forever! God offers us eternal life, too, when we turn away from our sins and trust in Jesus as our Savior.

Some Questions for You

1. What's the missing word to the Bible verse?
"For God so loved the world, that he gave his only Son, that whoever believes in him should not perish but have eternal _____ "
Answer: life.

2. Who did God give so that we might have eternal life? *Jesus!*

Let's Pray!

A   We praise You, God. You love us so much! You, Yourself, have chosen to send a Savior to save us!

C   God, in our heart, we know that You are God and that we should obey You, but many times we don't. We are all sinners who deserve Your punishment for disobeying You. Oh, how we need a Savior!

T   Thank You for sending Your dear Son, Jesus to be that Savior. Thank You for making the way for our sins to be forgiven.

S   Work deep inside our hearts. Help us to turn away from our sins and trust in Jesus as our Savior. Help us to know You and live for You. Help us to go and tell others the good news of the gospel, too. In Jesus' name we pray. In Jesus' name we pray. Amen.

Let's Sing Our Bible Verse!

Big Question 3 Bible Verse Song *from Hide 'n' Seek Kids ESV Songs 3, track 14,14T*

For God So Loved the World: John 3:16

For God so loved the world,
That He gave His only Son,
That whoever believes in Him shouldn't perish,
But have eternal life. (refrain)
John Three, sixteen.

Song Question: How does God give us eternal life? *Through Faith in Jesus Christ! That's the gospel!*

Go to the Hide 'n' Seek Kids Parent Resources for Unit 3 to get the Bible story and many more resources for this unit at www.praisefactory.org

Which of these three things did God use to spread the good news of Jesus?
Put an "X" in the box next to each of these.

☐ **Enemies**

☐ **Some Bags**

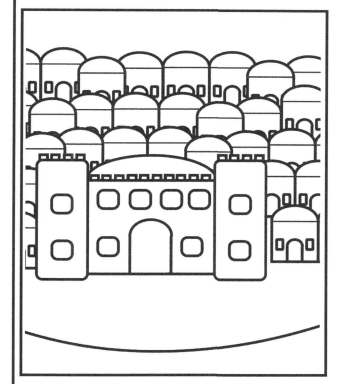

☐ **A New Country**

☐ **A Horse**

Answers: The horse was not in the story. The Christians packed their bags and left Jerusalem to get away from their enemies who wanted to hurt them. They went to live in many places, even other countries, and told the people there the good news of Jesus.

HSK BQ 3 L3 Coloring Sheet/Take Home pg.1

Hide 'n' Seek Kids Sneaky Seekers
hiding God's Word in our hearts, seeking to know God Himself

Big Question 3, Lesson 3 Take Home Sheet

Big Question 3: What Is the Gospel?
Answer: It's Salvation through Faith in Jesus Christ!

Meaning:

Gospel means "good news." In the Bible, the gospel is the good news that God sent His Son, Jesus, to save sinners like you and me from the punishment we deserve for our sins. Jesus did this when He suffered and died on the cross, giving His perfect life as the full payment for our sins. This salvation is for all who turn away from their sins and trust in Jesus as their Savior. It is a gift God offers to us, too. Now that is good news, indeed!

How do I know this is true? The Bible tells me so:

"For God so loved the world, that he gave his only Son, that whoever believes in him should not perish but have eternal life." John 3:16

Some Questions for You

1. Which of the three pictures belong in the story and which one does not? *The horse does not belong.*
2. How did God use the other three things to spread the good news of Jesus? *The Christians packed their bags and left Jerusalem to get away from their enemies who wanted to hurt them. They went to live in many places, even other countries, and told the people there the good news of Jesus.*
3. What was the good news that Philip and the others told? *God will forgive our sins when we turn away from our sins and trust in Jesus as our Savior.*
4. Who can help us believe the good news of Jesus? *God can! He loves to help us when we ask Him.*

Let's Pray!

A We praise You, God. You love us so much! You, Yourself, have chosen to send a Savior to save us!

C God, in our heart, we know that You are God and that we should obey You, but many times we don't. We are all sinners who deserve Your punishment for disobeying You. Oh, how we need a Savior!

T Thank You for sending Your dear Son, Jesus to be that Savior. Thank You for making the way for our sins to be forgiven.

S Work deep inside our hearts. Help us to turn away from our sins and trust in Jesus as our Savior. Help us to know You and live for You. Help us to go and tell others the good news of the gospel, too. In Jesus' name we pray. In Jesus' name we pray. Amen.

Let's Sing about Our Big Question and Answer!

Big Question 3 (Action Rhyme) Song *from Hide 'n' Seek Kids ESV Songs 3, track 13*

Refrain:
What is the gospel?   *Make question gesture with*
G-O-S-P-E-L?   *your arms (arms bent and palms*
What is the gospel?   *facing upward)*
Can anybody tell me?
What is the gospel?
Yes, I know what it is!
Salvation through faith in Christ,
That's what the gospel is.

Verse 1
"G" is for God, our good King and Creator,   *Make the letters*
O, we should obey Him,   *with your fingers!*
   but instead we're disobeyers,
So S, we need a Savior to save us from our sins,
That Savior is Jesus, who "P" took the punishment.

Verse 2
Yes, Jesus died upon the cross,   *Make a cross shape*
   the perfect sacrifice,   *with your fingers*
Then on day three, He rose again
To prove He'd won the fight,

Verse 3
And now "E" everyone who repents   *Make the letters*
   and believes in Him,   *with your fingers!*
He gives "E-L" eternal life:
   forever life with Him. Refrain

Song Question: What does each letter in the word GOSPEL stand for in our song? *G: God; O: Obey; S: Savior; P: Punishment and Perfect Sacrifice; E: Everyone; EL: Eternal Life.*

Go to the Hide 'n' Seek Kids Parent Resources for Unit 3 to get the Bible story and many more resources for this unit at www.praisefactory.org

HSK BQ3 L3 Coloring Sheet/Take Home pg.2

Forgive us, God!

Philip shared the good news of Jesus with the people of Samaria. Many people confessed their sins to God and asked God to forgive them...and He did! They trusted in Jesus as their Savior. How good God was to these people!

HSK BQ 3 L4 Coloring Sheet/Take Home pg.1

Hide 'n' Seek Kids Sneaky Seekers
hiding God's Word in our hearts, seeking to know God Himself

Big Question 3, Lesson 4 Take Home Sheet

Big Question 3: What Is the Gospel?
Answer: It's Salvation through Faith in Jesus Christ!

Meaning:

Gospel means "good news." In the Bible, the gospel is the good news that God sent His Son, Jesus, to save sinners like you and me from the punishment we deserve for our sins. Jesus did this when He suffered and died on the cross, giving His perfect life as the full payment for our sins. This salvation is for all who turn away from their sins and trust in Jesus as their Savior. It is a gift God offers to us, too. Now that is good news, indeed!

How do I know this is true? The Bible tells me so:

"For God so loved the world, that he gave his only Son, that whoever believes in him should not perish but have eternal life." John 3:16, ESV

Some Questions for You

1. What's something we can confess to God? *Our sins--the ways that we have each chosen to disobey Him.*
2. What does God promise to do when we turn away from our sins and trust in Jesus as our Savior? *To forgive our sins and make us His people forever!*
3. Who can help us do this? *God can! He loves to answers this prayer!*

Let's Pray!

A We praise You, God. You love us so much! You, Yourself, have chosen to send a Savior to save us!

C God, in our heart, we know that You are God and that we should obey You, but many times we don't. We are all sinners who deserve Your punishment for disobeying You. Oh, how we need a Savior!

T Thank You for sending Your dear Son, Jesus to be that Savior. Thank You for making the way for our sins to be forgiven.

S Work deep inside our hearts. Help us to turn away from our sins and trust in Jesus as our Savior. Help us to know You and live for You. Help us to go and tell others the good news of the gospel, too. In Jesus' name we pray. In Jesus' name we pray. Amen.

Let's Praise God Right Now!

Big Question 3 Hymn: And Can It Be *from Hide 'n' Seek Kids ESV Songs 3, track 17*

Refrain
Amazing love, how can it be?
That thou, my God, should die for me?
Amazing love, how can it be?
That thou, my God, should die for me?

Words: John Wesley   Music: Thomas Campbell

Song Question: What's something we can praise God for? *For His love! God's love is amazing! How He has loved sinners, like you and me! We all deserve God's full punishment for our sins. We all deserve to die and be separated from God forever. But Jesus came to die for the sins of all who would ever turn from their sins and trust in Him as their Savior. He died in their place. He took their sins. So that they could be forgiven and live as God's people forever. When we turn from our sins and trust in Jesus as our Savior, then His death pays for our sins, too. We, too, can know God now in our hearts, and one day, go to live with Him forever.*

Go to the Hide 'n' Seek Kids Parent Resources for Unit 3 to get the Bible story and many more resources for this unit at www.praisefactory.org

It seemed like nothing but bad news, when Philip and the others had to leave Jerusalem to escape from their enemies. But the Lord used it for good! Philip and the other Christians shared the good news of Jesus with everyone they met. Many turned from their sins and trusted in Jesus as their Savior. God is always up to good!

Hide 'n' Seek Kids Sneaky Seekers
hiding God's Word in our hearts, seeking to know God Himself

Big Question 3, Lesson 5 Take Home Sheet

Big Question 3: What Is the Gospel?
    Answer: It's Salvation through Faith in Jesus Christ!

Meaning:

Gospel means "good news." In the Bible, the gospel is the good news that God sent His Son, Jesus, to save sinners like you and me from the punishment we deserve for our sins. Jesus did this when He suffered and died on the cross, giving His perfect life as the full payment for our sins. This salvation is for all who turn away from their sins and trust in Jesus as their Savior. It is a gift God offers to us, too. Now that is good news, indeed!

How do I know this is true? The Bible tells me so:

"For God so loved the world, that he gave his only Son, that whoever believes in him should not perish but have eternal life." John 3:16, ESV

Some Questions for You

1. **Why was it bad news that the Christians had to leave Jerusalem?** *They had to leave their homes and their friends.*
2. **What good news did they share with people as they ran away to live in new places?** *They told them that they can become God's people when they turn away from their sins and trust in Jesus as their Savior.*
3. **Can Jesus be our Savior? How?** *Yes! Jesus came to save all who turn away from their sins and trust in Him as their Savior. If we do this, Jesus will save us, too. We can know the happiness of knowing God in our heart even today. And one day, He will take us to live with Him in heaven forever. That will be happiest of all!*

Let's Pray!

A We praise You, God. You love us so much! You, Yourself, have chosen to send a Savior to save us!

C God, in our heart, we know that You are God and that we should obey You, but many times we don't. We are all sinners who deserve Your punishment for disobeying You. Oh, how we need a Savior!

T Thank You for sending Your dear Son, Jesus to be that Savior. Thank You for making the way for our sins to be forgiven.

S Work deep inside our hearts. Help us to turn away from our sins and trust in Jesus as our Savior. Help us to know You and live for You. Help us to go and tell others the good news of the gospel, too. In Jesus' name we pray. In Jesus' name we pray. Amen.

Let's Praise God Right Now!

Big Question 3 Praise Song: I Have Decided to Follow Jesus *from Hide 'n' Seek Kids ESV Songs 3, track 18*

I have decided to follow Jesus,
I have decided to follow Jesus,
I have decided to follow Jesus,
No turning back, no turning back.

Song Questions:

1. **What do God's people praise Him for, when they decide to follow Jesus?** *For working in their hearts and helping them to do this. They are so grateful!*
2. **When we decide to follow Jesus, what does God want us to turn away from, and never turn back to?** *God wants us to turn away from living our life our own way. He wants us to turn away from sinning and be His people who love and obey Him. That's what it means to follow Jesus! God will help us do this, if we ask Him.*

Go to the Hide 'n' Seek Kids Parent Resources for Unit 3 to get the Bible story and many more resources for this unit at www.praisefactory.org

Hide 'n' Seek Kids Sneaky Seekers
hiding God's Word in our hearts, seeking to know God Himself

BIG QUESTION 3 BIBLE STORY & KEY CONCEPTS

Dear Parents,

Big Question #3 is: "What Is the Gospel? It's Salvation through Faith in Jesus Christ!"

Here's a copy of the Bible story they are learning along with the "Listening Assignment" for each lesson. These assignments provide a different teaching emphasis for each lesson, helping the children dig deeper into each Bible truth. They match up with your child's take home for each lesson. We hope that these resources help your family to further "Hide God's Word in your heart and SEEK to know God, Himself!" Happy hiding and seeking!

•many more resources for this Big Question came be found online at www.praisefactory.org•

Listening Assignments for Big Question 3 Bible Story:
"The Case of the Stranger's Very Good News"
Acts 8:1-8

NOTE: These questions are most suitable for older preschoolers and up.

Detective Dan's Lesson #1 Listening Assignment:

As you listen to the story, see if you can figure out:
1. Who ran away from Jerusalem went to Samaria?
2. What was the good news he brought with him and shared?

Detective Dan's Lesson #2 Listening Assignment:

Our Bible verse is John 3:16: "For God so loved the world, that he gave his only Son, that whoever believes in him should not perish but have eternal life."

As you listen to the story, see if you can figure out:
1. Who did God use to tell the world the good news about His Son, Jesus?
2. What happened when they shared the good news?

Detective Dan's Lesson #3 Listening Assignment:

I found four clues, but one of them is NOT in the story.
They are: Some enemies; some bags; some sick people; and a horse.
Hold up each of the four pictures for the children to see as you identify them. Better yet, put them up on your flannelgraph board, off to one side.

I need to know:
1. Which three pictures belong in the story and which one does not?
2. How did God use the other three things to spread the good news of Jesus?

Detective Dan's Lesson #4 Listening Assignment:

As you listen to the story, see if you can figure out:
1. Philip told the good news of Jesus to the people of what city?
2. What did they confess to God when they heard the gospel?

Detective Dan's Lesson #5 Listening Assignment:

As you listen to the story, see if you can figure out:
1. Why was it bad news that the Christians had to leave Jerusalem?
2. What good news did they share with people as they ran away to live in new places?

Read the questions, then say,

"Ok, Hide 'n' Seekers! Put on your best listening ears and see if you can find the answers these questions. When I finish reading the story, we will see if we can answer all the questions."

| Big Question 3 Bible Story | use with all FIVE lessons | p.2 |

"The Case of the Stranger's Very Good News"   Acts 8:1-8

*Story with lines separating paragraphs (**text in bold,** optional interaction cues in italics)*

"Run! Pack your bags! Get out of town!" The church leaders told the other Christians. "Jerusalem isn't safe anymore! The enemies of Jesus are after you! They will hurt you and put you in jail if they catch you!" the leaders warned. "So get out of town...NOW!"

How fast would you run if you had enemies trying to get you? Run in place and show me!

That's exactly what most of the Christians did. They packed their bags and ran, ran, ran out of town!

Oh, what bad news this was! Or was it? Yes, it was BAD news that these Christians had to leave their homes and their friends and everything they knew in Jerusalem. And, it was BAD news that they had enemies who wanted to hurt them. But.... it was GOOD news for the people of the world.

Why? Because when those Christians ran away, they took the gospel with them--that wonderful, marvelous, amazing good news about Jesus--and they shared it with everyone they met.

Some of the Christians went down the sea and made their home there. And what good news did they tell the people they met there? The gospel--the good news of Jesus!

Some went out to dry, deserty lands and made their home there. And what did they tell the people they met there? The gospel--the good news of Jesus!

Some went up to the tall mountains and made their home there.

Can you pretend to climb up a mountain...carrying your bags with you???

And what did they tell the people they met there? The gospel--the good news of Jesus!

Some even went far away to other countries. One of these people was a godly man named Philip. Philip went to the land of Samaria to live. And what did he tell the people he met there?

Can you tell me...the good news of who? Jesus!

You guessed it! The gospel--the good news of Jesus!

As Philip told the good news of Jesus, crowds of people gathered around and listened. There were poor people and rich people; sick people and well people; old people and young people. And to all of these people, Philip told the gospel, good news of Jesus. This is what he told them:

"God is the good King and Creator of the whole world. He created us and we should obey Him. But instead, we've all chosen to disobey Him. Disobeying God is what God calls "sin"; and, we deserve His punishment for our sins against Him. We need a Savior!" Philip told them.

"God sent Jesus to be that Savior. Jesus is God's perfect Son who came to earth to suffer and die on the cross to pay for our sins. Then, on the third day, Jesus rose from the dead, showing that He had beaten sin and death," Philip shared.

Big Question 3 Bible Story	use with all FIVE lessons	p.3

Story with lines separating paragraphs (text in bold, optional interaction cues in italics)

"Now, everyone who turns away from sinning and trusts in Jesus as their Savior will be saved. God makes them His people. And they will get to know God and live with Him forever! This is the gospel—God's good news to you. Come, turn from your sins and trust in Jesus as your Savior today!" Philip told them.

Have you heard this good news before? It is very good news, isn't it?

"What amazing things this stranger is saying," the Samaritans thought! "We haven't heard anything like this before. Could it really be true?" they wondered.

Then God did something marvelous to help them know this good news really was true. Philip prayed for God to heal the sick people listening to him preach. And right then and there, without any medicine, or doctor, or hospital, God made them well. By His great power alone!

The people of Samaria were even more amazed! God Holy Spirit worked in the hearts of many people as they heard the good news of Jesus and saw God's mighty power to heal the sick. "Surely this good news is true!" they exclaimed. They turned away from their sins and trusted in Jesus as their Savior. They were saved from their sins! God had made them His people!

Let's clap our hands and say, "Yay" for the good things God did in those people!

So, yes, maybe it had been bad news that made Philip run away from Jerusalem. But God had turned that bad news into good news for the people of Samaria. And that made Philip --and them --very, very happy!

Big Question 3 Bible Story
use with all FIVE lessons

Cracking the Case: (story wrap-up for Listening Assignments)

It's time to see how we did with our Listening Assignment.

Detective Dan's Lesson #1 Listening Assignment:
As you listen to the story, see if you can figure out:
1. Who ran away from Jerusalem and went to Samaria? Philip.
2. What was the good news he brought with him and shared? God forgives our sins and makes us His people when we turn away from our sins and trust in Jesus as our Savior..

For You and Me:
The good news Philip shared wasn't just for the people of Samaria. It's for us, too! God will forgive our sins and make us His people when we turn away from our sins and trust in Jesus as our Savior.. God will help us do this, if we ask Him to. What good news that is!

Detective Dan's Lesson #2 Listening Assignment:
Our Bible verse is John 3:16: "For God so loved the world, that he gave his only Son, that whoever believes in him should not perish but have eternal life."

As you listen to the story, see if you can figure out:
1. Who did God use to tell the world the good news about His Son, Jesus? His people--Philip and the other Christians.
2. What happened when they shared the good news? God worked in the hearts of many. They turned from their sins and trusted in Jesus as their Savior.

For You and Me:
God still uses His people today to tell others the good news about His Son, Jesus. God has even used them to tell us the good news of Jesus today! We can ask God to work in our hearts and help us to believe the good news of Jesus. We can ask Him to help us to turn away from our sins and trust in Jesus as our Savior.

Detective Dan's Lesson #3 Listening Assignment:
I found four clues, but one of them is NOT in the story. They are: Some enemies; some bags; another country; and a horse.

1. Which of the three pictures belong in the story and which one does not? The horse does not belong.
2. How did God use the other three things to spread the good news of Jesus? The Christians packed their bags and left Jerusalem to get away from their enemies who wanted to hurt them. They went to live in many places, even other countries, and told the people there the good news of Jesus.

For You and Me:
God has a wonderful plan to tell the whole world the good news of Jesus. He wants everyone to know how their sins can be forgiven and they can become one of His people. And God will use everything as part of this great plan--even very sad things like those believers having to leave them homes. How great is our God! How good and great are His plans!

Detective Dan's Lesson #4 Listening Assignment:
As you listen to the story, see if you can figure out:
1. Philip told the good news of Jesus to the people of what city? The city of Samaria.
2. What did many people confess to God when they heard the gospel? They confessed their sins and asked God to forgive their sins....and He did!

For You and Me:
Like the people of Samaria, we are sinners who need to confess our sins to God. Like them, we can ask Him to forgive our sins... and He can!

Detective Dan's Lesson #5 Listening Assignment:
As you listen to the story, see if you can figure out:
1. Why was it bad news that the Christians had to leave Jerusalem? They had to leave their homes and their friends.
2. What good news did they share with people as they ran away to live in new places? They told them the gospel--how they could become God's people by turning away from their sins and trusting in Jesus as their Savior.

For You and Me:
This good news is for us, too. Jesus can save us from our sins and make us God's people, too, when we repent of our sins and trust in Him as our Savior.

Big Question 3 Bible Story   use with all FIVE lessons   p.5

The Gospel (story wrap-up if NOT using Listening Assignments)

Our Bible Truth is:
What Is the Gospel?
It's Salvation through Faith in Jesus Christ!

Philip was so happy when the people of Samaria heard the good news of Jesus and believed. That good news is for us, too! We can ask God to work in our heart and help us to turn away from disobeying Him and trust in Jesus as our Savior. When we do, God will forgive our sins and save us! He will live in our heart, helping us to know Him right now. And one day, we will go to live with Him in heaven forever. That will be best of all!

Close in prayer.

Closing Unit 3 ACTS Prayer

A=Adoration   C=Confession   T=Thanksgiving   S=Supplication

A   We praise You, God. You love us so much! You, Yourself, have chosen to send a Savior to save us!

C   God, in our heart, we know that You are God and that we should obey You, but many times we don't. We are all sinners who deserve Your punishment for disobeying You. Oh, how we need a Savior!

T   Thank You for sending Your dear Son, Jesus to be that Savior. Thank You for making the way for our sins to be forgiven.

S   Work deep inside our hearts. Help us to turn away from our sins and trust in Jesus as our Savior. Help us to know You and live for You. Help us to go and tell others the good news of the gospel, too. In Jesus' name we pray.

    In Jesus' name we pray. Amen.

Big Question 3 Bible Story

HSK Sneaky Seekers: Big Question 3 Key Concepts   p.6

UNIT 3: The Good News of God, the Gospel

Unit Big Question (and Answer): "What's the Gospel? It's Salvation through Faith in Jesus Christ!"

Meaning:

Gospel means "good news." In the Bible, the gospel is the good news that God sent His Son, Jesus, to save sinners like you and me from the punishment we deserve for our sins. Jesus did this when He suffered and died on the cross, giving His perfect life as the full payment for our sins. This salvation is for all who turn away from their sins and trust in Jesus as their Savior. It is a gift God offers to us, too. Now that is good news, indeed!

Unit 3 Bible Verse: John 3:16

"For God so loved the world, that he gave his only Son, that whoever believes in him should not perish but have eternal life."

Meaning:

How great is God's love for sinners like you and me, that He would send His own Son, Jesus, to suffer and die for us! Now, all who turn from their sins and trust in Jesus as their Savior will not perish. They will not receive the punishment they deserve for their sins. Jesus has already paid for their sins when He died on the cross. Because of what Jesus has done for them, these people will enjoy eternal life with God. Here on earth, they will know God in their hearts and His care in their lives. And when they die, they will go to be with Him forever! God offers us eternal life, too, when we turn away from our sins and trust in Jesus as our Savior.

Unit 3 ACTS Prayer

A   We praise You, God. You love us so much! You, Yourself, have chosen to send a Savior to save us!

C   God, in our heart, we know that You are God and that we should obey You, but many times we don't. We are all sinners who deserve Your punishment for disobeying You. Oh, how we need a Savior!

T   Thank You for sending Your dear Son, Jesus to be that Savior. Thank You for making the way for our sins to be forgiven.

S   Work deep inside our hearts. Help us to turn away from our sins and trust in Jesus as our Savior. Help us to know You and live for You. Help us to go and tell others the good news of the gospel, too.

In Jesus' name we pray. Amen.

Unit 3 Story

The Case of the Stranger's Very Good News
Acts 8:1-8

Songs Used in Unit 3   *listen to or download songs for free at https://praisefactory.org: Hide n Seek Kids Music page*

Big Q & A 3 Song
Big Question 3 Song: What's the Gospel?
Big Question 3 Bible Verse Song: For God So Loved the World   John 3:16 ESV
Extra Unit 3 Bible Verse Song: For God So Loved the World John 3:16 ESV (other version)
Extra Unit 3 Bible Verse Song: For God So Loved the World John 3:16 ESV (other version)
Unit 3 Hymn: And Can It Be, v.1 Refrain
Unit 3 Praise Song: I Have Decided to Follow Jesus

Unit 3 Big Question and Answer Extra Craft

Coloring, Gluing and Sticking Activity

Craft Description
Children will color and decorate the number associated with the Big Question they are learning.

Supplies
White paper (cardstock is best)
Crayons, colored pencils, markers
Glue sticks
Small decorating items, such as glitter glue, colored paper dots (made with a hole punch), small fabric scraps, pom poms, sequins, small tissue or foil pieces, etc.

Preparation
1. Print out copies of the Big Question and Answer and the Number onto separate sheets of paper.
2. Cut out the circle around the number.
3. Set out coloring and decorating supplies.
4. Make an example of each card to show the children.

Directions
1. Show the children your example, telling them they are decorating and practicing the Big Question and Answer to go and tell their families and friends.
2. Have children first color their Big Question and Answer sheets,
3. Then have them use the additional decorating suppiles to fill in the space around their number.
4. Glue the number in place.
5. Write child's name on card.
6. Allow cards to dry.

If you don't want to use the extra decorating supplies, just have the children coloring in their numbers and glue them in place on their Big Question and Answer sheet.

Practice Telling
Have the children practice holding up the Big Question and saying it. You can have fun with this by having the children mimic when you raise it up, how you say it, etc. a sort of Simon Says element.

What Is the Gospel?

It's Salvation through Faith in Jesus!

Unit 3 Bible Verse Extra Craft: John 3:16

Heart Sticker Card

Bible Verse: "For God so loved the world, that he gave his only Son, that whoever believes in him should not perish but have eternal life." John 3:16

Craft Description
Children will decorate the Bible verse with hearts they glue in place.

Supplies
White paper or cardstock
Heart Pattern (or purchase heart stickers)
Red Construction paper
Glue
Scissors

Preparation
1. Print out onto the paper the Bible verse card.
2. Print out the heart pattern and cut 6 hearts out of red construction paper per child (or purchase heart stickers).
3. Set out glue.
4. Make an example of the craft for the children to see.

Directions
1. Show the children your example, telling them that they are making this so that can go and tell their parents and friends this week the Bible verse they are learning.
2. Have the children glue the hearts in place on card/stick the purchased stickers on the card.
3. Write child's name on card.

Practice Telling
Have the children practice telling the Bible verse by holding up the Bible verse card and saying the verse: "For God so loved the world, that he gave his only Son, that whoever believes in him should not perish but have eternal life." John 3:16. You also can play the Big Question 3 Bible Verse songs and practice as you sing.

"For God so loved the world, that he gave his only Son, that whoever believes in him should not perish but have eternal life." John 3:16

Heart Pattern

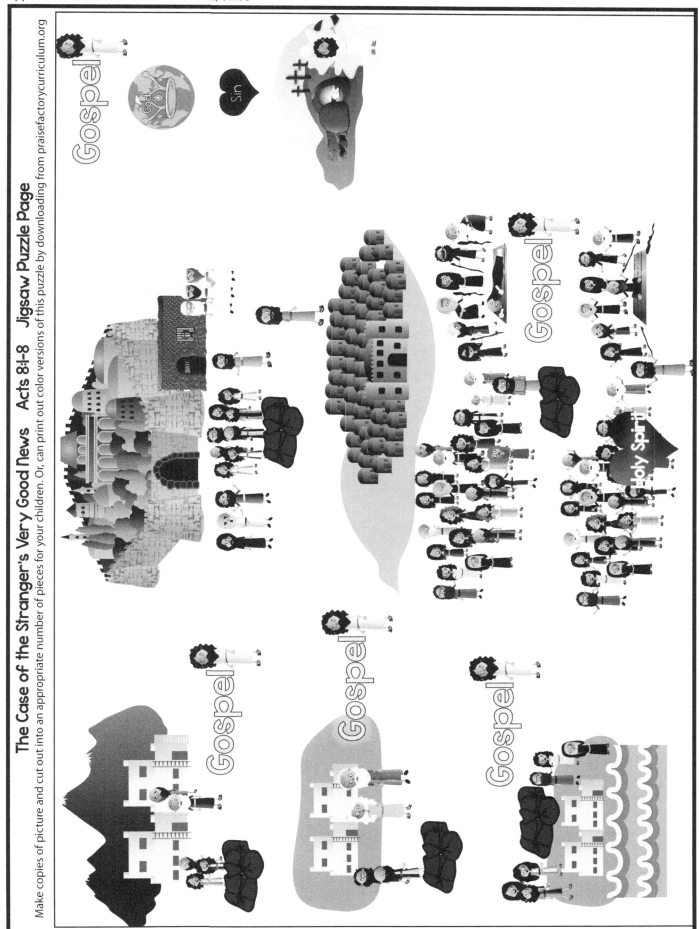

Hide 'n' Seek Kids

Unit 4 Take Home Resources
The God Like None Other

Can Anybody Tell Me What the LORD Is Like?

ANSWER:

He's Not Like Anyone Else!

Hide 'n' Seek Kids Sneaky Seekers
hiding God's Word in our hearts, seeking to know God Himself

Big Question 4, Lesson I Take Home Sheet

Big Question 4: Can Anybody Tell Me What the LORD Is Like?
    Answer: He's Not Like Anyone Else!

Meaning:

There are many gods that people worship, but none is like the LORD. He is the one, true God. He's not like anyone else! He's always been alive--and He will never die. He's completely good and loving. He's all-powerful and all-wise. And that's just the beginning of what the LORD is like. He is so great! There will always be more of Him to know.

How do I know this is true? The Bible tells me so:

"O LORD...there is no God like you, in heaven above or on earth beneath."

Some Questions for You

1. Can You Fix the Big Question and Answer?
Can Anybody Tell Me What the LORD Is Like? He's Just Like Everyone Else!
No. That's not right! Answer: Can Anybody Tell Me What the LORD Is Like? He's NOT Like ANYONE Else!

2. Who can help us know what the LORD is like? *The Bible, God's people and the LORD, Himself!*

3. What is the best first step we can ask God to do to help us know what He's like? *We can ask God to show us what He's like. We can ask Him to work in our heart, that we would turn away from our sins and trust in Jesus as our Savior. He delights to do these things!*

Let's Pray!

A   We praise You, God. You are the one, true God in heaven above and here on earth.

C   God, in our heart, we know that You are God and that we should obey You, but many times we don't want to. Please forgive us. We need a Savior!

T   Thank You for not just being good and great, but being so good and so great to people like us! Thank You for caring about us so much and for wanting us to know You. And thank You so much for sending Jesus to be our Savior.

S   Work deep inside our hearts. Help us to turn away from our sins and trust in Jesus as our Savior. Help us to know You and live for You. Help us to go and tell others what we've learned about You, the one, true God. In Jesus' name we pray. Amen.

Let's Sing Our Big Question and Answer!

Big Q & A 4 Song *from Hide 'n' Seek Kids ESV Songs 4, track 12*

Can anybody tell me,
Tell me, tell me,
Can anybody tell me,
What the LORD is like?
He's not like anyone else,
Anyone else, anyone else,
He's not like anyone else,
That's what the LORD is like.

Song Question: Can anybody tell me what the LORD is like?
    Answer: *He's not like anyone else!*

Go to the Hide 'n' Seek Kids Parent Resources for Unit 4 to get the Bible story and many more resources and songs for this unit at praisefactory.org
HSK BQ4 L1 Coloring Sheet/Take Home pg.2

"O LORD...there is no God like you....

in heaven above....

or on earth beneath." 1 Kings 8:23

Hide 'n' Seek Kids Sneaky Seekers
hiding God's Word in our hearts, seeking to know God Himself

Big Question 4, Lesson 2 Take Home Sheet

Big Question 4: Can Anybody Tell Me What the LORD Is Like?
Answer: He's Not Like Anyone Else!

How do I know this is true? The Bible tells me so:

"O LORD...there is no God like you, in heaven above or on earth beneath."

Meaning:

There are many gods that people worship, but none is like the LORD. He is the one, true God. He's not like anyone else! He's always been alive--and He will never die. He's completely good and loving. He's all-powerful and all-wise. And that's just the beginning of what the LORD is like. He is so great! There will always be more of Him to know.

Some Questions for You

1. What's the missing word to the Bible verse?
"O LORD...there is ___ God like you, in heaven above or on earth beneath."
Answer: No

2. Where is there no God like the LORD? *Not in heaven above or on earth beneath...No WHERE is there a God like Him!*

Let's Pray!

A   We praise You, God. You are the one, true God in heaven above and here on earth.

C   God, in our heart, we know that You are God and that we should obey You, but many times we don't want to. Please forgive us. We need a Savior!

T   Thank You for not just being good and great, but being so good and so great to people like us! Thank You for caring about us so much and for wanting us to know You. And thank You so much for sending Jesus to be our Savior.

S   Work deep inside our hearts. Help us to turn away from our sins and trust in Jesus as our Savior. Help us to know You and live for You. Help us to go and tell others what we've learned about You, the one, true God. In Jesus' name we pray. Amen.

Let's Sing Our Bible Verse!

Big Question 4 Bible Verse Song *from Hide 'n' Seek Kids ESV Songs 3, tracks 15, 15T*

O, O, LORD, there is no, no God like You,
O, O, LORD, there is no God like You.
O, O, LORD, there is no, no God like You,
First Kings Eight, twenty-three.

Song Question: How many gods are there like the LORD? *None! There is no God like the LORD!*

Go to the Hide 'n' Seek Kids Parent Resources for Unit 4 to get the Bible story and many more resources and songs for this unit at praisefactory.org

Which three things did God use to show He was the one, true God? Put an "X" in the box next to each of these. How did the LORD use these things to show He was the one, true God?

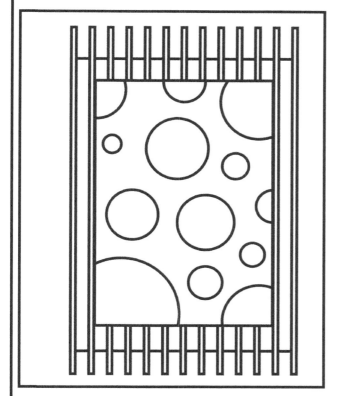

☐ **Rug**

☐ **A Frog**

☐ **A King (Pharaoh)**

☐ **Moses**

Answers: 1. The rug was not in the story. 2. Moses spoke God's words to the king, but the king refused to let the people go or admit that the LORD was God. The LORD used His mighty power and sent lots of frogs and many other things the king did not like until he admitted that the LORD really was the one, true God.

Hide 'n' Seek Kids Sneaky Seekers
hiding God's Word in our hearts, seeking to know God Himself

Big Question 4, Lesson 3 Take Home Sheet

Big Question 4: Can Anybody Tell Me What the LORD Is Like?
Answer: He's Not Like Anyone Else!

Meaning:

There are many gods that people worship, but none is like the LORD. He is the one, true God. He's not like anyone else! He's always been alive--and He will never die. He's completely good and loving. He's all-powerful and all-wise. And that's just the beginning of what the LORD is like. He is so great! There will always be more of Him to know.

How do I know this is true? The Bible tells me so:

"O LORD...there is no God like you, in heaven above or on earth beneath."

Some Questions for You

1. How did the LORD use Moses, frogs and the king to show He was the one, true God? *Moses spoke God's words to the king, but the king refused to let the people go or admit that the LORD was God. The LORD used His mighty power and sent lots of frogs and many other things the king did not like until he admitted that the LORD really was the one, true God.*
3. Who can help me know the LORD? *The Bible, God's people and the LORD, Himself can!*
4. What can I do to know the LORD better? *I can ask Him to work in my heart. I can ask God's people to help me know more about Him. I can listen to the Bible and learn about Jesus. I can turn away from my sins and trust in Jesus as my Savior.*

Let's Pray!

A We praise You, God. You are the one, true God in heaven above and here on earth.

C God, in our heart, we know that You are God and that we should obey You, but many times we don't want to. Please forgive us. We need a Savior!

T Thank You for not just being good and great, but being so good and so great to people like us! Thank You for caring about us so much and for wanting us to know You. And thank You so much for sending Jesus to be our Savior.

S Work deep inside our hearts. Help us to turn away from our sins and trust in Jesus as our Savior. Help us to know You and live for You. Help us to go and tell others what we've learned about You, the one, true God. In Jesus' name we pray. Amen.

Let's Sing about Our Big Question and Answer!

Big Question 4 (Action Rhyme) Song *from Hide 'n' Seek Kids ESV Songs 4, track 13*

Refrain:
Tell me, can anybody tell me,
Tell me, what the LORD is like?
Tell me, can anybody tell me,
Tell me, what the LORD is like?
He's not like anyone else,   *Shake head "no"*
He's not like anyone else,
He's not like anyone else,
He's not like anyone else,

Verse 1
He's Omniscient! *(He knows all things)*   *Touch head*
Omnipresent! *(He's everywhere you can be)*
Omni-benevolent! *(He's always good!)*
and Omnipotent! *(He can do all things!) Refrain*   *Flex arm*

Verse 2
He's Immutable! *(He never changes!)*   *Shake head "no"*
He's Infallible! *(He makes no mistakes!)*
He's Infinite! *(There's always more of Him to know!)*
And purely Righteous!

Song Question: What are four, big words about the LORD that start with an "O" in the song?
Answer: Omniscient; Omnipresent; Omni-benevolent; and Omnipotent.

Go to the Hide 'n' Seek Kids Parent Resources for Unit 4 to get the Bible story and many more resources and songs for this unit at praisefactory.org

HSK BQ4 L3 Coloring Sheet/Take Home pg.2

Help Us, O LORD!

God's people cried out to God to rescue them from the mighty, mean king. The LORD answered their prayers and saved them....and He did it in a way to show everyone that He is the one, true God. There is no one like Him!

HSK BQ 4 L4 Coloring Sheet/Take Home pg.1

Hide 'n' Seek Kids Sneaky Seekers
hiding God's Word in our hearts, seeking to know God Himself

Big Question 4 Lesson 4 Take Home Sheet

Big Question 4: Can Anybody Tell Me What the LORD Is Like?
Answer: He's Not Like Anyone Else!

Meaning:

There are many gods that people worship, but none is like the LORD. He is the one, true God. He's not like anyone else! He's always been alive--and He will never die. He's completely good and loving. He's all-powerful and all-wise. And that's just the beginning of what the LORD is like. He is so great! There will always be more of Him to know.

How do I know this is true? The Bible tells me so:

"O LORD...there is no God like you, in heaven above or on earth beneath."

Some Questions for You

1. What's something we can thank God for? *For letting us know Him, the great God who is not like anyone else!*

2. What is something I can ask God to do inside of me, if I want to know what He's like? *I can ask God to help me know more about Him. And, that He would work in my heart and help me to turn away from my sins and trust in Jesus as my Savior.*

Let's Pray!

A   We praise You, God. You are the one, true God in heaven above and here on earth.

C   God, in our heart, we know that You are God and that we should obey You, but many times we don't want to. Please forgive us. We need a Savior!

T   Thank You for not just being good and great, but being so good and so great to people like us! Thank You for caring about us so much and for wanting us to know You. And thank You so much for sending Jesus to be our Savior.

S   Work deep inside our hearts. Help us to turn away from our sins and trust in Jesus as our Savior. Help us to know You and live for You. Help us to go and tell others what we've learned about You, the one, true God. In Jesus' name we pray. Amen.

Let's Praise God Right Now!

Big Question 4 Hymn: Praise Him, Praise Him, All Ye Little Children *from Hide 'n' Seek Kids ESV Songs 4, track 19*

Praise Him, praise Him,
All ye little children,
God is love (powerful, holy),
God is love (powerful, holy),
Praise Him, praise Him,
All ye little children,
God is love (powerful, holy),
Praise Him, praise Him,
All ye little children,
God is love (powerful, holy).
Words: Carey Bonner   Music: Anonymous

Song Question: What's something we can praise God for? *That He is good, powerful and holy. And what is the greatest way He has used His goodness, power and holiness to care for us? He sent Jesus to be the Savior for all who would turn away from their sins and trust in Him as their Savior. He can be our Savior, too.*

Go to the Hide 'n' Seek Kids Parent Resources for Unit 4 to get the Bible story and many more resources and songs for this unit at praisefactory.org

Long ago, the LORD rescued His people from a mighty, mean king. We might not need to be rescued from a mighty, mean king like they did, but we do all need to be rescued from our sins. The LORD wants to rescue us. He sent His Son, Jesus to be our Savior. Jesus can save us from our sins and make us God's people, too, when we repent of our sins and trust in Him as our Savior.

Hide 'n' Seek Kids Sneaky Seekers
hiding God's Word in our hearts, seeking to know God Himself

Big Question 4, Lesson 5 Take Home Sheet

Big Question 4: Can Anybody Tell Me What the LORD Is Like?
Answer: He's Not Like Anyone Else!

Meaning:

There are many gods that people worship, but none is like the LORD. He is the one, true God. He's not like anyone else! He's always been alive--and He will never die. He's completely good and loving. He's all-powerful and all-wise. And that's just the beginning of what the LORD is like. He is so great! There will always be more of Him to know.

How do I know this is true? The Bible tells me so:

"O LORD...there is no God like you, in heaven above or on earth beneath."

Some Questions for You

1. **Who did the LORD save His people from in our story?** *The mighty, mean king.*
2. **What would He send Jesus to save His people from one day**? *Save them from their sins.*
3. **Can Jesus be our Savior? How?** *Yes! Jesus came to save all who turn away from their sins and trust in Him as their Savior. If we do this, Jesus will save us, too. We can know the happiness of knowing God in our heart even today. And one day, He will take us to live with Him forever in heaven. That will be happiest of all!*

Let's Pray!

A We praise You, God. You are the one, true God in heaven above and here on earth.

C God, in our heart, we know that You are God and that we should obey You, but many times we don't want to. Please forgive us. We need a Savior!

T Thank You for not just being good and great, but being so good and so great to people like us! Thank You for caring about us so much and for wanting us to know You. And thank You so much for sending Jesus to be our Savior.

S Work deep inside our hearts. Help us to turn away from our sins and trust in Jesus as our Savior. Help us to know You and live for You. Help us to go and tell others what we've learned about You, the one, true God.
In Jesus' name we pray. Amen.

Let's Praise God Right Now!

Big Question 4 Praise Song: God Is So Good *from Hide 'n' Seek Kids ESV Songs 4, track 19*

God is so good (powerful, holy),
God is so good (powerful, holy),
God is so good (powerful, holy),
He's so good (powerful, holy) to me.

Song Question: What are three things about the Lord does this song tell us about? *That He is good, powerful and holy. And what is the greatest way He has used His goodness, power and holiness to care for us? He sent Jesus to be the Savior for all who would turn away from their sins and trust in Him as their Savior. He can be our Savior, too.*

Go to the Hide 'n' Seek Kids Parent Resources for Unit 4 to get the Bible story and many more resources and songs for this unit at praisefactory.org

Hide 'n' Seek Kids Sneaky Seekers
hiding God's Word in our hearts, seeking to know God Himself

BIG QUESTION 4 BIBLE STORY & KEY CONCEPTS

Dear Parents,

Big Question #4 is: Can Anybody Tell Me What the LORD Is Like? He's Not Like Anyone Else!"

Here's a copy of the Bible story they are learning along with the "Listening Assignment" for each lesson. These assignments provide a different teaching emphasis for each lesson, helping the children dig deeper into each Bible truth. They match up with your child's take home for each lesson. We hope that these resources help your family to further "Hide God's Word in your heart and SEEK to know God, Himself!" Happy hiding and seeking!

•many more resources for this Big Question came be found online at www.praisefactory.org•

Listening Assignments for Big Question 4 Bible Story:
"The Case of the Big Showdown"
Exodus 1-12

Detective Dan's Lesson #1 Listening Assignment:

As you listen to the story, see if you can figure out:
1. A showdown is like a fight to see who's the best. Who won the showdown in this story?
2. What did He prove when He won?

Detective Dan's Lesson #2 Listening Assignment:

Our Bible verse is 1 Kings 8:23: "O LORD... there is no God like you in heaven above or on earth beneath."

As you listen to the story, see if you can figure out:
1. Who didn't believe the LORD was the one, true God in our story?
2. How did the LORD show that He really was the one, true God?

Detective Dan's Lesson #3 Listening Assignment:

I found four clues, but one of them is NOT in the story.
They are: A rug; A frog; A king (Pharaoh); and Moses.
Hold up each of the four pictures for the children to see as you identify them. Better yet, put them up on your flannelgraph board, off to one side.

I need to know:
1. Which three pictures belong in the story and which one does not?
2. How did the LORD use three things to show He was the one, true God?

Detective Dan's Lesson #4 Listening Assignment:

As you listen to the story, see if you can figure out:
1. Who did the LORD prove He was in our story?
2. What was something God's people asked the LORD for and He answered their prayers?

Detective Dan's Lesson #5 Listening Assignment:

As you listen to the story, see if you can figure out:
1. Who did the LORD save His people from in our story?
2. What would He send Jesus to save His people from one day?

Read the questions, THEN SAY,

"Ok, Hide 'n' Seekers! Put on your best listening ears and see if you can find the answers to Detective Dan's questions. When I finish telling the story, we'll see what we come up with."

Big Question 4 Bible Story	use with all FIVE lessons	p.2

"The Case of the Big Showdown" Exodus 1-12

*Story with lines separating paragraphs (**text in bold,** optional interaction cues in italics)*

God's people were very sad.

What do you look like when you are sad? Can you show me?

A mighty, mean king was hurting them. He made them work too hard. He didn't take care of them. He wouldn't let them go home.

"Help us, LORD! Help us! DO SOMETHING!" God's people cried out.

Can you help God's people cry out? Say, "Help, us, LORD! Help us! DO SOMETHING!"

The LORD heard the people. He saw what the mighty, mean king did. He knew how sad His people were and He DID something! He sent Moses and Aaron to rescue them.

"What do you think the LORD did?"

The LORD told Moses and Aaron to talk to the king. "The LORD says: 'Let My people go!' they told the king.

Can you tell the mean king the LORD's message? Say: "Let My people go!"

But the mighty, mean king did NOT think the LORD was any god at all. He said, "No!" to Moses. "I will not let them go! Instead, I will make the people sadder. I will make them work harder." And he did just that.

Now God's people were even sadder! They worked even harder and hurt even more! There was only one thing to do: "Help us, LORD!" Moses and the people cried out to God. "Help us! DOOOOOO SOMETHING!"

The people were really, REALLY sad now. Let's cry out to God even louder with them: "Help us, LORD! Help us! DOOOOO SOMETHING!"

The LORD heard the people. He saw what the mighty, mean king did. He knew how sad His people were... and He did something AGAIN!

"What do you think the LORD did now?"

The LORD sent sad things upon the mighty, mean king, his people, and his land... but He protected His people from them all. This would show EVERYONE that the LORD was the One, True God. This would make the king free God's people.

Story with lines separating paragraphs (text in bold, optional interaction cues in italics)

The LORD sent nasty flies and gnats that swarmed and buzzed all around the king and his people...but not a one bothered God's people!

Can you buzz like a fly?

He sent lots of slippery-slidey frogs to hop all around the king and his people... and even into their houses...and even into their beds! But not a one bothered God's people!

Can you hop like a grasshopper?

He sent hungry locusts to munch up all the food of the king and his people. He made itchy, scratchy, ouchy bumps pop out all over their skin. He made other sad things happen to the king and his people (and even to their animals and their plants. But not a one bothered God's people or their animals or plants!

The mean king and his people were very sad and miserable. They didn't like all the things the LORD had sent upon them.

What do you think they looked like?

What would the mighty, mean king do now? Would he believe that the LORD is the One, True God? Now would he let God's people go free? YES, HE WOULD!

"Go away! Go home! THE LORD IS GOD!" the mighty, mean king said. "We have had enough of these sad things. We will do what your God wants us to do," he said. "God's people can go free!"

What did the mean king say? "Go away! Go home! The LORD IS GOD!"

How HAPPY Moses and Aaron were! How happy God's people were! They praised the LORD, the one, true God. He loved them and had heard their cries. He had seen what the mighty, mean king did. He knew how sad His people were... AND HE DID SOMETHING!

God's people were so happy! The LORD rescued them from the mighty, mean king. Let's cheer for God! He's not like anyone else!

How great is the LORD! He is not like anyone else!

Big Question 4 Bible Story   use with all FIVE lessons   p.4

Cracking the Case: (story wrap-up for Listening Assignments)

It's time to see how we did with our Listening Assignment.

Detective Dan's Lesson #1 Listening Assignment:
1. A showdown is like a fight to see who's the best. Who won the showdown in this story? The LORD.
2. What did He prove when He won? The LORD showed that He was the one, true God.

For You and Me:
Long ago, the LORD showed He was the one, true God, and He is still the one, true God today. There's no one better to love and obey than Him. His good plans for His people and this world will always win! Let's ask Him to help us to put our trust in Him.

Detective Dan's Lesson #2 Listening Assignment:
Our Bible Verse is 1 Kings 8:23: "O LORD... there is no God like you in heaven above or on earth beneath."

1. Who didn't believe the LORD was the one, true God in our story? The mean, mighty king (Pharaoh) and his people.
2. How did the LORD show that He really was the one, true God? He rescued His people from the mean, mighty king, and did it in such great ways that even the king had to say that the LORD is God in heaven and on earth!

For You and Me:
The LORD is still the one, true God. There are none other like Him in heaven or on earth. And the amazing thing is, this great God wants us to be His people! Let's ask Him to help us to turn away from our sins and put our trust in His Son, Jesus, as our Savior. He loves to answer this prayer.

Detective Dan's Lesson #3 Listening Assignment:
I found four clues, but one of them is NOT in the story. They are: A rug; A frog; A king (Pharaoh); and Moses.

1. Which three pictures belong in the story and which one does not? The rug was not in the story.
2. How did the LORD use three things to show He was the one, true God? Moses spoke God's words to the king, but the king refused to let the people go or admit that the LORD was God. The LORD used His mighty power and sent lots of frogs and many other things the king did not like. At last, he admitted that the LORD really was the one, true God.

For You and Me:
The LORD is still the one, true God. He wants us all to love Him, know Him and obey Him. We can ask Him and He will help us. What a wonderful thing it is to be one of God's people!

Detective Dan's Lesson #4 Listening Assignment:
1. Who did the LORD prove He was in our story? The one, true God.
2. What was something God's people asked the LORD for and He answered their prayers? They asked God to rescue them.

For You and Me:
God is still the one, true God who wants us to know, love and obey Him. He still loves to rescue His people when they cry out to Him We can be His people when we turn from our sins and trust in Jesus as our Savior.

Detective Dan's Lesson #5 Listening Assignment:
1. Who did the LORD save His people from in our story? The mighty, mean king.
2. What would He send Jesus to save His people from one day? Save them from their sins.

For You and Me:
We might not need to be rescued from a mighty, mean king like God's people did long ago, but we do all need to be rescued from our sins. The LORD wants to rescue us. He sent His Son, Jesus to be our Savior. Jesus can save us from our sins and make us God's people, too, when we repent of our sins and trust in Him as our Savior.

Big Question 4 Bible Story	use with all FIVE lessons	p.5

The Gospel (story wrap-up if NOT using Listening Assignments)

Our Bible Truth is:
Can Anybody Tell Me What the LORD Is Like?
He's Not Like Anyone Else!

The LORD is the one, true God. We should all obey Him! But, like the mighty, mean king in our story, we all say "no" to God... and we deserve God's punishment! How sad!

But, oh, how kind is the LORD! If we turn away from our sins and ask Jesus to be our Savior, God will forgive us and save us!

What a wonderful beginning that will be! For then we will get to know God in our hearts. And one day, we will go to live happily with Him forever.

Let's thank God and praise God right now for sending Jesus to Let's ask Him to help us turn away from our sins and trust in Jesus as our own Savior.

Close in prayer.

Closing Unit 4 ACTS Prayer

A=Adoration C=Confession T=Thanksgiving S=Supplication

A   We praise You, God. You are the one, true God in heaven above and here on earth.

C   God, in our heart, we know that You are God and that we should obey You, but many times we don't want to. Please forgive us. We need a Savior!

T   Thank You for not just being good and great, but being so good and so great to people like us! Thank You for caring about us so much and for wanting us to know You. And thank You so much for sending Jesus to be our Savior.

S   Work deep inside our hearts. Help us to turn away from our sins and trust in Jesus as our Savior. Help us to know You and live for You. Help us to go and tell others what we've learned about You, the one, true God.

In Jesus' name we pray. Amen.

HSK Sneaky Seekers: Big Question 4 Key Concepts

UNIT 4: The God Like None Other

Unit Big Question (and Answer): "Can Anybody Tell Me What the LORD Is Like? He's Not Like Anyone Else!"

Meaning:

There are many gods that people worship, but none is like the LORD. He is the one, true God. He's not like anyone else! He's always been alive--and He will never die. He's completely good and loving. He's all-powerful and all-wise. And that's just the beginning of what the LORD is like. He is so great! There will always be more of Him to know.

Unit 4 Bible Verse: 1 Kings 8:23

"O LORD...there is no God like you, in heaven above or on earth beneath."

Meaning:

The LORD is God's name. He is the one, true God. There is no one like Him, in heaven or earth. Let's praise Him!

Unit 4 ACTS Prayer

A We praise You, God. You are the one, true God in heaven above and here on earth.

C God, in our heart, we know that You are God and that we should obey You, but many times we don't want to. Please forgive us. We need a Savior!

T Thank You for not just being good and great, but being so good and so great to people like us! Thank You for caring about us so much and for wanting us to know You. And thank You for sending Jesus to be our Savior.

S Work deep inside our hearts. Help us to turn away from our sins and trust in Jesus as our Savior. Help us to know You and live for You. Help us to go and tell others what we've learned about You, the one, true God. In Jesus' name we pray. Amen.

Unit 4 Story
The Case of the Big Showdown
Exodus 1-12

Songs Used in Unit 4   *listen to or download songs for free at https://praisefactory.org: Hide n Seek Kids Music page*

Big Q & A 4 Song
Big Question 4 Song: Can Anybody Tell Me What the LORD Is Like?
Inspector Graff's Rap: The ABC's of God
Unit 4 Bible Verse Song: O, O, Lord 1 Kings 8:23, ESV
Extra Unit 4 Bible Verse Song: In Heaven Above Kings 8:23, *ESV (short version)*
Extra Unit 4 Bible Verse Song: In Heaven Above Kings 8:23, *ESV (full version)*
Extra Unit 4 Bible Verse Song: In Heaven Above or Earth Beneath Kings 8:23, *ESV (other version)*
Unit 4 Hymn: Praise Him, Praise Him, All Ye Little Children
Unit 4 Praise Song: God Is So Good

Unit 4 Big Question and Answer Extra Craft

Coloring, Gluing and Sticking Activity

Craft Description
Children will color and decorate the number associated with the Big Question they are learning.

Supplies
White paper (cardstock is best)
Crayons, colored pencils, markers
Glue sticks
Small decorating items, such as glitter glue, colored paper dots (made with a hole punch), small fabric scraps, pom poms, sequins, small tissue or foil pieces, etc.

Preparation
1. Print out copies of the Big Question and Answer and the Number onto separate sheets of paper.
2. Cut out the circle around the number.
3. Set out coloring and decorating supplies.
4. Make an example of each card to show the children.

Directions
1. Show the children your example, telling them they are decorating and practicing the Big Question and Answer to go and tell their families and friends.
2. Have children first color their Big Question and Answer sheets,
3. Then have them use the additional decorating suppiles to fill in the space around their number.
4. Glue the number in place.
5. Write child's name on card.
6. Allow cards to dry.

If you don't want to use the extra decorating supplies, just have the children coloring in their numbers and glue them in place on their Big Question and Answer sheet.

Practice Telling
Have the children practice holding up the Big Question and saying it. You can have fun with this by having the children mimic when you raise it up, how you say it, etc. a sort of Simon Says element.

Can Anybody Tell Me What the LORD Is Like?

He's Not Like Anyone Else!

Unit 4 Bible Verse Extra Craft: I Kings 8:23

Bible Verse: "O LORD, there is no God like you...in heaven above or earth beneath." 1 Kings 8:23

Craft Description
Children will decorate the Bible verse, with special emphasis on the word "No."

Supplies
White paper (preferably) cardstock
Crayons/colored pencils/markers
Glue sticks/glue
Small decorating items, such as glitter glue, colored paper dots (made with a hole punch), small fabric scraps, pom poms, sequins, small tissue or foil pieces, etc. (choose one or two)

Preparation
1. Print out the craft page, one per child (preferably on cardstock).
2. Set out crayons/colored pencils/markers and other decorating supplies.
3. Make an example of the craft for the children to see.

Directions
1. Show the children your example, telling them that they are making this so that can go and tell their parents and friends this week the Bible verse they are learning.
2. Have the children color in their letters, then add the extra decorating items.
3. Write child's name on card.
4. Set aside to dry, if needed.

Practice Telling
With dried pictures, practice saying the verse, emphasizing the word No. You might want to sing the Big Question 4 Bible Verse Song. It emphasizes the word "No."

"O LORD...there is

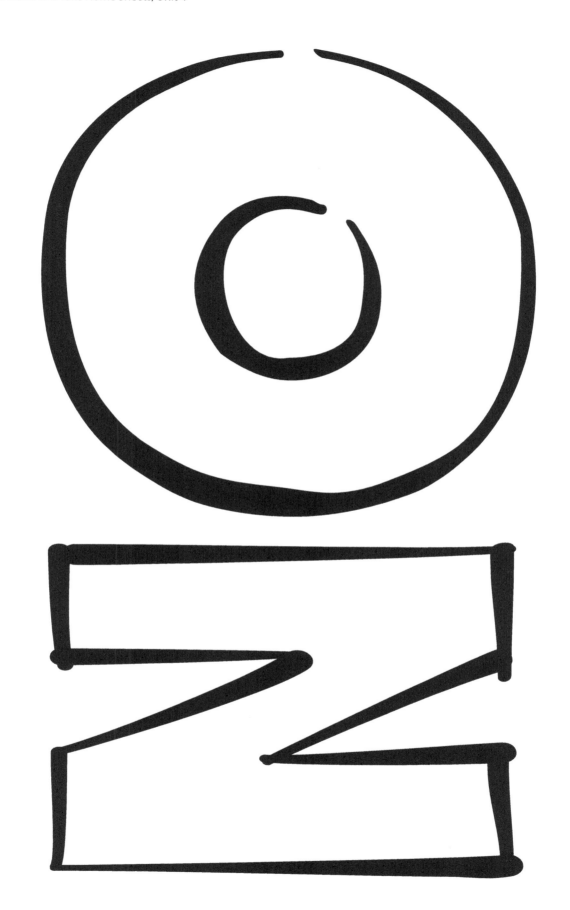

God like you...in heaven above or earth beneath." 1 Kings 8:23

The Case of the Big Showdown Exodus 1:1-12 Jigsaw Puzzle Page

Hide 'n' Seek Kids

Appendix D: Just for Fun Activities

Just-For-Fun Activities

The following are activities that you can incorporate into your free play time. While the activities, themselves, are just-for-fun, you can make them rich times of relationship building, and even use it as an opportunity to discuss what is being taught during Circle Time. Don't over do it, but you can use the Hide 'n' Seek Kids Discussion Sheet for question ideas.

Gluing and Sticking
Just for Fun Arts and Crafts

Directions
Teacher cuts out or draws a basic shape or shapes related to concept or story on cardstock or construction paper for children to stick stickers on or glue fabric or paper scraps (tissue, Gift wrap paper, construction paper, etc), beans, popcorn, buttons, cotton balls, foam shapes etc. onto. Use glue sticks rather than craft glue for these crafts. Cut fabric/paper scraps fairly large—about 1" or so.

Print-Making
Just for Fun Arts and Crafts

Directions
Children will make designs on a plain piece of construction paper or one with a simple shape drawn on it, using tempera paint (with a little dish soap added to it to make clean up easier) and any number of objects. Objects suggested in this curriculum: marbles, duplos, sponge shapes, empty thread spools, blocks with rick-rack glue-gunned to the bottom of them, cars and trucks, bubble wrap and cork.

Necklaces
Just for Fun Arts and Crafts

Directions
These are made with hollow pasta shapes and hole-punched shapes related to the story/concept. Children can string these onto a piece of yarn or string and have you tie the ends together when they are done.

Coloring (Really Scribbling)
Just for Fun Arts and Crafts

Directions
Children will use crayons or washable markers to draw on construction paper. If desired, the teacher can draw a picture or shapes related to the story on the paper for children to scribble on.

Puzzles
Just for Fun Arts and Crafts

Directions
A simple picture related to the story or concept is printed out onto cardstock and cut into a puzzle of 4 to 10 pieces. This can be done by enlarging one or a number of the people/objects from the story, in a Word, Power point or other program to the desired size, then printing out onto cardstock. Children can "color" in the picture, then you can cut it out for them into as many pieces as is fitting for the child.

Craft Dough
Just for Fun Arts and Crafts

Directions
Provide purchased or homemade play dough (recipe provided) along with various "tools" such as plastic knives (without teeth), small jar lids, keys, garlic presses, little rolling pins, plastic cookie cutters, etc.

Homemade Play Dough Recipe
2 cups flour
1 cup salt
4 tsp cream of tartar
2 tbsp oil
2 cups water

Combine the flour, salt and cream of tartar. Mix well. In a large pot, combine the oil and the water. Add food coloring, if desired. Add flour mixture to the pot, stirring as you add. Heat mixture over medium heat, stirring constantly. Continue to stir until mixture forms ball and pulls away from the sides of the pot. Remove ball and knead on plain surface (not floured) until the texture becomes like play dough. Store dough in an airtight plastic container. Keeps about 3 months. Makes about 5 cups. Allow at least a ½ cup per child.

Sandpaper Shapes and Patterns
Just for Fun Arts and Crafts

Directions
Use a glue gun to glue full 8 ½" by 11" sheets of sandpaper to foamboard or sturdy cardboard cut the same size. Give the children yarn pieces of various lengths, 4" to 12" long. Let them stick the yarn onto the sandpaper and make designs and pictures with them.

Dance Ribbons
Just for Fun Games

Supplies
3 4' ribbons per child
1 plastic shower curtain ring per child
CD player
CD of music

Preparing the Activity
1. Tie three 4' ribbons to a plastic shower curtain ring.

Directions
1. Give them to the children to run around with. Have music for them to dance to as they twirl their ribbons. If desired, you could have them sing the Big Question/Bible verse song.

Match the Shape with Objects
Just for Fun Games

Supplies
Common objects such as keys, cookie cutters, spoons, unsharpened pencils, etc.
Cardstock
Permanent marker
Shoe box

Preparing the Activity
1. Trace around common objects such as keys, cookie cutters, spoons, unsharpened pencils, etc., each on a separate piece of cardstock.
2. Put these and the objects in a shoe box.

Directions
Have the children take out the cardstock outlines and the shapes and match them up.

Match the Shape with Blocks
Just for Fun Games

Supplies
Shoe box
Different shape blocks
Duct tape

Preparing the Game
1. Cut the outline of different blocks from a child's building block set in the top of a sturdy shoe box.
2. Use duct tape to tape down one long side, making a hinge for the lid.

Directions
1. Have the children put the right shape block into the box through the hole of the same shape.

Ball 'n' Tube
Just for Fun Games

Supplies
Have the children match the block shapes and insert them into the shoe box.

Materials
4-6' length of PVC pipe with a 2"-3" diameter opening, found very inexpensively at home improvement stores
Various sizes of balls that will fit through the diameter of the PVC pipe

Playing the Game
1. Have the children take turns putting the ball down one end and watching it roll out the other.

Bowling
Just for Fun Games

Supplies
6 or so empty 2-liter soda bottles
A soft, foam ball
Optional: sand or beans, packing/duct tape

Preparing the Game
If desired, put sand or beans in all/some of the bottles. Seal with tape.

Directions
Line up empty 2 liter soda bottles and have the children try to knock them down by rolling a ball into them.

Color Sort
Just for Fun Games

Supplies
Various single colored objects, such as pom-poms, foam shapes, beads, etc. (Be careful to choose objects of a non-swallowable size)
1 Large container that fits all the objects in it at once
Smaller containers, one per color
Construction paper or markers

Preparing the Activity
1. Put all the objects in the large container. Mix up.
2. Put a piece of construction paper/paper colored with marker on the outside of each of the small containers that matches the color object to go in it.

Directions
Have the children separate out all the colored items into their proper container.

Pattern Post Office
Just for Fun Games

Supplies
Various scraps of Gift wrap paper or other colorful paper
Glue stick
Cardstock or cereal box
Shoe Box

Preparing the Activity
1. Cut out envelope-sized pieces of Gift wrap paper (or scrap booking paper) and glue them onto cardstock of the same size.
2. Have a shoe box with a letter slit cut in the top for each of the different paper types.
3. Glue a piece of the designated Gift wrap paper for each particular box on top of the box.

Directions
Have the children sort through the "mail" and put them in their right mail slot.

More Ideas for Activity Centers

Dress-up Clothes
Hats and Crowns
Simple Wooden Puzzles
Duplos
Blocks and Cardboard bricks
Peg Sets*
Magnet Sets (especially "Tall Stacks")*
(Large) Beads and Threading Laces
Small plastic people, animals, and vehicles*
Lacing cards
Housekeeping sets
Doctor's and nurse's sets
Tool sets
Simple Matching games
Dolls
Train sets
Sand or Rice Center with containers
Magnifying glasses and objects*
Shape and Color Sorters
Ring Stackers
Pull toys
Hammer and Peg sets
Tap a Tune pianos
Balls, everything from nerf balls to beach balls*

Great Idea Books
for homemade activity centers

The Wiggle & Giggle Busy Book: 365 Fun, Physical Activities for Your Toddler and Preschooler,
Trish Kuffner and Megan McGinnis
The Toddler's Busy Book, Trish Kuffner
Arts and Crafts Busy Book
The First Three Years of Life, Burton L. White
Creative Resources for Infants and Toddlers, Judy Herr and Terri Swim

Websites
Just for Fun Games for ordering activity centers activities and materials

christianbook.com
amazon.com
toysrus.com
growingtreetoys.com
orientaltrading.com

Big Question Box/Briefcase

What You Want
The Big Question Briefcase is a briefcase or other container with these characteristics:
- Ideally, this should be around 17" x 12", but needs to be at least big enough to fit a 8 ½" x 11" sheets of paper inside it.
- Have various pockets to put these sheets in
- Is attractive or curious looking to preschoolers
- Not necessary, but extremely fun, if is has a combination lock

Finding a Briefcase:
You can certainly buy one new, but you always may find a used one at a thrift shop. Or, someone may have one they want to donate. We use one that stores valuables in it and is the 17" x12" size. Very durable and has the lock feature that the kids love.

You also can move away from the briefcase idea and use a little trunk or other box for your substitute briefcase. Just change the name to the Big Question Box, if you use a box instead. A boot box or the cardboard box that 10 reams of copy paper comes in is a great size, if you are using a box.

If you use a box, but want a lock-like feature, that's easy to do. Simply cut "straps" out of felt or vinyl and glue in place to the top and bottom sides of the box on one side, with the top strap overlapping the bottom straps. Add velcro to the top and bottom pieces so that they meet and fasten. Make back "hinges" for the box with the felt/vinyl straps, too. Or, you can simply add a belt around the box that has to be unfastened before the box can be opened.

Here are some suggestions for decorating a box or even the outside of your briefcase to make it appealing.

Supplies
Your box/briefcase
Plain white contact paper or white cardstock
Colorful wrapping paper
Glitter glue
Markers
Sequins, fake jewels, buttons, rick rack, etc.
Other decorating supplies
Stickers
Glue
Clear packing tape

Directions
1. If you are using a box that has wording on it, you will first need to make plain surfaces for decorating and a hinge for the lid. Stick the white contact paper or white cardstock to each side of the box. On the other hand, you can also use colorful wrapping paper. Then, make a lid by sticking the clear packing tape along one long side of the box, attaching the lid to the box.

2. Use the craft decorating supplies to decorate the box. If desired, you can put a big question mark on top of the box, but remember that you are working with two and three year olds: the question mark symbol is not very meaningful to them yet.

Making a Flannelgraph Storyboard
for use in story-telling and in playing the story review games

While you may decide to use sticky tac and stick your storyboard pictures to a white board, it is very easy to make a flannelgraph board. The advantage to the flannelgraph board is that the pictures stick very easily and there is no messing with the sticky-tac.

Supplies
Large Format Pictures Board: AT LEAST a 36" x 48" foamboard or corkboard (We actually use a far bigger canvas and attach it to the wall) A science project board with the two sides that fold out makes a good 36" x 48" board.
Small Format Pictures Board: AT LEAST a 24" x 36" (to 36" x 48)" board
Large piece of neutral-colored felt to cover your board with extra to overlap over to the back, if desired.
Glue gun and glue sticks

Directions
1. Center felt on front side of board. Turn over. Secure in place with glue.

Making Durable Storyboard Pictures
for use in story-telling and in playing the story review games

Whether you purchase the Hide 'n' Seek Kids storyboard pictures from Amazon or print them off the website (included in the Hide 'n' Seek Kids Visual Aids book), you will want to find some way to make them more durable. They are used not only as a part of telling the story, but are integral in the story review games. Here's how we make ours durable enough to be used over and over again. **See note below for other simpler options for using these pictures.**

Supplies
Hide 'n' Seek Kids Visual Aids book (purchased or downloaded)
White cardstock or printer paper (if downloading pictures)
Sticky-back velcro, circles or cut pieces; or sticky tac putty
Laminator or Self-laminating sheets
Sturdy Sheet Protectors, preferably the "Secure Top" kind, like offered by Avery
Flannelgraph pictures for the Bible stories found at www.praisefactory.org with each unit's resources.

Directions
1. Purchase from Amazon or download and print out the storyboard figures.
2. Cut out flannelgraph figures.
3. Laminate the figures.

Special tip: When laminating the big background pictures that are two (and sometimes even three or four) pieces put together, leave a small gap between the two pieces before laminating together. This small space acts like a hinge and allows you to fold up pictures without hurting them into a manilla envelope that fits 8.5" x 11" sheets of paper along with all of the smaller, regular-sized storyboard pictures.

4. If using a flannelgraph board: Stick a piece of sticky backed velcro (ROUGH SIDE) onto the back of each figure. If using sticky tack and whiteboard: simply stick a small amount of sticky tack on the back of a picture when using it. Remove and store sticky tack in airtight container.

Note: Instead of using all of the pictures as separate flannelgraph pieces, you can choose to use only a few (helpful to have 10 for the story review game); you can clump them onto posterboard and make them into picture scenes; or, you can simply use the Storyboard Picture Guide as a single picture. At praisefactory.org, go to HSK Bits and Pieces for a 22" x 28" poster size jpg of this picture guide if you want to create a large version.

The Hide 'n' Seek Kids "Bible" Folder

This is a homemade folder that looks (kinda) like the cover of a Bible. You will use this to put the Bible verse, the Bible Story and storyboard pictures to help make the point that the truths you are teaching them come from the Bible.

Supplies
1 piece of 22" x 28" posterboard (white is fine. Green or brown is nice)
Glue
Stapler and staples or packing tape
The Bible Cover pictures (see online with resources for this unit or from the back of each Hide 'n' Seek Kids Visual Aids book.)

NOTE: The Bible Cover pictures included in the Hide 'n' Seek Kids Visual Aids books cannot be created larger than 8.5" x 11". That means that they will be under-sized for a Bible Folder of the dimensions you are making. However, you can go online to the Hide "n' Seek Kids curriculum and there is a pdf of a bigger version of these covers that will actually fit the size of this HSK "Bible" Folder.

Directions
1. Lay out poster board with long side along the bottom.

2. Fold in 2" on each side.

3. Take packing tape and tape the folded in 2" flaps to the main section of the posterboard, all the way down.

3. Fold up 8 1/2" on the bottom of the poster board.

4. Use packing tape to tape this flap in place, all the way down.

5. Take scissors and snip through the tape where the flap is attached to the folder. This will give you a bit more room in the folder.

6. Fold the poster board in the middle to make the center fold.

7. Cut out the Bible Cover Pictures. If possible, laminate these. They will last longer.

8.. Glue the two cover pieces to the outside of the folder.

28" side

22" side

2"   2"

8 1/2"

Made in the USA
Middletown, DE
19 September 2023

38787317R00212